Using Children's Literature To Learn About Disabilities and Illness

For Parents and Professionals Working with Young Children

(2nd Edition)

Using Children's Literature To Learn About Disabilities and Illness

For Parents and Professionals
Working with Young Children

(2nd Edition)

by

Joan K. Blaska

Educator's International Press, Inc.
Troy, NY

Blaska, Joan K.
Using Children's Literature To Learn About Disabilities and Illness—2nd ed.

Published by Educator's International Press, Inc.
18 Colleen Road
Troy, N.Y. 12180

Library of Congress Cataloging-in-Publication Data:

Blaska, Joan
   Using Children's Literature To Learn About Disabilities and Illness—2nd ed.
   p. cm.
   Includes bibliographical references and index
   ISBN 1891928-25-2 (alk. paper)—ISBN 1891928-24-4 (pbk. : alk. paper)
   1. Children—Books and reading—United States. 2. People with disabilities—Juvenile literature—Bibliography. 3. Chronically ill—Juvenile literature—Bibliography. 4. Children's literature—Bibliography. 5. Toleration—Study and teaching (Primary) 6. Toleration--Study and teaching (Preschool) 7. Education, Primary—Curricula. 8. Education, Preschool—Curricula. I. Title.

Z1037.A1B58225 2003
028.5'5—dc21   2003012702

ISBN   1891928-24-4 (pbk.)
          1891928-25-2 (cloth)

Manufactured in the United States of America

07   06   05   2   3   4   5   6

Table of Contents

Introduction

This book is designed for parents and early childhood professionals to help young children (birth through third grade) learn about disabilities and illness through children's literature. It is specifically designed for teachers in Nursery Schools, Montessori, Head Start, Early Childhood Family Education, Early Childhood Special Education, Early Intervention, Kindergarten, Primary Grades, Parent Education, as well as Child Care Providers, Librarians, Child-Life Specialists and Support Staff who work with children this age (i.e. Occupational Therapists, Physical Therapists, Speech/Language Clinicians).

All children need to have the opportunity to learn about diversity of ability much like they learn about cultural diversity. Yet, often this does not happen. When Blaska conducted an informal survey of parents and professionals about their knowledge and use of children's literature with characters with disabilities, she found that they didn't know what literature was available or how to use it. Many professionals indicated they would include literature about a disability only when a child with a disability became a member of their class. It is important that children learn about disabilities and illness throughout the curriculum and throughout time so when children have the opportunity to interact or be classmates with someone with a disability, they have some previous knowledge and understanding.

Most of the professionals who participated in the survey indicated they would be interested in using more books in their programs if they knew which ones were available and if they were provided methods for using them. This book was written to make the task of finding literature with characters with disabilities and illness easier for parents and professionals and to provide appropriate methods for including the books throughout the early childhood curriculum.

All of the books in the Annotated Bibliography have been reviewed using the *Images and Encounters Profile* in Appendix A. Each book was rated as outstanding, very good, fair, or not recommended. The books rated "not recommended" are not included in this collection. An Annotated Bibliography (See Chapter Five) was developed for each book to make it easier for you to choose books that include the type of information or characters that you want. Cross-referencing was done to facilitate the ease in which a title can be located.

The books include fiction and non-fiction, represent 11 disability areas and 10 chronic illnesses. All books are for the early childhood population. Early childhood includes children birth to age eight based on the definition of the National Association for the Education of Young Children (NAEYC). Most of the books are available at local book stores and libraries, however, in the event you are unable to locate a specific title, a list of publishers is provided in Appendix E. Anyone working with young children will find this book to be a valuable resource.

The first chapter emphasizes why it's important for all young children to learn about people with disabilities and illness. The influence of books and reading to young children and the importance of having a bias-free curriculum are also included. The chapter ends with a Diversity Quiz, which will provide insight into the reader's current practices related to diversity.

Chapter Two is intended to increase the reader's understanding of how to use books with young children and includes practices for reading aloud. Chapter Three is designed to help the reader understand how to teach about differences, which generally precedes teaching about disabilities. Included is a short annotated bibliography of books about differences and would be good choices when teaching the concepts of same and different.

Chapter Four provides information on how to help young children learn about disabilities and chronic illness. Strategies for teaching are outlined including how to spiral information throughout the curriculum. The philosophy of using "person first" language when talking about individuals with disabilities is presented. Many examples are provided encouraging the reader to adopt this philosophy. Demonstrating respect and dignity as you work with young children is also stressed. In order to answer children's questions about a disability or illness, it's necessary for the parent or professional to have some basic information. A brief overview of each of the disabilities and illnesses that are represented in this collection of children's books is provided. How to respond to young children's questions is included in the overview.

Chapter Five contains the Annotated Bibliography of children's books that have a character with a disability or illness in the story. The annotations provide a brief overview of the story plus additional information based on the review that will help you make appropriate selections for your child or students. Chapter Six contains a listing of the children's books cross-referenced by disability or illness. When you want a book about a specific disability or illness, this listing will make the task an easy one.

Chapter Seven provides information on curriculum planning using a theme or literature-based approach. The process for developing Text Sets to use with each theme is provided along with six examples that incorporate diverse literature. Unit development is outlined in this chapter, including how to incorporate children's literature. Several examples of teaching units or webs are included.

Chapter Eight has the books cross-referenced by theme. When teaching using a specific theme, merely turn to this listing to find which books can be used to incorporate disability or illness. Chapter Nine provides a Text Set Lesson Plan to help you organize the children's literature that you choose to use with each theme. The format of the lesson plan allows the reader to continually update the plan with newly found books. A Text Set Lesson Plan form is provided that can be copied for your use.

Six Appendices are included: Appendix A: *Images and Encounters Profile*; Appendix B: Children's Books That Include Persons with Disabilities or Illness Alphabetized by Title; Appendix C: Children's Books Cross-Referenced by Categories; Appendix D: Activities for Teaching Children About Disabilities; Appendix E: Publishers of Children's Books, and Appendix F: National Organizations and Agencies.

CHAPTER ONE

Why It's Important For Young Children To Learn About Disabilities and Chronic Illness

INTRODUCTION

Books serve as mirrors for children to see characters who look like themselves and have feelings and experiences similar to their own. Books also serve as windows through which children learn about their world by looking beyond their immediate surroundings and seeing characters and events that occur in other communities or other parts of the world (Rudman & Pearce, 1988). It is through books that children are able to learn about and make sense of what goes on in their world (Sawyer & Comer, 1991). The images of people and places that children form from their earliest literacy experiences are recognized as important for their overall development (Rudman & Pierce, 1988). In children's books it is important for young children to see characters with whom they can identify. Within stories, they need to see familiar experiences and a variety of emotions expressed by the characters.

In literature it is best for children to encounter a variety of role models that represent the diversity of people in the society and world in which they will grow up (Routman, 1988). Children with disabilities or illnesses need to see people similar to themselves. Perhaps no group has been as overlooked and inaccurately presented in children's books as individuals with disabilities. Most often they were not included in stories and when they were, many negative stereotypes prevailed such as characters who were pitiful or pathetic, evil or superheroes, or a burden and incapable of fully participating in the events of everyday life. Often the difference or disability was the main personality trait emphasized to the reader, not a balance of strengths and weaknesses (Blaska & Lynch, 1994).

Over the past fifteen years, authors, illustrators and publishers have made an effort to develop more positive role models. Included in these efforts has been the inclusion of characters from a variety of socioeconomic levels, life-styles and heritage. However, it should be remembered that diversity is not limited only to heritage. Characters with disabilities need be included to represent the population with varying abilities.

In 1992, a study by Blaska and Lynch reviewed 500 award-winning and highly recommended books for children, birth through age eight and published between 1987–1991, for the inclusion and depiction of persons with disabilities. Of the books that were reviewed, ten (2%) included persons with disabilities in the storyline or illustrations. Within the ten books, persons with disabilities were integral to the storyline in only six of the books. The limited presence of persons with disabilities points out the need for more stories that represent the diversity of society which includes persons with varying abilities. While more books with characters with disabilities are published today, the percentage is still very small when compared to the total number of children's picture books published each year.

INFLUENCE OF BOOKS AND READING

Attitudes can be changed by reading or being read stories according to recent research findings (Sawyer & Comer, 1991). Schrank and Engles (1981) reviewed the literature on bibliotherapy, which is sometimes called guided reading, and found that the research overwhelmingly supported the premise that guided reading can bring about attitudinal changes toward disabilities. Care should be taken in the appropriate selection of books and the presentation of the content.

Bibliotherapy means using books and subsequent discussion to address a variety of needs. During the discussion, the leader would ask questions and have discussion in the following areas:

Content of the story:	Retell the plot; highlight the characters, their feelings and situations within the storyline.
Probing questions:	Ask students questions that help them think about their feelings to better identify with characters and events in the story.
Transfer to real life:	Transfer situations from the story to real life situations; explore consequences of behaviors and feelings.
Conclusions & generalizations:	From actions in the story, draw conclusions and generalizations (McCarty & Chalmers, 1997).

This process can be used with all ages and can be effective with young children. There can be many benefits from the discussions such as clarifying misconceptions, understanding yourself and other people, and developing self-confidence. However, change should not be expected after the reading and discussion of only one story. The reading and discussion of a number of related books are needed for the best results (Fouse & Morrison, 1997).

A study by Salend and Moe (1983) challenged the notion that exposure to children's books about disabilities alone could affect a positive attitude change. They found that when book reading was paired with activities that highlight the critical information to be learned, books became highly successful in changing attitudes. The results of this study point out the importance of children participating in discussion or activities following the reading of stories to affect change.

Guided reading can be helpful when working with siblings of children with disabilities. When one child in a family has a disability or illness, it affects everyone including brothers and sisters. The siblings generally have a number of questions, concerns and fears, and often do not understand what is happening. In the stories that address the issues of living with a child with a disability or illness, siblings are able to see they are not alone with their questions and feelings. Siblings learn about themselves as well as their brother or sister. Reading stories such as these opens the door for healthy discussion where siblings can get their questions answered, heighten their understanding of the child with the disability, ease feelings of guilt and help the siblings feel better about themselves. When children read about others who are trying to make sense of a situation similar to their own, it brings hope. Children learn their feelings are typical, which helps them understand that they are okay people even if they experience some negative feelings. Through empathetic characters in literature, children learn tolerance for others and how to develop solutions to problems (Sawyer & Comer, 1991). Books can be inexpensive yet powerful tools for providing information to siblings.

Reading and discussing literature about disabling conditions can help children understand and accept persons with varying abilities. The Carnegie Corporation (1974) findings are still relevant today, "Books, perhaps children's books most of all, are powerful tools by which a civilization perpetuates its values—both proudest achievements and its most crippling prejudices. In books children find characters with whom they identify and whose aspirations and actions they might one day try to emulate; they discover, too, a way of perceiving those who are of a different color, who speak a different language or live a different life" (p. 1).

BIAS FREE CURRICULUM

Schools are making every effort to have bias free programs that use anti-bias curricula. An anti-bias curriculum reflects diversity of race and ability and non-stereotypic gender activities. This bias free philosophy is reflected in the materials used by having a balance among different groups of people, and a balance of men and women doing a variety of jobs that do not stereotype by sex. People with varying abilities are depicted as doing work and participating in recreational activities with their families being careful not to create images of dependency and passivity (Derman-Sparks, 1991). Today, publishers of children's books generally do not accept manuscripts with obvious bias toward race, religion, ability, sex or age. However, there are many books published in past years that do contain negative bias and some newer books with subtle bias. When using books with young children it is important that they be previewed for forms of bias, which may influence how the books are used.

Often collections of books have bias by omission. To determine if this is happening, simply count the number of books available, determine how many of the books represent the various kinds of people and then look at the number that represents the population that you are checking. You will be able to see if there are representative number of books. There is no magic number, but the ratio should tell you if there is a need for concern (Sawyer & Comer, 1991). It's important that all children see themselves in materials that are being used in the classroom. This includes children with disabilities or illnesses.

It's important that role models and activities in which children partic-ipate be inclusive, realistic and positive in order to foster positive relation-ships among children and enhance the self-esteem of children with disabilities. Society is changing and is becoming more accepting of peo-ple who are different. We can continue to promote this acceptance by carefully planning how we work with young children and with wise selec-tion of books and materials.

INCLUSIONARY PROGRAMS

Best practices currently dictate that young children with disabilities are to be educated with their peers who do not have disabilities (Sainto & Lyon, 1989). Several federal laws have provided the impetus to educate children with disabilities in the regular classroom. Positive attitudes about human differences can be promoted through inclusionary programming. This provides the opportunity for positively influencing societal attitudes towards people with disabilities (Safford, 1989).

The children of today are the future parents of children with disabili-ties or illness. They will become the future neighbors, doctors, teachers, coaches, and so forth. Children who learn about people with differences at an early age and learn to accept those differences will become citizens who are more sensitive, tolerant and understanding of people of all abil-ities. Children tend to be afraid of the unfamiliar. Once children have the opportunity to interact and be educated with children with disabilities they will be exposed to a variety of differences and common fears can be overcome.

There is a tendency for professionals to use books about a particular disability or illness when they have a child with that challenge in their pro-gram. While this has merit, books from the disability literature should be incorporated into every program and not be limited to classes where a child with a disability is a member. This is the only way to educate all chil-dren about a variety of abilities and disabilities. With exposure through literature, children will have the opportunity to ask questions and gain information prior to meeting a person with a disability or illness whether it occurs in school or in the community.

EMERGENT LITERACY

The emergent literacy approach is a dominant teaching strategy for young children with and without disabilities in integrated programs. The emergent literacy theory includes the development of listening, speaking, reading and writing. It is believed that the four areas develop concurrently and begin developing at birth. Children develop literacy skills through active engagement in real life situations such as "signing" their names to Grandma's birthday card. Through this active process children develop an awareness of print; the squiggles (letters) on paper mean something. They begin to understand the function of print; print says something important. They develop concepts of book print; books have a beginning and ending, there is a right side up, and you turn one page at a time. (Teale & Sulzby, 1986).

For optimum literacy development, the environment needs to be filled with print and countless opportunities to read, write, speak and listen. The children would have a multitude of opportunities to interact with adults in literacy activities. They would also have an excited, supportive adult who models and supports learning (International Reading Association, 1985). A strong research base emphasizes the benefits of reading regularly to young children. Those who have been read to regularly tend to be better readers, read earlier and have a greater enjoyment of reading.

With more and more early childhood programs adopting the theory of emergent literacy, early childhood programs are incorporating more books into the curriculum than ever before. It's important that the selection of books includes stories with characters with disabilities and illness. Exposure to this diversity in the early years provides the opportunity to eliminate old stereotypes. Through this exposure children will begin to develop sensitivity for people with differences.

Ten Tips: Literacy Development with Young Children

- Develop a philosophy that recognizes that the development of literacy skills is important for young children including those with special needs.
- Design an environment rich in literacy practices based on the latest research, providing daily opportunities for children to interact by speaking, listening, reading and writing.
- Interact with children within the literacy rich environment while modeling reading and writing in real life situations.
- Be supportive of children's efforts and get excited with them as they try new activities and learn new skills.
- Incorporate opportunities throughout the curriculum for children to write and see print in a meaningful way.

- Adapt literacy activities so that children with special needs can gain the most from each literacy activity.

- Use "teachable moments" to enhance children's learning about reading and writing helping them make the connection between the spoken and written word.

- Read to children each day and promote language development by talking about the stories and asking appropriate questions.

- Spiral diverse literature throughout the curriculum, including books that represent cultural differences and ones that have characters with disabilities or illness.

- Provide information to parents so they will understand how literacy develops with young children, their role in that development and the many literacy practices that can, and do, occur in homes (Blaska, 2000).

Because literacy development includes reading, writing, listening and speaking almost all children will develop some level of literacy. However, it is not easy to predict the literacy levels that will be achieved by young children with disabilities. Because of the unknowns, in early childhood it is critical that all young children with disabilities be exposed to early childhood programs rich in literacy practices so each child has an opportunity to learn all that he or she is capable of learning (Blaska, 2000).

DIVERSE CHILDREN'S LITERATURE & MATERIALS

During the past decade or so, an emphasis was made on the importance of exposing children to materials that represent diverse cultures. Many books have been written and Louise Derman-Sparks in her nationally acclaimed book, *The Anti-Bias Curriculum,* has provided guidelines for early childhood professionals (Derman-Sparks, 1989). Today, in most early childhood classrooms, materials representing diverse cultures can be seen (Blaska, 1998). Individuals with disabilities are also mentioned in Derman-Sparks book, but most programs have not done a very good job of including this group of diverse individuals into their curriculum. Professionals can complete the Diversity Self-Quiz to provide insight into their daily practices.

Diversity Self—Quiz

Directions: Please number your paper from 1 to 5. Answer "yes" or "no" to each of the following questions:

1. Do you routinely read books to your children that represent diverse cultures? (routinely means often or frequently)

2. Are books that represent diverse cultures routinely available for children to read independently?

3. Do you routinely have pictures and posters on the walls that represent diverse cultures?

4. Do you routinely have props in your learning centers that represent diverse cultures?

5. Do you spiral information regarding diverse cultures throughout your curriculum? (Spiraling means to introduce information, then periodically throughout the year that topic or information is talked about again and again.)

Directions: Now, please make a second column of numbers from 1 to 5. Again, please Answer "yes" or "no" to each question.

1. Do you routinely read books to your children that have characters with disabilities or chronic illness?

2. Are books that have characters with disabilities or illness routinely available for children to read independently?

3. Do you routinely have pictures and posters on the walls that represent people with disabilities or illness?

4. Do you routinely have props in your learning centers that represent people with disabilities or illness?

5. Do you spiral information about individuals with disabilities or illness throughout your curriculum?

Look at your answers in the two columns. Take time to analyze . . . do you see any trends? What are the strengths? Are there weaknesses? Usually, early childhood professionals do well in the first column asking about diversity of culture but do poorly in the second column which addresses individuals with disabilities or illness. (Blaska, 1998). The results of this Self-Quiz will point out areas that are strong and areas that are weak which need to be addressed.

References

Blaska, J. (2000). Emergent literacy with young children with disabilities. *Your Link,* Summer, 1–2.

Blaska, J., & Lynch, E. (1994). Inclusion and depiction of individuals in award-winning and highly recommended children's books. Unpublished manuscript.

Blaska, J. (1998). Focus issue: Promoting emergent literacy with young children. In J. Comeau, (Ed.) *Family Information Services* (pp. 73–84). Minneapolis, MN: Family Information Services.

Carnegie Corporation. (1974). Racism and sexism and children's books. *Carnegie Quarterly,* 22(4), 1–8.

Derman-Sparks, L. (1989). *Anti-bias curriculum: Tools for empowering young children.* Washington, DC: NAEYC.

Fouse, B. & Morrison, J.A. (1997). Using children's books as an intervention for attention-deficit disorder. *The Reading Teacher,* 50(5), 442–445.

International Reading Association (1985). *Literacy development and pre-first grade.* Newark, DE: IRA.

McCarty, H., & Chalmers, L. (1997). Biblio intervention prevention. *The Council for Exceptional Children,* July–August, 12–17.

Routman, R. (1988). *Transitions: From literature to literacy.* Portsmouth, NH: Heinamann.

Rudman, J.K., & Pierce, A.M. (1988). *For the love of reading: A parent's guide to encouraging young readers from infancy through age 5.* Mount Vernon, NY: Consumers Report Books.

Safford, P.L. (1989). *Integrated teaching in early childhood.* NY: Longman, Inc.

Sainto, D.M., & Lyon, S.R. (1989). Promoting successful mainstreaming transitions for handicapped preschool children. *Journal of Early Intervention,* 13(4), 305–314.

Salend, S., & Moe, L. (1983). Modifying nonhandicapped students' attitudes toward their handicapped peers through children literature. *Journal of Special Educators,* 19(3), 22–28.

Sawyer, S., & Comer, D.E. (1991). *Growing up with literature.* NY: Delmar.

Shrank, F.A., & Engles, D.W. (1981). Bibliotherapy as counseling adjunct: Research findings. *Personnel and Guidance Journal,* 60, 143–147.

Teale, W., & Sulzby, E. (1986). *Emergent literacy: Writing and reading.* Norwood, NJ: Ablex Publishing Corp.

CHAPTER TWO

Using Books with Young Children

INTRODUCTION

Reading books to young children has a number of benefits that have been identified throughout the years. Children learn about their world and try to make sense of it through the books they read. In addition, they learn about themselves and develop positive attitudes regarding many things they have learned through books. This includes learning about the variety of people in the world and through this learning they begin to develop an understanding and sensitivity toward differences. Another benefit, which is well documented in the literature, is that children develop an interest in reading and tend to be better readers when they have been read to consistently beginning at a young age (Sawyer & Comer, 1991).

It's important to have frequent and regular times for reading with young children. This should be a special time for a child to receive the undivided attention of a caring adult. Comfortably seated on your lap, or next to you, the story is shared, with the child participating whenever possible. Children associate these pleasurable times with reading which in turn influences their love for reading (Neuman, Copple, & Bredekamp, 2000).

The best way parents and teachers can help children become better readers is to begin reading to them when they are very young. Children who are read to regularly grow up with the idea that reading is a normal part of daily life. As language becomes more meaningful, reading can stimulate imaginations and provide a foundation for new knowledge (Sawyer & Comer, 1991). As children grow older, they can identify letters and words and talk about the meaning of words. They can discuss what happened in the story and the feelings displayed by the characters. When discussing stories, use questions that help children think, such as, "What do you think will happen next?"

Children should be read to on a daily basis. Sawyer and Comer (1991) stressed, "Each month that books are not read to infants is a month that is lost forever" (p. 17). There is no magic number of stories to be read daily but the more, the better. Every day books need to be available for children to use independently both at home, childcare, and in school.

READING TO INFANTS

According to Schickendanz (1986), a four-step approach is recommended when reading to infants:

1. Get the baby's attention or focus the baby's attention on a picture in the book. You might say, "Look!" or "Look at that!"
2. Ask the baby a labeling question such as, " What is that?"
3. Wait for the baby to respond, or when necessary, provide the answer yourself. The baby or adult answers by providing a label for the photograph or illustration.
4. Provide feedback to the baby. When the child is able to label the picture, provide feedback such as "Yes" or "You're right." If the label is difficult to understand, perhaps a new word or concept, the adult should repeat the label. If the child has pronounced the label incorrectly, the adult can repeat the label pronouncing it correctly. In this way the child hears and learns the correct pronunciation without being corrected, keeping learning fun. If the child labels the picture incorrectly, the adult should label it correctly such as "It looks like a dog, but it's a cat." This type of response keeps learning positive by eliminating the need to tell the child his or her label was incorrect.

When reading a book to young children, parents lead the dialogue because of the infant's limited language. Young infants like the sounds of a caring voice and the rhythm of the language even if they don't understand the story.

As children get older and are able to participate more and more, the adult can have the child take the lead. Participation in the reading experience and making it enjoyable is very important. The attitude of the person reading the book influences how much fun the child is having.

It's important that books are treated with respect and as something very special. With training and modeling, children will slowly learn how to treat books respectfully.

READING TO TODDLERS AND PRESCHOOLERS

Infants and toddlers like simple, colorful books and pictures. Photographs of simple objects found in their environment are good. They prefer to be close to an adult when reading, sitting on a lap or close by. They also show an interest in books with predictable repetitions within the storyline. They like to join in with the familiar and predictable lines in addition to pointing and naming pictures.

Older toddlers and preschoolers are ready for more sophisticated stories and rhymes. Preschoolers and kindergartners like a wider range of themes and are ready for more involved plots (Sawyer & Comer, 1991). They also like to talk about the story after it is read. Children are able to talk about the story in a more meaningful way when the adult uses open-ended questions such as 'What do you think about . . . ? "What would happen if . . . ?" This encourages the children to think about the story not merely parrot back details of the story (Jalongo, 1990).

It can be expected that preschoolers will sit through short stories. However, infants and toddlers should be allowed to stop after just a few pages. Toddlers like to leave, roam around and then may return to the person reading the story. They like to listen while in various positions and places; ideally reading should take place on the floor. This level of attending is developmentally appropriate and should be anticipated and expected. A child's ability to attend increases with age. To avoid frustration, it is important that our expectations for sitting and attending match the child's developmental stage.

READING ALOUD TO CHILDREN

It isn't necessary to be a professional storyteller in order to read stories to young children. While reading aloud does not come naturally to some people, anyone can practice and become an effective reader. Be sure to read books that you enjoy and you know the children will like. The reader's enthusiasm is contagious to the listeners. It's important that you become familiar with the books that you plan to read aloud. Reading books ahead of time makes it possible to become aware of parts of the story that may need to be explained or shortened.

Practice also gives you time to think about how you want to use your voice. If you are very unsure of reading aloud to children, the best way to learn is by listening to someone else reading stories. Listen to how they use their voice and watch facial expressions. Observe how they interact with the children as they read the story. Read the book to yourself and think of how you want to sound. Read books over and over to children. They love the stories more each time they are read (Dilks, 1992).

Before you read each story, practice using a variety of voice inflections and volume levels. The rate of reading is also important. Reading slower allows children to think about what is going to happen next. They can use their imaginations and form visual images. It also gives them time to enjoy the pictures. Speeding up when the action picks up can make it so exciting that the children can hardly wait to find out what happens. But, be careful not to read too fast, a common mistake when reading aloud. Pausing at appropriate times can also be extremely effectively in helping to set the mood or tone of the story. It also gives you time to ask an open-ended question about the story or talk about the illustrations.

Remember your voice is an important tool to be used when reading to children. Use your voice to differentiate between characters and to emphasize important parts of the story. Be careful not to get too carried away. The object is to read the book not to perform the story. Subtle changes in your voice can be very effective without getting overly dramatic. (Jalongo, 1990). Changing the intensity of your voice is also effective, like whispering as the child in the story drifts off to sleep. Practice reading each story so you are prepared to use your voice effectively.

The way the adult holds the book when reading to young children is very important in maintaining their interest. When reading to a group of children, the book should be held facing the group and at their eye level. With a group, the book needs to be moved slowly from side to side to make sure that all of the children see the words and illustrations. This slow scanning can occur during or after reading each page. It's easier to read from a book held in this manner when the reader is familiar with the story.

When children are sitting on the reader's lap or next to the reader, the book is held in front of the group with the thumb in the center of the pages. With this type of grouping, the children will be able to see without moving the book from side to side. Children will become restless and frustrated when they cannot see the words and illustrations. Next, they will lose interest in the story or in story time. Planning and practice can keep this from happening and ensure that story time is a fun learning experience.

ADDITIONAL HINTS FOR READING TO YOUNG CHILDREN

- Make if fun. Show enthusiasm; never turn reading into a chore.
- Read every day. Make it a part of your daily schedule; make it a priority.
- Begin reading to children as infants; the sooner, the better.
- Use rhymes to stimulate the infant's listening and language development.
- Select simple, brightly colored pictures as they arouse children's curiosity.
- Read in a comfortable area using plenty of softness such as pillows.
- Let the child hold the book and turn the pages when appropriate.
- Pause between pages so the children can enjoy the illustrations.
- Point to the pictures as you talk about them.
- Point to words you read; children learn the black marks (words) tell what to say.
- When reading a familiar book, leave out words for the children to fill in.
- Make deliberate mistakes as you read so the children can "catch" you.
- Whenever possible, add props to the story (stuffed animals, hats).
- When the children want the book read again and again, read it again! (Miller, 1984; Threlease, 1989)

References

Dilks, C. (1992). *Creating a classroom literacy environment.* Philadephia, PA: Children's Literacy Initiative.

Jalongo, M.R. (1990). *Young children and picture books.* Washington, DC: NAEYC.

Miller, K.M. (1984). *More things to do with toddlers and twos.* Chelsea, MA: Telshare Publishing, Inc.

Neuman, S.B., Copple, C., & Bredekamp, S. (2000). *Learning to read and write: Developmentally appropriate practices for young children.* Washington, DC: NAEYC.

Sawyer, W., & Comer, D.E. (1991). *Growing up with literature.* NY: Delmar Publisher.

Schickedanz, J.A. (1986). *More than the ABCs.* Washington, DC: NAEYC.

Threlease, J. (1995). *The new read-aloud handbook* (3rd ed.). NY: Penguin Books.

CHAPTER THREE

Learning About Likenesses and Differences

INTRODUCTION

This chapter contains an annotated bibliography of children's books about differences. The books can be used to help children learn about differences in the world. Besides using these books to promote discussion about similarities and differences, each annotation identifies additional themes where the books can be incorporated. A variety of differences are included such as differences in the way people look, the clothes we wear, the foods we eat, the houses we live in, and the transportation we use. It can be fun learning about differences within ourselves, our families and others. It's important to introduce the concept of different in a positive way. Help children see that it's natural to have differences in our lives. This helps promote the development of a positive self-image. We must all be reminded that it is the differences in our world that make it an exciting place to live. Help children celebrate differences.

CHILDREN'S AWARENESS OF DIFFERENCES

Children become aware of differences at a very early age. As young as toddlers, children learn to name physical characteristics such as skin and hair color. They notice location of body parts. It is at this age that they might develop fear or discomfort around unfamiliar attributes such as glasses, facial hair, skin color, and disabilities. Children who are three or four years of age base their thinking on how something looks, not on logic. Their thinking is limited and often distorted and inconsistent. This makes them very susceptible to believing in stereotypes. It is through the development of self-concept and self-esteem play that children learn to recognize and accept others. As intellectual development occurs during the preschool years, children develop the ability to see likenesses and differences. From this develops the awareness of how people are alike and different. Preschoolers are unable to understand that the inside of a person stays the same even though the physical appearance may change (York, 1991).

Derman-Sparks (1989) reminds us not to deny differences that children point out by saying, "She's just like you." Help children recognize how people are different and alike. In addition, don't criticize children for asking questions about differences with comments such as, "It isn't nice to look." This may teach children not to ask questions which can lead to misconceptions and fears.

HOW WE ARE ALIKE, YET DIFFERENT

When teaching children about likenesses and differences, be careful not to give the child any negative messages about differences. Begin with familiar things in their environment such as hair color, height and shoe size. While it's important to show how we are all the same (i.e. everyone has hair) it's just as important to show how we are different (i.e. my hair is brown, yours is red). While we may be different on the outside, children need to learn that we are alike on the inside with similar wants (we all want friends), needs (we all need food and drink), and feelings (we all get sad when we're teased).

Begin working on likenesses and differences that are concrete and the children can see such as hair or skin color. Later move to those characteristics that are more abstract. When an idea is abstract, such as feelings, try to make it more concrete by focusing on what the child can see. What do people do when they are happy? Smile or laugh? What do people do when they are sad? Cry. Smiling, laughing and crying are concrete behaviors children can see, which makes the abstract notion of feelings become more concrete and more easily understood.

We must discuss similarities as well as differences as this is how children are able to discover ways they are alike which helps build relationships. People can be alike yet different in many ways. Some of those characteristics that you can share with children are differences in people's appearance (i.e. My eyes are blue; your eyes are brown), feelings (i.e. I'm smiling because I am happy; she's crying because she is sad), abilities (i.e. I can ride my bike; you can print your name), homes (i.e. I live in an apartment; you live in a house), families (i.e. I have a family of five; you have three in your family), occupations (i.e. My mom's a police officer; your mom is a cashier at the supermarket). You will be able to think of many more ways people are alike and different. Talking about differences such as these helps set the stage for children to learn about differences in hearing, seeing, moving and other disabilities or illnesses. Differences about ourselves and our families are easier to understand and will lay the groundwork for understanding other types of differences which children will encounter throughout their lives.

Annotated Bibliography:
Children's Books About Likenesses And Differences

Badt, Karin Luisa. *Hair There and Everywhere,* **illus. and photo-graphs by a variety of people. Children's Press, 1994. ISBN 0-516-48187-8 [32 p]. Nonfiction, Gr. 1-5.**

The entire book is about hair. Included are fascinating history and hair styles from many different cultures and religions. The photographs and sketches are interesting with the text appropriate for children third grade and older. Younger children would enjoy the photographs. A wonderful book for talking about differences—we all have hair but there are many differences in how it is groomed and how it looks.

<u>Themes or Units</u>: **Body Awareness; Children & Families Around the World; We Are Alike, We Are Different.**

Baer, Edith. *This is The Way We Go to School,* **illus. by Steve Bjorkman. Scholastic, 1990. ISBN 0-590-43162-5 [36 p]. Nonfiction, Gr. PS-3.**

This book shows children from around the world and the many different ways they travel to school. Some children ride cable cars, others ride bicycles, trains, and even helicopters. The illustrations incorporate diversity and will capture the children's attention.

<u>Themes or Units</u>: **Children & Families Around the World; Friends & School; Transportation.**

Benjamin, A. H. *What If?* **Illus. by Jane Chapman. Little Tiger Press, 1996. ISBN 1-888444-00-2 [24 p]. Fiction, Gr. PS-2.**

All of the farm animals on Buttercup Farm are worried because a kangaroo is coming to stay. No one has ever seen a kangaroo so they imagine the worst. The animals are afraid that the kangaroo will take over their jobs on the farm and they will no longer be needed. When the kangaroo arrives, the animals discover what the kangaroo can do best—taking care of the young animals. This is an appealing story with vivid illustrations.

<u>Themes or Units</u>: **Farm & Farm Animals; Feelings; Zoo Animals.**

Caple, Kathleen. *The Longest Nose,* **illus. by author. Houghton Mifflin Co., 1985. ISBN 0-395-36894-4 [32 p]. Fiction, Gr. PS-3.**

This is a story about a family of elephants. Eleanor is teased at school because her nose is longer than anybody else. At home, Eleanor ties her nose in a knot to make it shorter. The rest of the story shows the imaginative methods her family uses to get Eleanor's nose untied. At school, she agrees that maybe she has the longest nose but questions who has the biggest mouth, as she looks at her friend the hippo. An entertaining story that points out what it feels like to be different.

Themes or Units: Body Awareness; Friends & School; We Are Alike, We Are Different.

Cheltenham Elementary School Kindergartners. *We Are Alike . . . We Are All Different,* **illus. by authors; photographs by Laura Dwight. Scholastic, 1991. ISBN 0-590-49173-3 [27 p]. Nonfiction, Gr. PS-2.**

This book was created by a kindergarten class to help children learn about diversity. They explored likenesses and differences among themselves. The children with the help of their teacher wrote the text and drew the illustrations; photographs were added. This book won the Cabbage Patch Kids/Scholastic "We Are Different . . . We Are Alike" Creative Teacher Awards Program. This is an excellent beginning book to talk about differences of all kinds.

Themes or Units: Families; Friends at School; We Are Alike, We Are Different.

Dorros, Arthur. *This is My House,* **illus. by author. Scholastic, Inc., 1992. ISBN 0-590-45303-3 [30 p]. Nonfiction, Gr. PS-2.**

This book shows the many different kinds of houses people live in around the world. "This is my house" is printed under the illustration of each house in the language of the country where the house is located. Nineteen countries are represented with a variety of houses from a highrise apartment building in Hong Kong to a houseboat in Thailand. People are all the same in that they all have houses, but they are also different by the kind of houses in which they live.

Themes or Units: Children & Families Around the World; Homes & Neighborhoods; We Are Alike, We Are Different.

Fox, Mem. *Whoever You Are,* **illus. by Leslie Staub. Voyager Books, Harcourt, Inc., 1997. ISBN 0-15-200787-3 [26 p]. Fiction, Gr. PS-2.**

This book illustrates little children all over the world. It shows how they are alike, playing and learning, eating and sleeping, and laughing and crying. The children may not look the same or speak the same language and their lives might be very different, but inside they are the same. Brightly colored illustrations add to the story.

Themes or Units: Children & Families Around the World; We Are Alike, We Are Different.

Hamanaka, Sheila. *All The Colors of The Earth,* illus. by author. Morrow Junior Books, 1994. ISBN 0-688-11131-9 [30 p]. Fiction, Gr. PS-3.

Superb illustrations include children from many cultures and shows the many ways children are alike and different. The story points out that people come in many different colors and hues. The book has limited text with outstanding illustrations in warm colors that really tell the story.

Themes or Units: Children & Families Around the World; Colors in My World; We Are Alike, We Are Different.

Holy Cross School Kindergartners, *What's Under Your Hood, Orson?* Illus. by Terry Kovalcik. Scholastic, 1993. ISBN 0-590-49247-0 [28 p]. Fiction, Gr. PS-1.

This book was written by a kindergarten class in New York and was a winner in a Scholastic Contest. The story is about two cars, Yellow and Blue, who are friends. Along comes Red who wants to be a friend. Blue and Yellow come to realize that Red might look different, but under the hood they are all alike. They wonder if people are the same way. This story points out there can be external differences yet internal similarities.

Themes or Units: Colors in My World (red, blue, yellow); Friendship; Transportation; We Are Alike, We Are Different.

Leventhal, Debra. *What Is Your Language?* Illus. by Monica Wellington. Dutton, 1994. ISBN 0-525-45133-1 [32 p]. Fiction, Gr. PS-3.

As a young boy visits countries around the world he asks, "What is your language? Please tell me now." Children from each country answer him and demonstrate how they say, "yes" in each of their languages. The text is an easy-to-learn song that children can enjoy singing as they learn about cultural similarities and differences.

Themes or Units: Alphabet; Children & Families Around the World; We Are Alike, We Are Different.

Macdonald, Maryann. *Little Hippo Gets Glasses,* **illus. by Anna King. Dial Books, 1991. ISBN 0-8037-0964-1 [24 p]. Fiction, Gr. PS-2.**

Children often perceive themselves as different when they need to wear glasses. This was the case with Little Hippo who needed glasses to see television and the blackboard at school. He feels better about wearing glasses when he finds that Sophia his friend needs glasses too. A delightful book that may help children feel better about wearing their glasses. The anthropomorphic approach is very effective.

<u>Themes or Units</u>: **Dentists, Doctors, Nurses & Hospitals; Feelings; Friends at School; Safety; Sense of Sight; We Are Alike, We Are Different.**

Martin, Bill, & Archambault, John. *Here Are My Hands,* **illus. by Ted Rand. Henry Holt & Company, 1987. ISBN 0-8050-1168-4 [24 p]. Fiction, Gr. PS-K.**

Children from different cultures show various body parts and explain their purpose. "My hands are for catching and throwing. My feet for stopping and going." The illustrations and text point out how we are the same, i.e. everyone has these same body parts. Yet, we are different people.

<u>Themes or Units</u>: **Body Awareness; We Are Alike, We Are Different.**

McDonald, Megan. *The Potato Man,* **illus. by Ted Lewin. Orchard, 1991. ISBN 0-531-088514-7 [32 p]. Fiction, Gr. PS-3.**

Potato Man comes to town selling vegetables. The children call him Potato Man because he has only one eye with skin lumpy as a potato. They were afraid of him but it was just old Mr. Angelo who had lost his eye in the war. This is an excellent story that could promote good discussion about fears children might have when someone looks different. The colored illustrations do an outstanding job of representing life in the early 1900s.

<u>Themes or Units</u>: **Feelings; Giving & Sharing; Grandmothers & Grandfathers; Holidays Around the World (Christmas); We Are Alike, We Are Different.**

Morris, Ann. *Bread Bread Bread,* **photographs by Ken Heyman. Scholastic, 1989. ISBN 0-590-46036-6 [29 p]. Nonfiction, Gr. PS-2.**

Colorful photographs show the many varieties of bread that are eaten by people throughout the world. The shape, texture, and how it's made may be different, but it is all bread. Bread is also toasted in different ways—from a fancy toaster to an open fire.

Themes or Units: Foods in My World; Shapes, Sizes & Weights; We Are Alike, We Are Different.

Morris, Ann. *Hats Hats Hats,* **photographs by Ken Heyman. Scholastic, 1989. ISBN 0-590-44878-1 [29 p]. Nonfiction, Gr. PS-2.**

People around the world model many kinds of hats all captured in beautiful colored photographs. Included are fun hats, work hats, play hats, warm hats and much more. All people wear hats, but specific hats are worn in different parts of the world.

Themes or Units: Children & Families Around the World; Hats; We Are Alike, We Are Different.

Morris, Ann. *On The Go,* **photographs by Ken Heyman. Scholastic, 1990. ISBN 0-590-45995-3 [29 p]. Nonfiction, Gr. PS-3.**

This book includes the many different kinds of transportation used in various parts of the world. Colorful photographs show a variety of vehicles. The story begins with people transporting goods, then the goods are moved by vehicles with wheels that are pushed or pulled by people. Finally there are vehicles that are fueled to run by themselves.

Themes or Units: Transportation; We Are Alike, We Are Different; Wheels.

Nikola-Lisa, W. *Bein' With You This Way,* **illus. by Michael Bryant. Lee & Low Books, 1994. ISBN 1-880000-05-9 [27 p]. Fiction, Gr. PS-3.**

As a group of children play at the park, they discover that despite their physical differences such as straight hair, curly hair; brown eyes, blue eyes; light skin, dark skin; they are all really the same. The narrative is written in an entertaining verse which the author calls "playground rap." Illustrations show the diversity of children having fun together. An entertaining book that points out differences in a way that shows the reader that differences are okay.

Themes or Units: Friendship; Homes & Neighborhoods; Summer; We Are Alike, We Are Different.

Penn, Audrey. *Sassafras,* **illus. by Ruth E. Harper. Child & Family Press, 1995. ISBN 0-87868-578-2 [29 p]. Fiction, Gr. PS-3.**

Sassafras is a shy skunk and is sad because some of the other animals call her names like smelly-old or funky-old skunk. Father skunk tells the young skunk that every animal in the woods has a special way to be safe and the smell is part of being a skunk. By the end of the story all of the young forest animals are playing together—in spite of their differences. The story points out how it feels to be different and called names and how good it feels when everyone accepts each other.

<u>Themes or Units</u>: **Friendship; We Are Alike, We Are Different; Wild Birds & Animals.**

Pinkney, Sandra L. *Shades of Black: A Celebration of Our Children,* **photographs by Myles C. Pinkney. Scholastic Inc., 2000. ISBN 0-439-14892-8 [24 p]. Nonfiction, Gr. PS-3.**

Exquisite photographs tell the story of how black children are all unique in the color of their skin, the texture of their hair and the color of their eyes. It shows children that all children who are black are not the same just as children in any other race are not the same. The author makes lots of fun comparisons, i.e. "my hair is the soft puff in a cotton ball."

<u>Themes or Units</u>. **Sense of Sight; Sense of Touch; We Are Alike, We Are Different.**

Quincy, Mary Beth. *Why Does That Man Have Such A Big Nose?* **Illus. by author. Parent Press, 1983. ISBN 0-943-990-25-4 [32 p]. Gr. PS-3.**

This book answers questions innocently asked by young children about people who children see as different. The photographs show a variety of differences in people's appearance including size, choice of clothing, skin color, facial features, and disability. The text provides responses to each question while helping the child empathize with the person. This is an amusing book with photographs that would promote discussion and would be an excellent choice when learning about differences.

<u>Themes or Units</u>: **Feelings; We Are Alike, We Are Different.**

Ross, Tom. *Eggbert: The Slightly Cracked Egg,* **illus. by Rex Barron. Putnam & Grosset Group, 1994. ISBN 0-698-11444-2 [29 p]. Fiction, Gr. PS-3.**

Eggbert loves to paint beautiful pictures and decorates the refrigerator with them. Then one day the fruits and vegetables notice that Eggbert is slightly cracked. He is told he can no longer live in the refrigerator because of his crack. Eggbert travels to find a place where he can live—in these travels he notices that the world is full of cracks such as the sun shining through a crack in a cloud. He decides it is not bad to have a crack and continues his travels and painting. Another story that points out how sad it is to be different and not be accepted by your peers. This is an excellent story to promote discussion about differences.

Themes or Units: Feelings; Friendship; Fruits & Vegetables; We Are Alike, We Are Different.

Spier, Peter. *People,* **illus. by author. Delacorte Press, 1980. ISBN 0-385-13181-X [38 p]. Fiction, All Ages.**

This book is about the many people who live in the world. With few words and many pictures, it points out differences in how people look, dress, live, the languages they speak and write and much, much more. It's a book that needs to be looked at many times because of the many pictures. The story ends by illustrating how boring the world would be if everyone would look, think, eat, dress and act the same.

Themes or Units: Children & Families Around the World; Hats; Homes & Neighborhoods; Pet Animals; We Are Alike, We Are Different.

Swain, Gwenyth. *Eating,* **photographs by a variety of photographers. First Avenue Editions, Lerner Publishing, 1999. ISBN1-57505-369-1 [19 p]. Nonfiction, PS-2.**

This small book takes you around the world with photographs showing foods that people eat and how they prepare it. In the back they provide additional information about the photographs including where they were taken,

Themes or Units: Children & Families Around the World; We Are Alike, We Are Different.

Takeshita, Fumiko. *The Park Bench,* **illus. by Mamoru Suzuki. Kane/Miller Book Publishers, 1989. ISBN 0-916291-21-9 [32 p]. Fiction, Gr. K-2.**

This book was originally published in Japan. The narrative is provided in both English and Japanese. The story is about "a day in the life of a park bench." The reader is introduced to the different people who use the park bench including a grandpa, mothers, children, friends and all of the reasons they use the park bench, i.e. to meet friends, to rest and to sit in the sunlight. This story provides a unique way of looking at differences.

Themes or Units: **Community Helpers & Occupations (park worker); Summer.**

References

Derman-Sparks, L. (1989). *Anti-bias curriculum.* Washington, DC: NAEYC.

York, S. (1991). *Roots & wings.* Minneapolis, MN: Redleaf Press.

CHAPTER FOUR

Talking About Disabilities and Chronic Illness with Young Children

INTRODUCTION

When presenting information about disabilities or illness to young children it is important to be open and honest. It's best to answer their questions when they are asked using simple, respectful language while providing clear, accurate information. Providing information about disabilities is much like teaching young children about sex. Give enough information to answer their questions but not enough to overwhelm them. A young child needs a brief answer while an older child requires more in depth information. By being aware of the child's age and developmental level, you can present information in a way that the child will understand. Use accurate terminology. Children can learn what terms mean if you introduce new words slowly. With information such as this, you will be establishing a base of knowledge, which can be built upon throughout the upcoming weeks, months and years.

Encouraging and answering questions is the most natural way for children to learn. This openness will help them feel it's okay to ask questions.

Remember, no question is a "dumb" question. Children should not be made to feel embarrassed about any questions they might ask. For example, a young child may want to know how someone in a wheelchair goes to the bathroom. Questions such as this reflect the natural curiosity of young children and need to be answered openly and honestly. As children get older their questions will become more complex since they will have developed a greater level of understanding. Your answers will need to reflect this change in development by providing more complete information.

Children often express fears about a disability or illness. Some common fears are that they will catch the disability or fear of the equipment that is used by some children. With honest information it's possible to dispel such fears. Children are sometimes confused about what a child with a particular disability can and cannot do. It's difficult for them to grasp what having a disability really means because they have not had first hand experience. It's important for children to see that with the use of aids (i.e. wheelchair, sign language) and adapting how to do things, people with disabilities can do many of the activities they do even if it's done in a somewhat different way.

Remember, it's the unknown that frightens children. If they do not ask questions, parents and professionals should facilitate question asking and discussion. One way to do this is by reading stories that include a character with a disability or illness. In order to answer children's questions, parents and professionals need to have basic information about disabilities and illnesses. A brief overview of the disabilities and chronic illnesses that are represented in this collection of children's literature is provided in this chapter.

RESPECT AND DIGNITY

Respect means that you talk and interact with children with disabilities or illness much like you would any other child. Professionals and parents demonstrate this respect in their behaviors toward the child. For example, by being a good listener to a child whose speech comes slowly, by allowing children to become independent, assisting them with tasks only when it's needed.

Sometimes it is necessary to teach children to be respectful of those who are different from themselves. Rejection might happen for a number of reasons such as fear, anxiety, impatience, stereotyping or lack of skills for interacting with the child with the disability (Derman-Sparks, 1989). It may be that children don't know how to act or don't understand what is expected of them. If children use name-calling or demonstrate any other inappropriate behavior (make faces) interrupt their language or behavior, and through modeling and verbalizing show them appropriate ways to interact. Teaching children how to be respectful of others is most effectively done through positive modeling. When children see their teachers and parents modeling respectful behaviors they will begin to imitate those same behaviors.

Being respectful means the professional or parent does not talk about the disability to another adult or child in front of the child with the disability. Sometimes adults do this because they forget or think the child can't hear or won't understand what they are saying. Sometimes a child doesn't understand all that is being said, but may understand some words and pick up on the tone of the conversation. It's also possible that children understand more than you think. Even very young children can tell when people are talking about them. Talking in front of children demonstrates a lack of respect to them as people. A more respectful strategy would be to step into the hall or another room to discuss or share necessary information.

When talking to children about a disability, invite the child with the disability to help explain, if he or she is capable and if the child wants to participate. This gives children the opportunity to participate when they feel comfortable and decline if they feel uncomfortable. Participating should be their choice and whatever choice they make should be accepted.

When talking to individuals with disabilities, it is not necessary to speak loudly to them. Sometimes people talk more loudly to children or adults with disabilities when they don't seem to understand what is being said. Increasing the intensity of your voice does not increase the person's ability to understand. Instead, it would be helpful to simplify some of your words or shorten your sentences in an effort to help the person understand. When you are not sure, ask the person, "Do you understand?" Most often they will be able to tell you. These actions demonstrate respect.

USING "PERSON FIRST" LANGUAGE

"The words or phrases people speak and write plus the order in which they are sequenced greatly affects the images that are formed about individuals with disabilities and the negative or positive impressions that result" (Blaska, 1993, p. 25). To demonstrate respect when talking about individuals with disabilities, use "person first" language. "Person first" means that you refer to people first as individuals and then to their disability when needed, using words that are descriptive yet respectful. If you use "person first" language when talking to young children about individuals with disabilities, they will learn to use appropriate words by modeling your language. This will help eliminate stereotypic language.

Use this:	Instead of this:
Child with a disability	Disabled child
Child with Down syndrome	Down syndrome child
Child with retardation	Retarded child
Boy with a physical disability	Crippled
Person with epilepsy	Epileptic

To keep this philosophy in perspective, think about how you might introduce a friend who does not have a disability. You would first use that person's name and then tell where he or she works or lives. Should it be any different for someone with a disability? Everyone is made up of many characteristics and most people don't want to be identified by only one of them (PACER, 1989).

The "person first" philosophy was first adopted by (TASH) The Association for Persons with Severe Handicaps (Bailey, 1992). Many advocacy organizations and disability groups have published similar information to educate the public. Perske (1988) tells about a woman who stood up at a meeting and said, "We are tired of being seen first as handicapped, or retarded, or developmentally disabled. We want to be seen as people first" (p. 5). When we use the expression "the blind child" it makes the disability the most important characteristic about the child, while saying, "the child who is blind" takes the focus away from the disability, making it but one of the descriptors. This order of reference is often more awkward, but it is more respectful of persons with disabilities (Blaska, 1993).

Examples of "Person First" Language
Disability vs. Handicapped

There has been much debate whether to use "disability" or "handicap." Generally, a disability is defined as a condition of the person, which might be emotional or physical, while a handicap is the result of environmental or societal barriers (Hadley & Brodwin, 1988). In reality, a disability does not have to be a handicap. A disability may mean "that a person may do something a little bit differently from a person who does not have a disability, but with equal participation and equal results" (Kailes, 1985, p. 68).

Use this:	Instead of this:
The boy with a disability	The handicapped boy
Children with disabilities	Handicapped children
Children without disabilities	Non-handicapped children
Disabling conditions	Handicapping conditions

Normal vs. Abnormal

The problem with using the term "normal" when referring to a person without a disability is the inference that a person with a disability is "abnormal" or "not normal." A person with a disability may have some abnormal development but he or she is not an "abnormal" person. When using terms such as these, it's important that you are talking or writing about development and not about a person or program (Blaska, 1993).

Use this:	Instead of this:
Normal development	Normal child
Child without a disability	Normal child
Mainstream classroom	Normal classroom
Children without disabilities	Normal children or normal peers

Words to Avoid

There are a number of words that should be avoided because they have a negative or judgemental connotation (Tyler, 1990). Words such as these do not demonstrate respect and fail to recognize the person's strengths and abilities. They create images of people who are to be pitied and perpetuate negative stereotypes of people with disabilities.

Avoid using words such as:

Victim	Disease
Suffers from	Unfortunate
Stricken	Poor
Crippled	Drain or burden
Afflicted	Confined

Additional Suggestions

Using the verb "to have." The most effective way of expressing the link between a person and a disability is to use a form of the verb "to have" (Hadley & Brodwin, 1988). Tyler (1990) says, "A person is a human being and should not be confused with a condition" (p. 65). We should say, "the child has autism" instead of "is autistic." " The child has mental retardation" instead of "is retarded." "The child has spastic muscles" instead of "is spastic."

Disability or Disease. A disability is not a disease. People with disabilities are often very healthy. Words such as symptoms, cases or patients should be avoided unless talking or writing about someone's health or medical condition.

Portrayal. People with disabilities should be portrayed as actively going about the business of living as other people do, not as passive victims, tragic figures or super-heroes (Hadley & Brodwin, 1988).

Special. "Special" is a word that is routinely used when referring to persons with disabilities. Pershe (1988) shed some light on using this term. "Being seen as special might not be so bad, if you're a top celebrity or the national champion. But, if you've been singled out as not normal, given a label, excluded from full participation, exist in out of the way residences, or attend "out of the real world programs" when you felt you wanted to live "in the middle of things," calling you special might only add to the wound you already feel" (p. 59). All persons with disabilities may not be offended by using the term "special." However, let Pershe's comments serve as a reminder to all of us to choose our words carefully and always speak with respect to all people (Blaska, 1993).

SPIRALING CONCEPTS THROUGHOUT THE CURRICULUM OR THROUGHOUT TIME

Learning about disabilities or illness is not a one-time event. Information should be spiraled throughout the curriculum or throughout time to enhance learning. This means that information about a disability or illness is introduced to children with time for discussion and ample opportunity to have questions answered. In the future, the parent or professional talks about the disability or illness when another opportunity naturally occurs. The child may ask a question, or you may see something in the newspaper, on television, or in a book that sparks a conversation. Using these teachable moments you then talk about the disability or illness or related issues building on the information previously provided to the children. In the event opportunities such as these do not occur, the parent or professional should periodically re-introduce the topic in order to create the need for further discussion. Using children's books can be a very effective strategy. In early childhood and primary programs, disability and illness should become part of the ongoing curriculum, not a one week unit during "Disability Awareness Week" which we know is not effective for optimal learning.

OVERVIEW OF DISABILITIES AND CHRONIC ILLNESSES WITH RESPONSES TO CHILDREN'S QUESTIONS

Autism or Autistic Like Behavior

Autism is a disorder of the brain, which causes severe impairment of the way sensory input is assimilated into the brain (Milota, et al., 1991). It is a serious brain-based developmental disability. The major characteristics are a global language disorder, abnormal behavior patterns, social isolation and, most often, mental retardation (Batshaw & Perret, 1992). Autism differs from mental retardation in that the characteristic feature of autism is not a developmental delay rather it is a series of deviations from normal development that is apparent by age three. Behaviors often noted with these children include sing-song, monotonous speech (for those who have language), parroting or repeating words or phrases which is referred to as **echolalia**, a limited behavioral repertoire, a lack of tolerance to environmental change, self-stimulating behaviors (e.g. hand flapping), self-abusive behaviors and obsessive rituals and routines (Batshaw & Perret, 1992).

Many professionals define autism and pervasive developmental disorders (PDD) using the *Diagnostic and Statistical Manual of Mental Disorders,* a diagnostic manual printed by the American Psychiatric Association. According to the *DSM-IV,* the term **PDD** is an umbrella term under which the following specific diagnoses are defined: Autistic Disorder, Asperger's Disorder, Childhood Disintegrative Disorder, Pervasive Developmental Disorder Not Otherwise Specified (PDDNOS), and Rett's Disorder (American Psychiatric Association, 2000).

The primary feature of all children with PDD is impairment in social reciprocity as well as impairments in communication, and problems with repetitive behaviors, narrow interests, and rituals or stereotypic movements (i.e. hand flapping). Because of the limitations in social skills and emotional recognition children with PDD usually have profound limitations in play skills. Children with PDD have a neurogenetic disorder, which may occur with other developmental disabilities such as mental retardation, inattention, hyperactivity, and epilepsy (Batshaw, 2002).

Autism is often referred to as a spectrum disorder, which means the symptoms and characteristics of autism occur in a wide variety of combinations—mild to severe. Any combination of behaviors can occur with any degree of severity. Which means that two children both diagnosed as having autism might behave very differently from one another (CFL, 1997).

When children have severe behaviors they are referred to as having **autism**. These children are almost always non-verbal. Those with moderate behaviors or characteristics have differences in the way they interact verbally and socially and are referred to as having **autistic-like behaviors** or having **pervasive developmental disorder (PDD)**. Children with mild characteristics often resemble someone with a severe learning disability (Milota, et al., 1991). Therapy for children with autism is interdisciplinary including psychiatry, speech and language therapy, behavior management, and social work to provide assistance to the family.

Children may ask about unusual behaviors particularly any self-stimulating or abusive patterns or about the child's ability to communicate. Answer simply and honestly such as: "He likes the movement of his hands as they flap, but he is working on remembering not to do that." "She has a hard time understanding what she sees or hears because her brain works differently than yours and mine." "Learning to talk has been hard for Suzy, but she is learning some new words. We need to learn sign language so we can communicate with her. Remember, there are different ways to communicate and that's okay." Your answers should always be honest while respectful and positive.

Blind or Partially Sighted

A child who has a visual disability has a visual impairment, which, even with correction, adversely affects a child's educational performance (IDEA, 1997). These children are unable to use their vision to learn in the same way that children with normal vision are able to use their sight.

When talking about low vision or blindness, the concern lies in **visual acuity,** which is the ability to see something at a specified distance. Visual acuity is measured by having the person discriminate objects or read letters at a distance of 20 feet. This is most often done with the **Snellen Chart**. Visual acuity is then expressed as a fraction or ratio, which tells how well the person can see. For example, the expression 20/20 which is familiar to most people means that the person reads letters or discrimi-nates objects at 20 feet that a person with normal vision can read or dis-criminate at 20 feet. The ratio 20/90 means that the person can read or discriminate at 20 feet what a person with normal vision can read or dis-criminate at 90 feet, etc. (Deiner, 1999).

Having **low vision** or being **partially sighted** refers to a loss of visual acuity in the range of 20/70 to 20/200 with correction. The American Federation for the Blind prefers using the term partially sighted to iden-tify children with some degree of visual impairment. These children have enough useable vision to learn with the help of magnifiers and large print books (Deiner, 1999).

Being **blind** refers to children who have no vision or have only light perception. Being legally blind means having visual acuity in both eyes of less than 20/200 after the best correction with glasses. Many children who are identified as legally blind have light perception which means they are still able to distinguish between varying shades of light (Batshaw, 2000). Children who are blind need to rely on their senses of touch and hearing in order to learn. Aids used by this group include Braille, guide dogs or white canes, talking books, computers, as well as other technology.

The most common congenital causes of blindness or partial sighted-ness in children are intrauterine infections, such as German measles, and malformations. Other causes are retinopathy of prematurity, head trauma, anoxic events, tumors, and eye infections (Batshaw, 2000). **Retinopahty of Prematurity (ROP)** is a disease of the retina where scar tissue forms behind the lens and develops a mass that causes detach-ment of the retina from the optic nerve. It usually occurs in both eyes and causes complete loss of sight. The major cause of this condition is the high concentration of oxygen, which is needed to keep premature infants alive (Batshaw, 2000).

Young children have difficulty understanding what it's like to be blind. Depending on their ages, these children may have limited ability to imag-ine being blind. For this reason, it is helpful to have children actively par-ticipate in activities, which makes the abstract notion of being blind become more real. See Appendix D for suggested activities.

Children will be naturally curious and have many questions. Answers might be: "She can't see because her eyes don't work like ours." "The nerves behind her eyes don't work so she's not able to see." "Her eyes are open but she sees darkness." "No, her eyes don't hurt." "No, you can't 'catch' being blind." "He can see but his eyes work differently than ours so it's hard for him to see things that are small or far away."

Chronic Illness or Other Health Disabilities

Children who have chronic illnesses that affect their learning are considered by federal law to have a health disability. Public Law 102-119, Individuals with Disabilities Education Act (IDEA—formerly P.L. 94-142) describes "other health impaired" as having "limited strength, vitality or alertness, due to chronic or acute health problems such as heart condition, tuberculosis, lead poisoning, leukemia or diabetes, which adversely affects a child's educational performance" (IDEA, 1997). Children with chronic illnesses that affect learning are entitled to all of the rights afforded students with disabilities according to special education law.

Acquired Immune Deficiency Syndrome (AIDS). AIDS is a communicable viral disease that is life threatening and has no known cure or vaccine. The human immunodeficiency virus (HIV) itself does not kill but weakens the immune system making the body unable to defend itself against other diseases. **Acquired** means the disease is transmitted through direct contact with blood, semen, or breast milk. An infant may contract AIDS from the mother while in utero. **Immune** is the system of the body that is affected and **Deficiency** describes how the immune system is unable to fight off harmful organs that invade it. **Syndrome** refers to the group of symptoms that make up the disease (Deiner, 1999). In addition to chronic health needs, AIDS may also cause psychotic behavior, mental retardation, seizures, and neurological impairments (Hallahan & Kauffman, 1991).

An increasing number of children are contracting the disease through their mothers in utero or through the birth process. Some researchers are predicting that as the numbers of children with HIV infection continues to grow, the virus will become the leading infectious cause of mental retardation and developmental disability in children (Hallahan & Kauffman, 1994).

It is not always possible to know if any of the children with whom you work have AIDS, therefore, universal cleaning and disinfectant procedures should be routinely used which includes appropriate hand washing, cleaning, and disposal of contaminated items. Good hygiene is important for everyone at home and in programs to help prevent the spread of infection and to ensure a safe environment for children.

What to tell young children about AIDS is a difficult question. For children functioning under eight years of age, information about AIDS would probably be beyond their cognitive abilities and serve only to frighten them. Should a child ask a question, be sure to provide an honest yet simple answer. If a young child asks: "What is AIDS?" Your answer might be, "It is a serious disease but you don't have to worry about catching it." Children need to feel safe at home and in school environments.

Allergies. An allergy is a sensitivity to something in the environment that is harmless to most people. Allergies are the most common health impairment in children. Four categories of allergic substances have been identified: airborne or inhalants (e.g. plant pollen), foods and drugs which are ingested, direct contact with the skin (e.g. soap), and some drugs and chemicals which are injected (e.g. penicillin) (Deiner, 1999).

It is possible that allergies can affect a child's development, ability to learn, behavior, and interpersonal relationships. One side effect of some medications is drowsiness and may effect the child's ability to concentrate. It's important to know if any of the children with whom you work have allergies. Find out from parents what the child is allergic to, common reactions, what you should do, and if medication is administered, are there any side effects. Have emergency procedures in place for children who might have their first allergic reaction when they are with you.

Children may ask why a friend doesn't eat a particular food. An answer might be, "His body doesn't work like yours and mine and if he eats that food it will make him sick."

Asthma. Asthma is a respiratory problem caused by a swelling of the bronchial tubes or membrane lining. This swelling causes an obstruction of the small bronchial tubes, which can result in difficulty breathing, coughing, or wheezing. The most common cause of asthma is allergies. Attacks can be triggered by excitement, overexertion or even ordinary activity. Children with asthma usually have medication in pill or inhaler form to take when attacks occur. These children are frequently absent from school which may affect their rate of learning (Deiner, 1999). Other children may be curious about the inhalers that are used. An answer that explains how the medicine in the inhaler helps the child breathe more easily will satisfy most children.

Cancer. Cancer is a term that describes a group of diseases that produce malignant tumors in some part of the body. It is usually treated with surgery, radiation, chemotherapy, or a combination of these methods. The most common form of cancer in young children is **leukemia**, which is a cancer of the body's blood-forming tissues. In persons with leukemia, an overabundance of white cells are produced that are not effective in fighting infection and disrupt red blood cell production and prevent blood from clotting properly. Once leukemia is diagnosed, intensive treatment is ordered which is often followed by a period of remission when the child looks and acts healthy. Medications may take away the child's appetite, which makes good nutrition very important at this time. The causes of leukemia are unknown. (Larson, 1996).

Cardiac. There are many types of congenital heart defects. Most can be treated successfully. If a child has a heart condition the parents must provide information from the doctor regarding any restrictions. Some children may need limitations in their activity level. Be responsive to a child with a heart condition; provide periodic rest periods as needed. It is important for children to be included and participate in activities with the other children at a level appropriate for each child. Quiet activities may need to be made available (Diener, 1999). Children may ask why a child is resting. You might say, "Sammy needs rest times because his heart works differently than yours and mine and it makes him get tired."

Diabetes. Diabetes is a metabolic disorder of the pancreas. **Insulin** is a hormone made by the pancreas and is needed to help the body use glucose. With diabetes, the pancreas is unable to produce enough insulin or the insulin being produced is ineffective. Because the pancreas is not working properly, excess fatty acids can poison the body. If this occurs and goes untreated, **diabetic coma** and death can occur. To prevent this from happening, insulin therapy is necessary. While insulin can't cure diabetes, it can control the disease. To be successful, a proper balance is needed between the insulin and food sugar. A well-rounded diet free of sugar is prescribed in order to maintain this balance. Exercise is also very important because it helps the insulin work appropriately. Some adults can control their diabetes with diet, however children usually require insulin injections in order to control their disease (Milota, et al., 1991). Common symptoms of diabetes in young children include frequent urination and increased thirst (Larson, 1999).

Young children are generally unable to recognize the warning signs of an **insulin reaction.** The child may be dizzy, trembling, shaky, or might have an emotional outburst just before the insulin reaction (Larson, 1996). Find out in advance what you should do if an insulin reaction occurs. Generally you need to have some quick-burning sugar available to give to the child. The key is to be prepared ahead of time. Snacks and lunches should also be discussed with the parents to ensure the timing and content are appropriate for the child. When children ask questions, explain how Suzy's body doesn't work like yours and if she eats sweets like candy, she'll get very sick.

Epilepsy or Seizure Disorder. Epilepsy is a disorder of the brain and is not a disease. It is characterized by **seizures,** which are caused by abnormal discharges of electrical energy in certain brain cells (Deiner, 1999). During the time when these electrical charges are occurring, the seizures can cause a temporary loss of consciousness or some temporary changes in behavior, bodily functions, sensations, or motor activity (Milota, et al., 1991).

Seizures can take many forms, however there are two major types. **Generalized** seizures, sometimes referred to as grand mal seizures, involve the entire body because the discharge of cells is in a large portion of the brain. Whereas, **partial** seizures involve only a small or localized part of the brain causing only a small part of the body to be involved. Seizures can last several minutes or for just a few seconds. Likewise, they can occur frequently or once a year. Some seizures can be totally controlled by medications while other types, only partially controlled. After a seizure occurs, the child will be tired and need an opportunity to rest (Hallahan & Kauffman, 1991). Persons working with children with seizures must have the necessary background information to understand what type of seizures a child has, if the seizures are controlled by medication, what medication the child takes and any side effects. In addition, you need to know first aid procedures in the event a seizure does occur.

Seeing someone have a seizure can be scary to young children. Stay calm and answer their questions openly and honestly with as much information as they want and can understand. Responses might be: "Sometimes her brain gets extra energy and it causes her body to move around. When it's over she is tired and needs to rest." "No, it doesn't hurt." "No, it won't happen to you because your brain has a different amount of energy."

Juvenile Rheumatoid Arthritis. Juvenile rheumatoid arthritis affects children and resembles rheumatoid arthritis that affects adults. Children may experience swelling and stiffness in the joints, fever and rash, fatigue and irritability and associated inflammation of the eyes. Generally the symptoms disappear after several months or years. About half of the children with acute juvenile rheumatoid arthritis recover completely while the other half develop a chronic disease. The causes are unknown.

Therapy includes a balance between regular activity while providing appropriate rest to avoid fatigue and excessive stress on joints. For both psychological and physical reasons, children should not be isolated from their regular routines (Larson, 1996). Children may ask why a friend is unable to participate in a physical activity. A response might be, "He needs to rest because his knees are hurting him. With rest his legs will get better but it may take awhile."

Muscular Dystrophy. Muscular dystrophy is a name given to a group of diseases characterized by the chronic, progressive degeneration and weakening of voluntary muscles (e.g. those in the arms and legs). **Duchene** muscular dystrophy is the most common form, which affects only male children. It is inherited and transmitted through a defective gene, usually between the ages of two and six.

There is no cure for Duchene muscular dystrophy. There isn't any medication or treatment that can slow or stop this progressive degeneration of muscle tissue. The first symptoms might be that parents notice the child becoming clumsy and falling down a lot due to muscle weakness. Tip-toe walking occurs. As the disease progresses, the child may have difficulty getting up from a sitting or lying position. A waddling gait may appear. There is a continued weakening and decline in muscle strength and health. Some of the child's muscles may appear enlarged which is due to the replacement of healthy tissue with fat and fibrous tissue. Over time orthopedic devices are needed and sometimes surgery to continue mobility. Eventually a wheelchair is needed. The disease itself is painless and does not effect intellectual functioning. As the disease progresses, there is increased disability and ultimately death most often before adulthood from pneumonia or other chest infections (Larson, 1999). Children may ask why someone uses a wheelchair or walker. A response such as, "His legs get tired very quickly so the wheelchair helps him get around," may be appropriate.

Sickle Cell Disease. Sickle cell disease is the most common inherited **blood disorder** and effects primarily African Americans. It can be detected at birth through blood screening which is offered to all families. In this disease, the red blood cells are rigid and shaped like sickles or crescents rather than being round and flexible. Children may experience fatigue, breathlessness, rapid heartbeat, delayed growth and development, susceptibility to infections, skin ulcers on lower legs, and vision problems affecting the retina. Sickle cell is a chronic condition that makes the body susceptible to infections. The progression of the disease can be limited by avoiding infections and by getting infections treated early (Larson,

1999). Children with this disease need frequent blood transfusions to replace the red blood cells that have been destroyed. The children will need a great deal of fluids each day and they will tire easily (Deiner, 1999).

Classmates may question if the child is sick. Answer to the developmental level of the children such as, "Sammy has a disease that makes him tired so he needs some extra rest." "No, you can't catch what Sammy has." It is important to reassure children that they are safe and will not catch this disease.

Deaf or Hearing Loss

Being **deaf** describes a severe hearing loss, which prevents people from understanding speech through just their hearing. They must rely on visual methods such as lip-reading or sign language to communicate. **Hearing loss** or **hard of hearing** refers to a loss that is not severe enough to interfere with hearing as the primary modality for understanding speech and learning (Milota et al., 1991). A hearing loss occurs when part of the hearing structure is malformed or malfunctions. While this affects hearing, it also may hinder a child's speech and language development, especially if this damage occurs prior to two years of age, the period of rapid language acquisition (Batshaw, 2000).

Hearing is measured with special equipment that is administered by a trained **audiologist.** The hearing loss is expressed in terms of **decibels (dBs).** Degrees of hearing loss are determined by measuring the softest sound that can be heard at three different frequencies, and then averaging these measurements (Bradshaw, 2000). With new technology, it is now possible to test newborn babies for hearing loss. Most states conduct newborn screening tests before the babies leave the hospital.

There are two types of hearing impairments classified according to their location in the hearing process. **Conductive loss** is when the outer or middle ear prevents sound from getting into the inner ear. This reduces the child's ability to hear speech sounds and is most often caused by an object lodged in the ear canal, excessive ear wax, or **otitis media** which is fluid in the ear. Most often this type of hearing loss can be corrected through surgery. **Sensorineural loss** occurs when there is damage to either the inner ear, the nerve to the brain stem or both. This type of loss is usually congenital, caused by high fevers or some medicines that are used. This type of loss cannot be treated surgically. A hearing aid is prescribed which makes sounds louder but they remain distorted and unclear to the child (Deiner, 1999).

One percent (1%) of all children have a persistent hearing loss. Of these losses, 40% are mild, 20% moderate, 20% severe, and 20% profound. A child with a **mild hearing loss** has trouble hearing distant sounds or soft speech. Their speech is usually normal. Those with a **moderate loss** have difficulty hearing even loud conversation. They usually have a limited vocabulary, errors in their speech and some abnormal voice quality. Children with **severe hearing loss** hear loud environmental sounds but not words. If this loss has occurred prior to age two, their language and speech does not develop spontaneously, however speech can be taught with amplification. Children with a **profound hearing loss** may hear some loud environmental sounds but hearing will not be their primary modality for learning as they will not comprehend speech (Batshaw, 2000). The effect of hearing loss on the development of speech and language development depends on the severity of the loss, the age of onset, the age when the loss was discovered, and the age when intervention occurs.

There are three main causes of deafness in infants: **genetic** which passed from parents to child, **diseases** such as German measles or meningitis, and **trauma** or injury. However, the cause of hearing loss in many children remains unknown (Milota et al., 1991). The causes of **acquired** hearing loss in children includes otitis media (middle ear infection), prenatal and postnatal infections, anoxia, prematurity, some antibiotics, and trauma. Ninety-five percent (95%) of all acquired hearing losses are due to middle ear infections (Batshaw, 2000).

Young children have a difficult time imagining what it would be like if you couldn't hear or if you could only hear some environmental sounds. Simulation activities can help children realize what it might be like. See Appendix D for suggested activities. Responses to children's questions might be: "He can't hear because his ears don't work like yours or mine." "The thing in his ear is part of his hearing aid. It makes sounds louder to help him hear." "Jimmy isn't able to say words so he 'talks' with his hands by signing." "Because his ears don't work, he wasn't able to hear and learn to say the words people were using." "No, you can't catch being deaf. Mindy was born this way." OR "Mindy was very sick when she was little and it caused her to lose some of her hearing."

Developmental Delay

Developmental delay is a term that includes a variety of disabilities that affect how a child grows and learns. While most infants and young children develop skills such as sitting and crawling at about the same age, some children develop much slower. Signs of a significant delay may become evident yet a specific diagnosis may not be clear. With the label of developmental delay, children are able to receive services without the concern of an unsure diagnosis or an inaccurate label. With early intervention, many at-risk children diagnosed as having a developmental delay will grow up without a disability, others will have a disability diagnosed by the time they are five or six years of age (Deiner, 1999).

People who have mental retardation are referred to as having a developmental delay. It is important to understand that even though persons with mental retardation have a developmental delay, not all people who have a developmental delay have mental retardation. Some common developmental delays are mental retardation, cerebral palsy, and autism.

Emotional and Behavioral Disorders

Emotional or behavioral disorders means an established pattern of one or more of the following emotional or behavioral responses: A) withdrawal or anxiety, depression, problems with mood, or feelings of self-worth, B) disordered thought processes with unusual behavior patterns and atypical communications styles, or C) aggression, hyperactivity or impulsivity.

The pattern of emotional or behavioral responses must adversely affect educational or developmental performance, including interpersonal, academic, vocational, or social skills; be significantly different from appropriate age, cultural, or ethnic norms; and be more than temporary, expected responses to stressful events in the environment.

To determine if the behavior is a disorder it's necessary to look at the length, severity, and unacceptableness of it. Behavior that is disturbed involves significant changes in the child's mood and behavior and is displayed across many situations and settings. These behaviors interfere with the child's overall learning and the development of interpersonal relationships and may also be harmful to the child or others (Deiner, 1999).

Some of the behaviors listed above are common for children during certain stages of development. When the behaviors appear during these expected times, they are considered normal behaviors. If the behaviors become excessive or persist beyond the expected age or developmental stage, the behaviors would be considered emotional or behavioral problems. Programming for children with emotional and behavioral problems include behavior management plans that can make the environment safe, secure and predictable for the child and his or her peers. **Behavior analysts** are trained to assess behavior and design intervention plans.

Children will question why a child behaves in a certain way. Explaining about the behavior without degrading the child is very important. For example, "David acts out when he is angry. He is working on ways to express his anger in school that are appropriate but it will take awhile for him to learn."

Attention Deficit Hyperactivity Disorder (ADHD). ADHD is not a disease, it is the way the brain works which includes a short attention span, impulsivity, distractibility and sometimes hyperactivity. Studies have shown that individuals with ADHD may have less chemical activity and blood flow in parts of the brain, which may explain these behaviors (Kajander, 1995). When children have these symptoms but do not have hyperactivity they are sometimes referred to as having **ADD**—attention deficit disorder. Children with ADD are often under diagnosed because usually they are not disruptive.

Children with ADHD seem to have little tolerance for frustration, often having rapid mood changes. Because of their short attention span, they appear to have random, erratic behavior and may "flit" about the environment. This combination of behaviors reduces the child's ability to engage in activities that promote learning (Peterson, 1987). An effective approach for working with children with ADHD is the use of behavior management techniques. These techniques build in structure, which these children lack, and help them remember what they should and should not do. The children learn they have to deal with the consequences of their behavior when it is inappropriate and receive reinforcement for behavior that is appropriate (Batshaw, 2000).

Children may ask about inappropriate behavior or behavioral outbursts. It's important to help children understand that the child with ADHD is working hard to act appropriately, the behavior is difficult to manage and it's the behavior we don't like, not the child.

Specific Learning Disability

The definition used nationwide is from Public Law 105-17 Individuals With Disabilities Education Act of 1997 (IDEA):

> 'Specific learning disability' means a disorder in one or more of the basic psychological processes involved in understanding or in using language, spoken or written, which may manifest itself in an imperfect ability to listen, think, speak, read, write, spell, or to do mathematical calculations. The term

includes conditions such as perceptual handicaps, brain injury, minimum brain dysfunction, dyslexia and developmental aphasia. The term does not include children who have learning problems which are primarily the result of visual, hearing or motor handicaps, of mental retardation, of emotional disturbance, or or environmental, cultural, or economic disadvantage.

Many of the descriptors of a learning disability are related to reading, writing, spelling and mathematics. Because of the criteria for learning disabilities and the assessment process that is used, it is not possible to qualify for a learning disability as a preschool child. However, some young children may have difficulty learning and exhibit patterns suspicious of a learning disability, which may be diagnosed as the child becomes older. The exact label isn't as important as understanding the child's learning problems and providing appropriate adaptations so the child can experience success in learning. At the present time a committee is looking at the definition and criteria of learning disability. The intent is to make some major changes.

Mental Retardation

The definition most widely used is from the American Association of Mental Deficiency. According to this definition, a person with mental retardation has the following: 1) significantly sub-average general intellectual functioning which is assessed by a standardized intelligence test, 2) impairment in adaptive behavior which includes functional skills for daily living which lead to personal independence and social responsibility, and 3) the age of onset occurred during the developmental years (i.e. between birth and 18 years).

There are three levels of retardation which generally indicate the type and intensity of services needed. **Mild** mental retardation occurs with an IQ 50–55 to 70–75. These children learn more slowly and may not be noticed during the preschool years. They tend to be immature and develop their language more slowly. Most often these individuals will be able to live independently and have a job after completing school. **Moderate** mental retardation is when the person has an IQ of 35–40 to 50–55. These children will have a significant delay in all areas of development. Their training focuses mostly on self-help and functional skills. In adulthood they usually live in supervised settings. People with **severe** mental retardation have an IQ of 20–25 to 35–40 and **profound** mental retardation have an IQ below 20 to 25. These children have severe delays, few communication skills and need intensive services (Deiner, 1999).

Characteristics that occur in children with mild mental retardation more often than children with normal development are: sensory and motor coordination disabilities, low tolerance for frustration, poor self-concept, short attention span, below average language ability, below average ability to generalize and conceptualize, and play interests younger than those of peers. It's unlikely that all of these characteristics would be present (Milota, et al., 1991).

Mental retardation affects a child's ability to learn, to understand and get along in the environment. Children who have mental retardation learn more slowly and may not be able to learn some of the things other children learn. Children may ask why another child is unable to do a specific task. Your answer might be; "Peter needs some more time at this activity before he's ready to move on to the next." OR "Peter learns, he just learns more slowly."

Down Syndrome. Down syndrome is present at birth. Children with Down syndrome can be identified by the **simian crease** in the palms of the hands and the "Asian" **eyefolds** as well as other physical anomalies. A genetic workup is done to confirm the diagnosis of Down syndrome. Children with Down syndrome are considered at risk as this condition is known to result in mental retardation, physical abnormalities, and delays in other areas of development such as speech and language, and motor development. In the past there were low expectations and negative self-fulfilling prophecies for individuals with Down syndrome. Today with early intervention and better medical and educational services, children with Down syndrome are functioning at increasingly higher levels in school and in the community.

Multiple Disabilities

Public Law defines multi-disabled as "those children with more than one serious disability (e.g. mental retardation and blind, deaf and blind), the combination of which causes such severe educational problems that they cannot be accommodated in special education programs solely for one of the impairments" (Milota, et al., 1991, p. 84). Children with multiple disabilities have very special needs and present a great challenge for educators and parents. Educational programs are designed with a team of parents and specially trained professionals who can address the variety of special needs.

Physical Disabilities

Physical impairments are classified according to three criteria: 1) the severity, 2) the clinical type, and 3) the parts of the body that are affected.

Mild impairment refers to children who are able to walk (with or without aids), communicate to make their wants and needs known, and use their arms. Their problems are mostly with fine motor tasks. They can do what most other children can do with appropriate adaptations. **Moderate** impairment refers to children who need help with movement and assistance with self-help skills and communication. **Severe** impairment refers to children who are usually unable to move around without the use of a wheelchair and need considerable assistance with self-help skills and communication. **Occupational therapists** work with children in the development of fine motor skills which includes eating and dressing. **Physical therapists** work with children in the development of gross motor skills including mobility with the use of aids as is needed (i.e. wheelchair, leg braces).

Children will ask about the boy or girl who uses aids. They may be fearful of "catching" whatever the child has. Some might be curious how the equipment works, others may be frightened. Whenever possible, let the children examine the equipment and even try it out, always with the permission of the child who uses the equipment, his or parents and with close supervision. Keeping in mind the cognitive levels of the children asking questions, help them understand the disability and why the equipment is being used. This information will help reduce or eliminate fears they may have. You could use comments such as: "Joey uses a wheelchair because his legs don't work so he can't walk and using the chair is how he gets around." "No, Joey's legs don't hurt." "Joey makes his wheelchair move by pushing a switch because his hands aren't strong enough to move the wheels."

Cerebral Palsy. Cerebral palsy is caused by damage to the brain before it is mature. It is a non-progressive condition and involves various types of impairment in fine and gross motor development. **Anoxia** or lack of oxygen to the brain and brain injury at birth are the most frequent causes of cerebral palsy (Deiner, 1999).

Cerebral palsy is classified according to seven different types: 1) **spastic**—loss of voluntary muscle control is the most common type. Muscles are tight (hypertonic) from too much muscle tone; 2) **athetosis**—excessive involuntary, purposeless movements of the limbs; 3) **rigid**—severe spasticity; the affected limbs are rigid and extremely difficult to bend; 4) **ataxia**—lack of balance, uncoordinated movement and lack of a sense of position in space; 5) **tremor**—shakiness of the affected limbs apparent only when a specific movement occurs; and 6) **hypotonia**—lack of muscle tone and inability to move or maintain postural control; child is floppy (Peterson, 1989).

The following terms are used to indicate which limbs are affected: **Hemiplegia**: one side of the body is involved; **Diplegia**: legs more involved than arms: **Quadriplegia**: all four limbs are involved; **Paraplegia**: only the legs; **Monoplegia**: only one limb; **Triplegia**: three limbs are involved (Deiner, 1999).

Cerebral palsy is no longer considered to be just a motor problem rather a multidimensional disorder. Neurological, cognitive and perceptual dysfunction are the underlying and associated impairments. All areas need to be considered during intervention (Peterson, 1989).

Spina Bifida. Spina bifida is a congenital malformation of the spinal cord that is present at birth. The most common form and most serious causing lasting effects is **myelomenigocele**. The spinal cord does not close and protrudes looking like a bubble or sac on the baby's back. This is surgically closed shortly after birth. In recent years, some doctors have been successful operating in utero to make the closure. This has resulted in less severe complications for the child.

The opening can occur anywhere along the spinal cord from the head to the lower end, however, most occur toward the lower end. The severity of the condition depends upon the location of the opening on the spine. The higher the opening, the greater the number of body parts affected. A weakness or complete paralysis of the legs, feet, bladder, and bowels, each affected in varying degrees is possible. Often there is no feeling in the buttocks and legs. When the opening is higher on the spinal cord it can affect bowel and bladder control. A high percentage of these children also develop **hydrocephalus** also known as water on the brain. This requires a **shunt**, inserted surgically, to drain the fluid. This surgery is usually done the first week after the birth. There can be some cognition problems as a result of the hydrocephalus. (Milota, et al., 1991). In recent years doctors have recommended that pregnant women add folic acid to their diet. This is based on the results of studies of women who took **folic acid** during the first twelve weeks of pregnancy and had a significant decrease in babies born with neural tube defects (Liptak, 1997).

Loss of Limb. Children can be missing an arm or leg as a result of accidents, infections, or diseases such as cancer. In addition, sometimes children are born without a limb as a result of congenital malformations. Preschool children are generally not fitted for an artificial limb, as physicians prefer to wait until they are older and better able to learn how to use the device (Peterson, 1989). As children get older, most are fitted with a **prosthesis,** which is an artificial hand, arm, foot or leg. With therapy, children can learn most self-help skills and become very independent at home and school. Other children will be curious and want to know how the limb was lost and how the artificial limb works. The child with the prosthesis can be invited to share how the prosthesis works, always make it a choice (in private), in case the child doesn't feel comfortable sharing. Explain to children that the child was born without a limb, or the child was in an accident. But remember only share the information with the children that you have permission to share.

Dwarfism or Short-Limbed. The most common type of Dwarfism is **achondroplastic dwarf.** This is caused by a genetic abnormality that affects the skeletal system (Riggs, 2001). Dwarfism occurs when there is an abnormality of the bones causing all of the long bones to be short and stubby resulting in the child having shortened arms and legs with a disproportionately large head. While motor development is often delayed, cognitive development is usually not impaired (Bradshaw, 2000).

Dwarfism does not limit a person's life span nor does it affect their intellectual capabilities. However, persons with dwarfism are susceptible to physiological problems relating to the skeletal and nervous systems. The Little People of America is a support group for people with dwarfism (Kuklin, 1986).

Children will ask why someone is shorter or looks differently. Remind children that everyone grows differently, we all look different and that is okay. When a question is asked about a child with dwarfism you might say: "Annie's body grows differently than ours so she will never grow to be tall." "No, you can't catch dwarfism, Annie was born this way." "Annie will be short but will be able to do many of the same things you do."

Speech and Language Impairments

Speech problems exist when children have difficulty with the production of sounds which includes the planned shaping of sounds into specific vowel and consonant utterances (Deiner, 1999). Speech disorders generally come under three types: 1) **articulation** disorders are irregularities in the production of vowels and consonants, 2) **voice** disorders are problems with appropriate pitch, volume or voice quality, and 3) **fluency** disorders are irregularities in the flow or rhythm of speech (Peterson, 1989). Language problems exist when children have difficulty understanding what others say, which is **receptive** language, or have difficulty expressing ideas in words and sentences, which is **expressive** language.

Speech and language problems can be present without any other type of disability or in combination with a number of disabilities. Many children with speech and language problems receive intervention in early childhood and elementary school and end up without any disability. Other children have such severe speech and language disorders that they cannot learn to speak and manual communication (i.e. sign language, finger spelling) or technology become the preferred methods of communication. For those who are unable to sign, communication boards and microcomputers present other options.

Children will ask why another child is unable to speak. Give the children as much information as needed depending on their cognition. Let children know there are other ways to communicate. If a classmate uses sign language, be sure that the teacher has all of the children learn some signing so peers are able to communicate with each other.

Cleft-lip-Palate. Cleft lip is a narrow division in the lip and cleft palate is a narrow division in the roof of the mouth. These occur when two parts of the lip or palate fail to join properly. A cleft palate leaves a gap between the mouth and nasal cavity, which may vary in size and involvement. Children with this birth defect have difficulty articulating some speech sounds. Corrective surgery is done to close the division in the lip and the gap between the mouth and nasal cavity, which will reduce or eliminate speech difficulties. Many of these children need to have therapy to correct their speech (Deiner, 1999).

Elective Mutism. Elective mutism occurs when a child who has the ability to talk chooses not to speak. The child elects to be mute. This is an emotional problem and usually occurs when a child is anxious or fearful. Professionals would need to evaluate and work with a child who is electively mute.

Stuttering. Stuttering is a **fluency disorder**, which is defined as an abnormal flow of speech that is interrupted by repetitions, hesitations and prolongations of some sounds and syllables. Normal dysfluency does occur between the ages of two and five years. As children learn language rapidly they sometimes struggle to say the correct word. Attention should not be given to these children. Give them time to speak without any correction or reaction. Much of this is developmental and will disappear over time. For children who continue to have dysfluency problems beyond early childhood, Speech and Language therapists should conduct assessment and intervention. Therapy can help children overcome some stuttering problems (Deiner, 1999).

References

American Psychiatric Association. (2000). *Diagnostic and statistical manual of mental disorders* (4ᵗʰ ed.). Washington, DC: American Psychiatric Association.

Bailey, D. (1992). Guidelines for authors. *Journal of Early Intervention, 15*(1), 118-119.

Batshaw, M. (2000). *Children with disabilities* (4ᵗʰ Ed.). Baltimore, MA: Paul H. Brookes.

Batshaw, M. (2002). *Children with disabilities* (5ᵗʰ Ed.). Baltimore, MA: Paul H. Brookes.

Batshaw, M., & Perret, Y. (1992). *Children with disabilities: A medical primer (3ʳᵈ Ed.)* Baltimore, MA: Paul H. Brookes.

Blaska, J. (1993). The power of language: Speak and write using "person first." In M. Nagle (Ed.), *Perspectives on disability* (pp. 25-32). Palto Alto, CA: Health Markets Research.

Children, Families & Learning (CFL). (1997). *Autism and Related Pervasive Developmental Disorders.* St. Paul, MN: Metro ECSU/Metro SPLISE Project.

Deiner, P. (1999). *Resources for teaching children with diverse abilities (3rd Ed.).* New York: Harcourt Brace Jovanovich College Publishers.

Derman-Sparks, L. (1989). *Anti-bias curriculum.* Washington, DC: NAEYC.

Hadley, R. & Brodwin, M. (1988). Language about people with disabilities. *Journal of Counseling and Development,* 67, 147-149.

Hallahan, D., & Kauffman, J. (1994). *Exceptional children: Introduction to special education.* Englewood Cliffs, NJ: Prentice-Hall.

Individuals with Disabilities Education Act (1997). Pub. L. No.105-17 111 Stat. 37-157. 20 U.S.C. 1400.

Kailes, J. (1985). Watch your language, please! *Journal of Rehabilitation, 51*(1), 68-69.

Kajander, R. (1995). *Living with ADHD: A practical guide to coping with attention deficit hyperactivity disorder.* Minneapolis, MN: Park Nicollet Medical Foundation.

Kuklin, S. (1986). *Thinking big.* New York: Lothrop, Lee & Shepard Books.

Larson, D. (1996). *Mayo clinic family health book (2ⁿᵈ Ed.).* New York: William Morrow and Company, Inc.

Liptak, G. (1997). Neural tube defects. In M.L. Batshaw (Ed.), *Children with disabilities (4th Ed.)*, pp. 529-553. Baltimore: Brookes Publishing.

Milota, C., Goldberg, M., Goldberg, P., Skaalen, J., Dahl, L., Jordan, D., Binkard, B., Edmunds, P., Leaf, R., & Steeber, B. (1991). *Count me in: Resource manual on disabilities.* Minneapolis, MN: PACER Center, Inc.

PACER. (1989, September). It's the 'person first'—Then the disability. *Pacesetter.* Minneapolis, MN: Parent Advocacy Coalition for Educational Rights.

Perske, R. (1988). *Circle of friends.* Nashville, TN: The Pathenon Press.

Peterson, N. (1987). *Early intervention for handicapped and at risk children.* Denver, CO: Love Publishing Co.

Riggs, Stephanie. (2001). *Never Sell Yourself Short.* Morton Grove, IL: Albert Whitman & Co.

Tyler, L. (1990). Communicating about people with disabilities: Does the language we use make a difference? *TheBulletin of the Association for Business Communication,* 53(3), 65-67.

CHAPTER FIVE

Annotated Bibliography: Children's Books That Include Characters with Disabilities or Chronic Illness

INTRODUCTION

An annotated bibliographic entry is provided for each book in this collection. Each entry contains the following information: author, title, illustrator, publisher, year of publication, ISBN number, number of pages, fiction or nonfiction, grade level, disability or illness, rating, category, annotation and theme/s.

<u>Author, Title, Illustrator</u>. The books are listed in alphabetical order by author. Sometimes parents or professionals may be more familiar with a book by its title. To assist in this type of search, the books have also been alphabetized by title. See Appendix B for this listing. Following the author's name is the book's title and illustrator. This collection of books consists of picture books with the illustrations an integral part of the story. Thus, the illustrators and photographers are identified by name.

<u>Publisher, Year Of Publication, ISBN</u>. Next is the publisher and the year of publication. The majority of these books having been published since 1985. Most of them can be located through your library, its loan system or your local bookstore. However, in the event you have difficulty finding a particular book, you may contact the publisher directly. See Appendix E for a list of publishers of the children's books in this collection. The ISBN number, which is the book's identification number, is included for each book. If you choose to order any of the books, it makes it easier when you have this number.

<u>Pages, Fiction or Nonfiction, Grade Level</u>. The number of pages is identified, whether the book is fiction or nonfiction, and the grade level for which the book is recommended. This information was obtained from the publisher or published book lists and will be helpful when selecting books appropriate for the age and developmental level of the children who will be using the books.

Keep in mind that some children's books may be used appropriately with children older or younger than are recommended. Books that have lots of words may be indicated for older children but can be used for younger ones as well if you tell the story while looking at the illustrations. Books may be used for children older than indicated when a book gives a particular message and it is used to generate discussion. In addition, children's books can be used very successfully in parent groups to introduce topics or ideas that will then be discussed. Many children's books contain wonderful messages which allows them to be used successfully in a number of ways.

<u>Disability Or Illness</u>. The disability or chronic illness is then listed. In the event that more than one disability or illness is present in the story, all are identified. Any aids that are used in the story or illustrations are also listed (i.e. wheelchair, cane). For physical disabilities, the type of disability is listed if it's available and for chronic illnesses, the type of illness is identified.

<u>Book Rating</u>. Each book was given one of three ratings based on the results of the review using the *Images and Encounters Profile* (See Appendix A). In the annotations, strengths are mentioned and concerns described when they are present.

	Ratings
OUTSTANDING	****
VERY GOOD	***
FAIR	**

<u>Book Categories</u>. The last part of the reference is the category of the book which is determined by the way in which the author presents the disability or illness and how it is incorporated into the story. The books fit into one of three categories:

Category A: Books provide factual information about a disability or chronic illness. These books do not have plot development. The intent of the book is to gain information about a particular disability or illness and may be used at home or in school.

Category B: Books provide information about a disability or chronic illness in a story format with character development and a plot. The person with the disability or illness is integral to the storyline. The intent is to learn about the disability or illness or related issues (i.e. attitudes, feelings). These stories provide an entertaining or interesting way for children to learn about a disability or illness. Books in this category are useful for children with and without disabilities or illnesses and can be used in home and school environments.

Category C: Books provide stories that have a character with a disability or chronic illness. The character may be integral or peripheral to the storyline. The story does not provide specific information about a disability or illness. However, the reader may incidentally gain some information and insight. The intent of the story is enjoyment. The author has included a character with a disability or illness to add diversity to the story. Blaska refers to these stories as inclusionary literature. For children without disabilities or illness, the stories expose them to a variety of people similar to those in our society, and opens the door for questions and discussion. Children are able to see what individuals with disabilities and illnesses can do and how they are like themselves yet different. This is a very natural way for children to learn about people with disabilities and illnesses who are integrated into our society. For children with disabilities and chronic illness, stories like these allow them to see themselves as part of the mainstream society. This inclusion can provide a boost to their self-esteem. Inclusionary stories can be used in both home and school settings.

<u>Annotation</u>. The annotation briefly summarizes the storyline. Strengths and concerns are highlighted based on the criteria that were used in the review process. See Appendix A for the Images and Encounters Profile.

<u>Theme Or Unit</u>. Each entry ends with the theme(s) or unit(s) into which the book can be appropriately incorporated based on the theme analysis. When a book is appropriate to use with more than one theme, multiple themes are listed.

A curriculum theme is a general idea or concept to which a variety of materials relate. All of the activities for the day or several days reflect the chosen theme including the selection of books.

Annotated Bibliography:
Books That Include Characters
With Disabilities or Chronic Illness

Ratings	Categories
OUTSTANDING ****	A—Information About Disability or Illness
VERY GOOD ***	B—Story About Disability or Illness
FAIR **	C—Story with Character[s] with Disability or Illness

Addabbo, Carole. *Dina the Deaf Dinosaur,* **illus. by Valetine. Hannacroix Creek Books, 1998. ISBN 1-889262-04-8 [26 p]. Nonfiction, Gr. PS-3. Disability: Deaf. (***) (Cat B).**

Dina is a dinosaur who is deaf and runs away from home because her parents won't learn sign language. She befriends animals in the woods who sign with her. In the end, the parents are reunited with Dina and they all use sign language. This is a good story for families to help them understand the importance of signing in order to communicate with their child. This book has the appearance of a self-published book.

Themes or Units: Dinosaurs; Families; Sign Language

Adler, David A. *A Picture Book of Helen Keller,* **illus. John & Alexandra Wallner. Holiday House, 1990. ISBN 0-8234-0818-3 [29 p]. Nonfiction, Gr. K-2. Disability: Blind and deaf. (***) (Cat B).**

This is a short story about Helen Keller's life, how Anne Sullivan was her teacher and ultimately taught Helen to read Braille. The story gives hope for the future to others who are blind. A good story to show children that persons who are blind can still live productive lives.

Themes or Units: Senses; Sense of Touch; We Are Alike, We Are Different.

Aldape, Virginia Totorica. *Nicole's Story,* **photographs by Lillian S. Kossacoff. Lerner Publications, 1996. ISBN 0-8225-2578-X [40 p]. Nonfiction, Gr. 1-4. Illness: Juvenile rheumatoid arthritis (wheelchair, walking sticks). (***)(Cat A).**

This books provides complete information about juvenile rheumatoid arthritis. In addition, an eight year old girl tells about her life with this disease. She describes the many challenges she faces and how she copes every day. This story does a good job of balancing what this girl can and cannot do. She wants everyone to know that she is "just a kid." This is a good resource for this disease.

Themes or Units: Health.

Alden, Joan. *A Boy's Best Friend*, illus. by Catherine Hopkins. Alyson Publications, 1992. ISBN 1-55583-203-2 [28 p]. Fiction, Gr. PS-2. Illness: Asthma. (****) (Cat B).

Willy wants a dog for his birthday but every year he is told that he can't have one because of his asthma. This year his special gift is LeDogg, a wooly stuffed dog with Willy's name on his collar. Willy takes LeDogg everywhere, including school where he is teased by bullies who throw LeDogg up into a tree. Some magic happens and Willy is able to get his LeDogg down. All children would enjoy this story but it would be special for children like Willy who aren't able to have pets.

Themes or Units: Families; Fantasy & Imagination; Health; Pet Animals.

Alexander, Sally Hobart. *Mom Can't See Me*, photographs by George Ancona. Macmillan Publishing Co., 1990. ISBN 0-02-700401-5 [45 p]. Nonfiction, Gr. K-3. Disability: Blind. (****) (Cat A)

A young girl tells what it is like to have a mother who is blind. Leslie explains what she and her mother do together such as canoeing, dance lessons, shopping and camping. Leslie explains that her mother is a writer and reads using Braille. Humorous events are also described such as the time her mother hugged a man at the airport who sounded like her brother! This is a very positive story as it points out all of the things this mother can do as well as the adaptations she makes because of her blindness. The author does not use "person first" language (i.e."handicapped person" and "blind parent"). This is a very realistic and heartwarming story.

Themes or Units: Families; Families at Work (writer); The Sense of Sight; Sense of Touch; We Are Alike, We Are Different.

Alexander, Sally Hobart. *Mom's Best Friend*, illus. by George Ancona. Macmillan Publishing Co., 1992. ISBN 0-02-700393-0 [45 p]. Nonfiction, Gr. K-3. Disability: Blind. (****) (Cat A)

This story is about Sally and her experiences as she receives training to have a new guide dog. Black and white photographs allow the reader to see the training episodes that prepare the guide dog who will eventually be able to work with Sally. In the end, the entire family gains a pet. This is a very informative and sensitive story that will help children understand blindness and the use of guide dogs. It promotes a positive image as Sally is shown being independent and capable.

Themes or Units: Pet Animals; Sense of Sight.

Allen, Anne. *Sports for the Handicapped*. Walker Publishing Co., 1981. ISBN 0-8027-6436-3 [78 p]. Nonfiction, Gr. 1-3. Disability: Physical, blind, mental retardation, deaf. (***) (Cat A)

The introduction provides a short history of people with disabilities participating in sports. Each chapter describes one of six sports in which persons with disabilities participate: skiing, wheelchair basketball, swimming, track and field, football, and horseback riding. Most participants have physical disabilities, however, blind, mental retardation, and deaf are also represented. The emphasis is on what individuals with disabilities can do and could provide hope to children with disabilities that they, too, may one day participate. The story does not use "person first" language.

Themes or Units: Sports.

Althea. *I Have Diabetes*, illus. by Angela Owen. Dinosaur Publications, 1991. ISBN 0-851-22809-7 [30 p]. Nonfiction, K-3. Chronic Illness: Diabetes. (****) (Cat A)

This is a story about a young girl who has diabetes. The reader learns about diabetes and the human body's need for insulin. The young girl is very independent giving herself her own shots, testing her blood and staying overnight with friends. This is an excellent book for helping children learn about diabetes. The story promotes a positive image and stresses the attitude of "one of us."

Themes or Units: Health.

Althea. *I Have Epilepsy*, illus. by Nicola Spoor. Dinosaur Publications, 1993. ISBN 0-85122-818-6 [31 p]. Nonfiction, Gr. K-3. Illness: Epilepsy. (**) (Cat A).

This is a story about a little boy who has epilepsy and is told from his perspective. This book was first published in England so they refer to the seizures as fits and refer to his mother as mum, which are terms used in England. Complete information is provided to help the reader understand what it is like to have epilepsy. The story is positive as it does tell what the little boy can do as well as his limitations.

Themes or Units: Health.

Amadeo, Diane M. *There's A Little Bit Of Me In Jamey*, illus. by Judith Friedman. Albert Whitman & Co., 1989. ISBN 0-8-75-7854-1 [32 p]. Fiction, Gr. 1-4. Chronic Illness: Cancer (bone morrow transplant). (****) (Cat B)

Brian wakes up and finds that his little brother, who has leukemia had become very ill during the night and was taken to the hospital. Jamey is very sick and needs a bone morrow transplant. The only possible donor is Brian who wants to donate but is scared. With assurance from his parents, he donates his bone morrow. Afterwards Brian's hip hurts a little but he doesn't mind because now a little bit of him is in Jamey. This is a very moving story, sensitively written. The warm pencil sketchings add to the beauty of this story.

Themes or Units: Brothers & Sisters; Dentists, Doctors, Nurses & Hospitals; Feelings; Giving & Sharing; Health.

Amenta, Charles A. *Russell is Extra Special: A Book About Autism for Children*, photographs by author. Magination Press, 1992. ISBN 0-945354-44-4 [27 p]. Nonfiction, Gr. Ps-2. Disability: Autism. (****) (Cat A)

Russell who has autism lives with his two brothers, his mom and dad. The story describes what it is like to have autism by talking about Russell, his behaviors, what he likes and dislikes, and how he plays and communicates. This is an excellent book for children to learn about autism. While it discusses Russell's behaviors and his many challenges, it also points out what he can do and clearly shows Russell as an important member of his family. The story has black and white photographs. The author does not use "person first" language.

Themes or Units: Families; We Are Alike, We Are Different.

Amer, Kim, & Brill, Marlene. *Short Mort and the Big Bully*, illus. by Lous. American Association. For the Care of Children's Health, 1996. ISBN 0-937821-93-4 [22 p]. Fiction, Gr. 1-5. Disability: Physical (growth deficiency). (***) (Cat B).

Mort was very, very short for his age. It was difficult at school to be so short and one of the kids bullied him by calling him names. His parents have him checked by a doctor and find that in all other ways he is healthy. The story describes his challenges and how he handles the bully with the help of his teachers. This is an important story as there are not many books about children who have growth problems.

Themes or Units: Feelings; Friends at School; We Are Alike, We Are Different.

Ancona, George and Ancona, Mary Beth. *Handtalk Zoo*, **photographs by Maureen Galvani. Macmillan, 1989. ISBN 0-02-700801-0 [28 p]. Nonfiction, Gr. PS-1. Disability: Deaf. (★★★★) (Cat B)**

This story shows Mary Beth and a group of children as they visit the zoo. The children sign and finger spell the names of the animals and places that they visit. Vibrant colored photographs capture the fun the children are having. The story demonstrates how all children can enjoy using sign language or finger spelling to express themselves.

Themes or Units: The Sense of Sight; Sign Language; Zoo animals.

Arnold, Caroline. *A Guide Dog Puppy Grows Up*, **photographs by Richard Hewett. Harcourt Brace Jovanovich, 1991. ISBN 0-15-232657-X [48 p]. Nonfiction, Gr. 1-3. Disability: Blind. (★★★★) (Cat B)**

This book tells the story of how a guide dog is selected, socialized and trained. Honey, a golden retriever puppy lives with a 4-H family for 15 months to be socialized and then undergoes two years of training at the guide dog school. The final portion of the training takes place with the dog's future partner who is bind. During the graduation ceremony, the family who socialized the puppy, passes the leash to the dog's new owner. This book provides interesting, factual information about training guide dogs that children would enjoy. "Person first" language is not used.

Themes or Units: Giving & Sharing; Pet Animals; Sense of Sight; We Are Alike, We Are Different.

Aseltine, Lorraine, Mueller, Evelyn, & Tait, Nancy. *I'm Deaf and It's Okay*, **illus. by Helen Cogancherry. Albert Whitman, 1986. ISBN 0-8075-3472-2 [34 p]. Fiction, Gr. K-4. Disability: Deaf. (★★★★) (Cat B).**

This is a story about a young boy who is deaf. He uses aids so he can hear a little. The story describes the many feelings he experiences throughout the day at school and when he spends time with friends. A teenage boy who is also deaf befriends him and gives him hope for the future. A very realistic account of what it is like to be deaf.

Themes or Units: Feelings; Friends at School.

Atkinson, Mary. *Why Do Some People Use Wheelchairs? Questions Children Ask About Disabled People,* photographs by multiple photographers. DK Publishing, 1997. ISBN 0-7894-2057-0 [16 p]. Nonfiction, Gr. K-3. Disability: Variety of disabilities. (***) (Cat A).

This book answers the "Why" question about a variety of disabilities and illnesses. Photographs show children and adults using a wheelchair, reading Braille, walking with a guide dog, using an inhaler, etc. A good book to promote a discussion about disabilities and chronic illness. It presents so much information that the entire book may be overwhelming for a young child. The story does not use "person first" language.

Themes or Units: We Are Alike, We Are Different.

Bahan, Ben & Dannis, Joe. *My ABC Signs of Animal Friends,* illus. by Patricia Pearson. DawnSign Press, 1994. ISBN 0-915035-31-6 [26 p]. Nonfiction, Gr. PS-2. Disability: Deaf (sign language). (****) (Cat A).

This is a cute alphabet book of animal signs. Each page presents one letter of the alphabet and a hand showing the sign for that letter. In addition, an animal whose name begins with the letter shows how to make the sign. The signs are represented clearly so that children could learn signing from the pictures.

Themes or Units: Alphabet; Sign Language; Wild Birds & Animals; Zoo Animals.

Baker, Pamela J. *My First Book of Sign,* illus. by Patricia Bellan Gillen. Kendall Green Publications, 1986. ISBN 0-930323-20-3 [75 p]. Fiction, Gr. PS-3. Disability: Deaf (sign language). (**) (Cat A).

The signs in this book follow the alphabet. For each letter, there are several pictures of items or actions that begin with that letter. An illustration of a child showing how to sign is next to each item. In addition, there is a section in the back of the book with descriptions of each sign. The illustration for horse shows a child dressed as a Native American sitting on the horse and demonstrating the sign for horse which promotes a stereotype. Otherwise, the illustrations are clear and represent a good selection of items and actions.

Themes or Units: Alphabet; Sign Language.

Barrett, Mary Brigid. *Sing To The Stars*, illlus. by Sandra Speidel. Little, Brown & Co., 1994. ISBN 0-316-08224-4 [30 p]. Fiction, Gr. PS-3. Disability: Blind. (****) (Cat C)

Young Ephram is taking violin lessons. On his way home, he sees his neighbor, Mr. Washington, walking his guide dog. Later he discovers that Mr. Washington is a famous pianist but hasn't touched a piano since becoming blind. Ephram convinces Mr. Washington to play music with him at the neighborhood get-together. This is a heart-warming story with African-American characters. Pastel illustrations help set the mood and promote a positive image.

Themes or Units: Friendship; We Are Alike, We Are Different.

Beatty, Monica Driscoll. *My Sister Rose Has Diabetes*, illus. by Kathy Parkinson. Health Press, 1997. ISBN 0-929173-27-9 [27 p]. Fiction, Gr. 1-4. Illness: Diabetes. (***) (Cat B).

This is a story about ten-year-old Rose who has diabetes. It describes her concerns and feelings about diabetes management, which are the same for most boys and girls. The story is told by her brother who is in seventh grade. He describes his feelings and how her illness has impacted their family. This is a good story to help children learn about diabetes. The story does stress that Rose is a "regular kid."

Themes or Units: Dentists, Doctors, Nurses & Hospitals; Feelings; Health.

Bergman, Thomas. *Going Places: Children Living with Cerebral Palsy*, photographs by author. Gareth Stevens Children's Books, 1991. ISBN 0-8368-0199-7 [41 p]. Nonfiction, Gr. PS-3. Disability: Cerebral palsy (wheelchair) and deaf (signing). (****) (Cat A).

Mathias is a six-year-old boy with cerebral palsy. Mathias has additional challenges, as he is also deaf and learning sign language. The story points out the importance of technology as Mathias practices on a computer and becomes more independent as he moves around in his new electric wheelchair. This is an excellent book for helping children gain an accurate understanding of cerebral palsy. Black and white photographs give the reader a clear picture of daily events in Mathias's life.

The book has a short section containing answers to questions most often asked about cerebral palsy.

Themes or Units: We Are Alike, We Are Different.

Bergman, Thomas. *We Laugh, We Love, We Cry: Children Living with Mental Retardation,* **photographs by author. Gareth Stevens Inc., 1989. ISBN 1-55532-914-4 [45 p]. Nonfiction, Gr. K-3. Disability: Mental retardation. (****) (Cat A)**

This book is about 5-year-old Asa and her sister, six-year-old Anna. Both children have mental retardation with some physical problems. Neither can speak but are learning to communicate by using sign language. Photographs at school, play and home depict daily events but focus mostly on the girl's therapy. It's important for children to understand that many persons with mental retardation are able to speak. Bergman is Sweden's best-known children's photographer and has captured the feelings of these little girls, their parents and the professionals who work with them.

Themes or Units: We Are Alike, We Are Different.

Berry, Steve. *The Boy Who Wouldn't Speak,* **illus. by Deirdre Betteridge. Firefly Books, 1992. ISBN 1-55037-230-0 [29 p]. Fiction, Gr. PS-3. Disability: Speech and language. (***) (Cat B).**

Owen is a young boy who doesn't talk. No one can figure out why. His mother keeps saying he will talk when he is ready. Meanwhile two giants move into his neighborhood. They are very good to Owen, but no one else visits the giants. One day neighbors come to tell the giants to leave because they are afraid of them. Owen takes this opportunity to talk so he can tell the neighbors wonderful things about the giants. This is a fantasy story that could be used when talking with children about selective mutism.

Themes or Units: Fantasy & Imagination; We Are Alike, We Are Different.

Booth, Barbara. Mandy, **illus. by Jim Lamarche. Lothrop, Lee & Shepard Bks., 1991. ISBN 0-688-10338-3 [31 p]. Fiction, Gr. PS-2. Disability: Deaf. (****) (Cat C)**

Even though Mandy is deaf, she and her grandmother do many things together. During their walk in the woods, Grandmother loses a small pin that is very special. Mandy sees her Grandma's tears. With lightening in the distance, Mandy goes out to look for the pin. She returns to a worried Grandma who is very grateful that Mandy found her pin. This story shows a wonderful relationship between a grandmother and her granddaughter. It promotes a positive image by showing all the fun they have together. The illustrations are outstanding and capture the emotions of the story.

<u>Themes or Units</u>: Day & Night; Grandmothers & Grandfathers.

Borden, Louise. *Good Luck, Mrs. K.!* illus. by Adam Gustavson. McElderry Books, 1999. ISBN 0-689-82147-6 [29 p]. Fiction, Gr. 1-4. Illness: Cancer. (****) (Cat C).

Mrs. K is a third grade teacher. The story describes all of the fun things she does with her students and how special she makes them all feel. Then Mrs. K. gets sick with cancer. The students and their substitute teacher write Mrs. K. notes. Before school is out for the year, the students have a party and Mrs. K. comes as a surprise! This is a realistic story that can help children understand illness.

<u>Themes or Units</u>: Community Workers/Occupations; Friends at School; Health.

Borton, Lady. *Junk Pile!* illus. by Kimberly Bulcken Root. Philomel Books, 1997. ISBN 0-399-22728-8 [29 p]. Fiction, Gr. K-3. Disability: Physical (wheelchair). (***) (Cat C).

Jamie was too young for school but she helps her brother get to and from the school bus by pushing his wheelchair. Jamie's father runs a junk yard, and with Jamie's wonderful imagination she makes flowers and other creative things out of junk parts. The new boy on the bus teases her, but when the bus breaks down, it is Jamie who retrieves the parts to fix it. Finally, the new boy gets to know Jamie and enjoys her imagination. One major theme of this story is when people live differently they are sometimes judged. It is a strength of the story that the author built in disability as well.

<u>Themes or Units</u>: Fantasy & Imagination; Friendship; Homes & Neighborhoods; We Are Alike, We Are Different.

Bouwkamp, Julie A. *Hi, I'm Ben! . . . And I've Got a Secret,* photographs by author. Band of Angels Press, 1995. ISBN 0-96477137-4-8 [23 p]. Nonfiction, Gr. PS-2. Disability: Down syndrome. (***) (Cat B).

This is a small book with photographs and limited text. It could be used with young children in early childhood or families of children born with Down syndrome. The story points out that children with Down syndrome play an active part within the community. The story describes all of the things that Ben does and does not like to do and not until page nineteen does the reader find out his secret—he has Down syndrome.

Themes or Units: We Are Alike, We Are Different.

Bove, Linda. *Sesame Street Sign Language ABC*, illus. by Tom Cooke & photographs by Anita & Steve Shevett. Random House, 1985. ISBN 0-394-87516-8 [28 p]. Nonfiction, Gr. PS-2. Disability: Deaf (sign language). (****) (Cat A).

This is an alphabet book of signing. For each letter of the alphabet there are illustrations of items that begin with that letter. There is a photograph of Linda Bove signing the letter plus additional words that begin with that letter. This is a fun book to learn about signing the alphabet. The colorful illustrations would keep it interesting for young children.

Themes or Units: Alphabet; Sign Language.

Brearley, Sue. *Talk to Me*, photographs by Jenny Matthews. A & C Black Limited, 1996. ISBN 0-7136-4410-9 [25 p]. Nonfiction, PS-2. Disability: Speech and language. (***) (Cat A).

This is a small book that describes the many reasons why a child may have trouble speaking. The book looks at alternative ways young children might communicate when they are unable to speak. The book was published in London.

Themes or Units: We Are Alike, We Are Different.

Brink, David. *David's Story: A Book About Surgery*, photographs by author. Lerner Books, 1996. ISBN 0-8225-2577-1 [30 p]. Nonfiction, Gr. 2-4. Disability: Facial malformation. (****) (Cat A).

David is born with a malformation of his nose and eyes. The doctors do surgery for facial reconstruction. This story describes the entire process of planning for the reconstruction, preparation for surgery, the surgery itself, and how he looks and feels afterwards. The author does a wonderful job of writing about this sensitive topic. David's friends realize that even though he looks different, he is the same David inside.

Themes or Units: Dentists, Doctors, Nurses & Hospitals; Friendship; Health.

Brown, Tricia. *Someone Special, Just Like You*, photographs by Fran Ortiz. Henry Holt & Company, 1984. ISBN 0-8050-0481-5 [55 p]. Nonfiction, Gr. PS-2. Disabilities: Hearing, vision, physical, & Down syndrome. (****) (Cat A)

Beautiful black and white photographs of children in preschool settings introduce what it is like to have a visual or hearing impairment, a physical disability or mental retardation. The message is that children with disabilities are children first who enjoy doing usual things like eating ice cream, singing, dancing, going down a slide, blowing bubbles, etc. The story emphasizes what children can do even though they have different capabilities and may experience life a bit differently. The photographs include children from diverse cultures.

<u>Themes or Units</u>: Friends at School; Friendship; Safety; We Are Alike, We Are Different.

Bunnett, Rochelle. *Friends at School*, photographs by Matt Brown. Star Bright Books, 1995. ISBN 1-887734-01-5 [29 p]. Nonfiction, Gr. PS-1. Disability: Variety of disabilities. (****) (Cat B).

This is a delightful story about children in a preschool, six of whom have disabilities. With beautiful colored photographs it shows children with and without disabilities engaged in a variety of outdoor activities. It is a wonderful book to see children playing and having fun together regardless of ability or race.

<u>Themes or Units</u>: Friends at School; We Are Alike, We Are Different.

Bunnett, Rochelle. *Friends in The Park*, photographs by Carl Sahlhoff. Checkerboard Press, 1992. ISBN 1-56288-347 [33 p]. Nonfiction, Gr. PS-1. Disability: Physical, Down syndrome. (****) (Cat B)

This book illustrates a typical day at the neighborhood park with children from diverse cultures and of varying abilities. In all, twenty children are photographed as they participate in activities such as: blowing bubbles, going down the slide, crawling through a tunnel, and having juice. Children with physical disabilities and others with Down syndrome are integrated with children without disabilities in a very natural setting. The photographs capture activities which illustrate what the children can do and promotes the feeling of "one of us."

<u>Themes or Units</u>: Friendship; Homes & Neighborhoods (park); Summer; We Are Alike, We Are Different.

Bunting, Eve. *The Sunshine Home*, illus. by Diane De Grout. Clarion Books, 1994. ISBN 0-395-63309-5 [32 p]. Fiction, Gr. K-3. Disability: Physical (wheelchairs & walker). (****) (Cat B)

Tim and his parents visit Grams at the nursing home. Grams looks great and seems happy, but when they get outside, Tim's mother starts to cry. When Tim runs back in to give Gram his picture, he finds Gram crying too! Through Tim's efforts, they all share and become honest about their feelings. This story is very heartwarming and realistic. Through the story children can become aware of the challenges of caring for the elderly. The illustrations capture the many emotions experienced by the characters.

Themes or Units: Dentist, Doctors, Nurses & Hospitals; Families; Feelings; Grandmothers & Grandfathers; Health.

Bunting, Eve. <u>The Wall</u>, illus. by Ronald Hilmer. Clarion Books, 1990. ISBN 0-395-51588-2 [32 p]. Fiction, Gr. PS-3. Disability: Physical (wheelchair). (****) (Cat C)

A father and son visit the Vietnam Memorial Wall in Washington D.C. to find the name of the boy's grandfather who was killed in the war. While at the wall, they see other people including a veteran with a physical disability. The watercolor illustrations support the simple text and capture the many feelings associated with this experience. The story provides a wonderful opportunity to discuss what it might be like to have a disability promoting empathy and disability awareness. The character with the disability is in illustration only.

Themes or Units: Feelings; Peace Education; We Are Alike, We Are Different.

Burns, Kay. *Our Mom*, photographs by Rick Reil. Franklin Watts, 1989. ISBN 0-531-10677-2 [46 p]. Nonfiction, Gr. PS-3. Disability: Physical (wheelchair). (****) (Cat A)

The mom in this story uses a wheelchair because her legs are paralyzed. Her daily routines of dressing, transferring into the wheelchair, cleaning house, cooking, driving and shopping are all briefly described and illustrated with excellent black and white photographs. She even pretends to take a shower (clothes on!) to show the reader how it's done. With her children, she plays at the park, watches a soccer game and in the evening sits on the couch and reads them a story. This story promotes acceptance and a positive image by pointing out all this mother can do, much like any other mom.

Themes or Units: Families; Transportation; We Are Alike, We Are Different.

Cairo, Shelley. *Our Brother Has Down's Syndrome*, photographs by Irene McNeil. Annick Press LTD., 1985. ISBN 0-920303-31-5 [21 p]. Nonfiction, Gr. K-3. Disability: Down syndrome. (***) (Cat A)

Two older sisters describe what it means to have Down syndrome and lovingly tell about their brother pointing out all of the things that Jai likes such as eating ice-cream, wading in the water and getting into his sister's things. The message is that Jai may be a little different but we all have differences about us. The story is sensitively written and promotes a positive attitude about a child with Down syndrome. The story does not utilize "person first" language and incorrectly refers to Down syndrome as Down's syndrome.

Themes or Units: Brothers & Sisters; Families; We Are Alike, We Are Different.

Calmenson, Stephanie. *Rosie: A Visiting Dog's Story*, photographs by Justin Sutcliffe. Clarion, 1994. ISBN 0-316-08224-4 [47 p]. Nonfiction, Gr. PS-3. Illness and Disability. (***) (Cat A)

Rosie is a working dog or also called a Therapy Dog. This is a story about how she is trained and what Rosie does when she is working. In this story, Rosie visits young and old people with disabilities and illnesses and helps cheer them up. Vivid colored photographs capture Rosie's personality and the many emotions expressed by the people she visits. This story clearly shows that people with disabilities and illness have feelings just like anybody else.

Themes or Units: Feelings; Giving & Sharing; Pet Animals.

Carlson, Nancy. *Arnie and the New Kid*, illus. by author. Viking Penguin, 1990. ISBN 0-14-050945-3 [28 p]. Fiction, Gr. PS-3. Disability: Physical (wheelchair). (****) (Cat B)

Philip is a new boy at school who uses a wheelchair. Sometimes he needs help, but many other times he does not. An anthropomorphic approach is used in this story with Philip and the other children depicted as animals. Arnie teases Philip until one day Arnie falls and breaks his leg, twists a wrist, and sprains his tail. With these injuries, Arnie is not as fast and capable as he had once been. After the accident, the boys become friends and do everything together. The story promotes friendships between children with and without disabilites.

Themes or Units: Feelings; Friends at School; Friendship; Giving & Sharing; We Are Alike, We Are Different.

Carlson, Nancy. *Sit Still!* illus. by author. Viking, 1996. ISBN 0-670-85721-1 [30 p]. Fiction, Gr. PS-2. Disability: Attention Deficit Hyperactivity Disorder (ADHD). (***) (Cat B).

Patrick is on the go and everyone is always telling him to, "Sit still!" After a visit to the doctor, they discover that Patrick really can't sit still. His mother plans lots of activities to keep him busy. A fun, short story with whimsical illustrations. The story shows respect for children who have trouble slowing down and could help children understand this challenge.

Themes or Units: Friends at School; We Are Alike, We Are Different.

Carter, Alden R. *Big Brother Dustin*, illus. photographs by Dan Young with Carol S. Carter. Albert Whitman, 1997. ISBN 0-8075-0715-6 [29 p]. Nonfiction, Gr. PS-3. Disability: Down syndrome. (****) (Cat C).

A delightful story of how parents prepared their son with Down syndrome for the birth of their new baby. When the baby is born, Dustin names her Mary Ann and participates in caring for the baby. A very positive story of including their child with Down syndrome in the exciting event of adding a new baby to the family.

Themes or Units: Brothers & Sisters; Families.

Carter, Alden R. *Dustin's Big School Day*, photographs by Dan Young and Carol S. Carter. Albert Whitman, 1999. ISBN 0-8075-1741-0 [30 p]. Nonfiction, Gr. PS-2. Disability: Down syndrome. (****) (Cat C).

Dustin's first day at school is filled with a multitude of fun learning activities. The story shows him actively participating with children without disabilities. Dustin enjoys his first day at school and is clearly accepted by his teachers and peers promoting the attitude of "one of us."

Themes or Units: Friends at School.

Carter, Alden R., & Carter, Siri M. *I'm Tougher Than Asthma,* photographs by Dan Young. Albert Whitman, 1996. ISBN 0-8075-3474-9 [22 p]. Nonfiction, Gr. PS-3. Illness: Asthma. (****) (Cat B).

This is a story about Siri who has asthma. The story provides information about asthma and all of the treatments but also shows Siri as a typical little girl who likes the outdoors and playing with friends. Since many children have asthma, this would be a good book to help children learn about this illness.

Themes or Units: Friends at School; Health.

Carter, Alden R. *Seeing Things My Way,* photographs by Carol S. Carter. Albert Whitman, 1998. ISBN 0-8075-7296-9 [29 p]. Nonfiction, Gr. K-3. Disability: Blind. (****) (Cat A).

This book provides complete information about children who are blind or have visual impairments. The story shows how Amanda and her second grade friends use a variety of methods and equipment as they cope with their visual impairments. The information is very positive as it shows what people can do even though they have visual impairments or are blind.

Themes or Units: Friends at School; Sense of Sight; We Are Alike, We Are Different.

Carter, Alden R. *Stretching Ourselves: Kids with Cerebral Palsy,* photographs by Carol S. Carter. Albert Whitman, 2000. ISBN 0-8075-7637-9 [35 p]. Nonfiction, Gr. K-5. Disability: Physical (cerebral palsy). (****) (Cat A).

This book does an excellent job of explaining cerebral palsy by focusing on three children with varying degrees of this disability. Wonderful photographs show the challenges these children face as well as the many activities they can do with peers at school or in the community. An excellent resource for children to learn about cerebral palsy.

Themes or Units: Friends at School; We Are Alike, We Are Different.

Caseley, Judith. *Apple Pie and Onions,* illus. by author. Greenwillow Books, 1987. ISBN 0-688-06763-8 [27 p]. Fiction, Gr. K-3. Disability: Physical (wheelchair). (****) (Cat C)

During one of Rebecca's visits to Grandma's, they go for a walk. Grandma is excited to see Hatti, a friend who is in a wheelchair. Hattie talks loudly in Yiddish and Rebecca is embarrassed. Grandma trys to help Rebecca by telling her a story about a time when she was embarrassed. Afterwards Rebecca and Grandma make an apple pie and have tea. This is a sensitive story about the relationship between a granddaughter and her grandmother. The story promotes a positive image of a person with a disability as Grandma treats Hattie special and is so excited to see her.

Themes or Units: **Apples, Feelings; Grandmothers & Grandfathers.**

Caseley, Judith. *Harry and Willy and Carrothead*, illus. by author. Greenwillow Books, 1991. ISBN 0-688-09492-9 [20 p]. Fiction, Gr. K-3. Disability: Physical (prosthesis for left hand). (****) (Cat B)

When Harry was born, his left arm ended at the elbow. At school the children ask questions about his prosthesis. They soon learn that Harry can play and eat like a "regular kid." Eventually, Harry, Willy and Carrothead become best friends. This story illustrates that children are teased for many reasons (i.e. disability, differences such as hair color). The story takes place in an integrated program and promotes a positive image of someone with a physical disability by illustrating the many things Harry is able to do. The illustrations are colorful and include children from diverse cultures.

Themes or Units: **Feelings; Friends at School; Friendship; We Are Alike, We Are Different.**

Chaplin, Susan Gibbons. *I Can Sign My ABCs*, illus. Laura McCaul. Kendall Green Publisher, 1986. ISBN 0-930323-19-X [52 p]. Fiction, PS-2. Disability: Deaf, hearing loss. (****) (Cat A)

This book is an introduction to the alphabet in sign language. On each set of two pages, the left page shows a hand demonstrating the manual handshape for a letter of the alphabet while the right page has a picture of a child demonstrating the sign for a common object. Large, brightly colored illustrations help the reader learn the signs. This would be a good book for children just learning to sign. The colorful illustrations add to its appeal.

Themes or Units: **Alphabet; Sense of Sight; Sign Language.**

Charlip, Remy. *Handtalk Birthday*, photographer by George Ancona. Mac Millan, 1987. ISBN 0-02-718080-8 [44 p]. Nonfiction, Gr. K-3. Disability: Deaf. (****) (Cat B)

A group of Mary Beth's friends surprise her with gifts and a party for her birthday. Mary Beth dresses outrageously which adds humor to the story. The colorful photographs show the reader how to sign and fingerspell.

Themes or Units: Giving & Sharing; Sign Language; We Are Alike, We Are Different.

Coerr, Eleanor. *Sadako*, illus. by Ed Young. G.P. Putnam's Sons, 1993. ISBN 0-399-21771-1 [45 p]. Nonfiction, Gr. 2-6. llness: Leukemia. (****) (Cat B)

Sadako is a twelve year old Japanese girl who develops leukemia, the "atom bomb disease," ten years after the bomb was dropped on Hiroshima. The story tells of Sadako's struggles to survive including the legend of a sick person folding 1,000 paper cranes so the gods will grant that person a wish to be well again. Because of the historic significance of this story, children will want to read Sadako, which is a very moving story.

Themes and Units: Health; Holidays Around the World; Peace Education.

Cohen, Miriam. *It's George*, illus. by Lillian Hoban. Greenwillow Books, 1988. ISBN 0-688-06812-X [29 p]. Fiction, Gr. PS-3. Disability: Mental retardation or learning disability. (**) (Cat B)

George is in first grade. Because reading and writing are difficult for him, some of the children call him "dumb." Each day on his way to school George stops at his friend's house, 79 year old Mr. Emmons. One morning Mr. Emmons has fallen out of his chair so George calls 911 and help comes. Now all his classmates like George. This story perpetuates the hero theme for persons with differences; George should be accepted for who he is without needing to become super-human. George's schooling takes place in an integrated setting with children from diverse cultures.

Themes or Units: Friendship; Safety.

Cohen, Miriam. *See You Tomorrow, Charles,* **illus. by Lillian Hoban. Dell Publishing, 1983. ISBN 0-440-40162-3 [28 p]. Nonfiction, Gr. PS-2. Disability: Blind. (***) (Cat B)**

Charles is in first grade and is blind. The story describes many school activities in which Charles participates and the feelings and perceptions of his classmates. Charles is very capable and one day is successful in guiding his friends out of a dark basement. This story portrays Charles as a "hero." The story does take place in an integrated setting and stresses what Charles can do as well as what he cannot do. The story incorporates diversity of ability as well as cultural diversity.

Themes or Units: Friends at School; We Are Alike, We Are Different.

Collins, Harold S. *The Beginning Sign Language Series,* **illus. by Kathy Kifer & Dahna Solar. Garlic Press, 1994. The series includes the following books:**

An Alphabet of Animal Signs **ISBN 0-931993-65-2 [13 p]**
Foods **ISBN 0-931993-87-3 [15 p]**
Fruits & Vegetables **ISBN 0-931993-88-1 [13 p]**
Pets, Animals & Creatures **ISBN 0-931993-89-X [29 p]**
Mother Goose in Sign **ISBN 0-931993-66-0 [13 p]**
Signing at School **ISBN 0-931993-47-4 [29 p]**
Songs in Sign **ISBN 0-931993-71-7 [16 p]**
Fiction, Gr. PS-4. Disability: Deaf (sign language). (****) (A)

The books are filled with colorful photographs. Each photograph is accompanied by an illustration of a person demonstrating the sign for the object in the photograph. Arrows accompany the sign so the reader knows how to move the hand or fingers when making the sign. This collection of books could be used to teach simple signs.

Themes or Units: Alphabet; Fantasy & Imagination; Fruits & Vegetables; Pet Animals; Sign Language; Wild Birds & Animals; Zoo Animals.

Condra, Estelle. *See The Ocean,* **illus. by Linda Crockett-Blassingame. Ideals Children's Books, 1994. ISBN 1-57102-005-5 [29 p]. Fiction, Gr. K-3. Disability: Blind. (****) (Cat C)**

Each year, Nellie, her parents and two older brothers travel across the mountains to their beach house at the ocean. The children always try to be the first to see the ocean from the top of the mountains. This year it's cloudy and misty and no one can see but Nellie. She describes the ocean but her brothers feel it's unfair because after all, she can't see. Her mom tells the boys, "Though your sister's eyes are blind, she can see with her mind." A sensitive story about this family's relationship. The illustrations are exquisite incandescent oil paintings.

Themes or Units: **Families; Oceans, Lakes & Sea Animals; Sense of Sight; Sounds in the Environment; Summer; We Are Alike, We Are Different.**

Corman, Clifford L., & Trevino, Esther. *Eukee The Jumpy Jumpy Elephant,* illus. by Richard A. DiMatteo. Specialty Press, 1995. ISBN 0-962129-8-1 [22 p]. Fiction, Gr. PS-2. Disability: Attention deficit hyperactivity disorder (ADHD). (****) (Cat B).

Eurkee gets into trouble in school. He explains to his mom that he feels all jumpy inside. The parents take Eurkee to the doctor who runs tests and diagnosis that Eurkee has ADHD. After getting help from the doctor and his parents, Eurkee has some success at school. This story is written very sensitively and may help children understand peers who also feel jumpy inside.

Themes or Units: **Friends at School; We Are Alike, We Are Different.**

Cowen-Fletcher, Jane. *Mama Zooms,* illus. by author. Scholastic, Inc., 1993. ISBN 0-590-45774-8 [29 p]. Fiction, Gr. PS-2. Disability: Physical (wheelchair). (****) (Cat C)

This is a story about a little boy and his mom who zoom everywhere in her zooming maching which in reality is her wheelchair. As they zoom around, the little boy imagines he's on a train, driving a race car, riding a racehorse, etc. The mom zooms him around until it's bedtime. This is a very positive story showing the mom zooming everywhere in her wheelchair, rarely needing help. She is perceived as being able to do many things which negates the old stereotype of being "confined" to a wheelchair.

Themes or Units: **Families; Fantasy & Imagination; Transportation; We Are Alike, We Are Different.**

Craig, Lori. *One Step at a Time*, illus. by Jim Gummerson. Children's Spirit Publishing, 1999. ISBN 1-55056-702-0 [24 p]. Nonfiction, Gr. PS-2. Disability: Physical (hip dysplasia & foot deformities; braces & walker). (***) (Cat B).

This story is narrated by Camille, a little girl who was born with hip dysplasia and deformed feet. The story tells about the surgery and treatments that Camille has had and her efforts to overcome her physical disability through laughter and imagination. This story is very positive emphasizing all the things Camille can do and how some activities help strengthen her legs so one day she will be able to walk.

Themes or Units: Families; Health; We Are Alike, We Are Different.

Crunk, Tony. *Big Mama*, illus. by Margot Apple. Farrar, Straus and Giroux, 2000. ISBN 0-374-30688-5 [28 p]. Fiction, Gr. PS-2. Disability: Physical (wheelchair). (***) (Cat C).

Billy Boyd lives with his grandmother, Big Mama, who is very special because she makes fun activities out of junk. Mama joins in all kinds of games, and turns a trip through town to get ice cream into a fun adventure. The story is very inclusive as one of the neighborhood children who joins in all the fun uses a wheelchair. Soft colored illustrations help tell the story.

Themes or Units: Homes & Neighborhoods; Grandmothers & Grandfathers.

Damrell, Liz. *With The Wind*, illus. by Stephen Marchesi. Orchard Books, 1991. ISBN 0-531-05882-4 [25 p]. Fiction, Gr. PS-2. Disability: Physical (leg braces & wheelchair). (****) (Cat C)

A young boy goes horseback riding. As he rides he feels the strength of the horse beneath him. He feels freedom, joy and power. When he returns from his ride, his parents are waiting and his father helps him off the horse and into his wheelchair. The text of this story is a poem that reflects the sense of freedom the boy imagines as he rides. The boy's disability undoubtedly influences his feelings of freedom. The mood is set with soft colors in the illustrations.

Themes or Units: Fantasy & Imagination; Farm & Farm Animals; Feelings; Pet Animals; We Are Alike, We Are Different.

Davis, Patricia. *Brian's Bird,* illus. by Layne Johnson. Albert Whitman, 2000. ISBN 0-8075-0881-0 [27 p]. Fiction, Gr. PS-3. Disability: Blind. (****) (Cat C).

Brian who is blind receives a parakeet from his family as he celebrates his eighth birthday. This is a fun story about his escapades with his bird and how he teaches it to talk. When his bird gets outside Brian successfully finds it with the help of his brother. A sensitive story stressing all that Brian is able to do including caring for his new pet.

Themes or Units: Brothers & Sisters; Giving & Sharing; Pet Animals.

DeBear, Kirsten. *Be Quiet, Marina!* Photographs by Laura Dwight. Star Bright Books, 2001. ISBN 1-887734-79-1 [21 p]. Nonfiction, Gr. PS-3. Disability: Down syndrome & cerebral palsy. (****) (Cat B)

This is a story about two little girls, one with Down syndrome and the other with cerebral palsy. At first they aren't successful in playing together because one is loud and the other is quiet. But, by the end of the story they have become good friends even with their differences. This book has simple text and lots of expressive black and white photographs. A nice addition to the literature on making friends.

Themes or Units: Friends at School; Friendship; We Are Alike, We Are Different.

Delton, Judy. *I'll Never Love Anything Ever Again,* illus. by Rodney Pate. Albert Whitman & Co., 1985. ISBN 0-8075—3521-4]32 p]. Fiction, Gr. PS-3. Illness: Allergies. (****) (Cat B)

This is a touching story about a young boy who finds that he must give up his dog, Tinsel, because he has become allergic to dogs. He is terribly upset but finally begins to think about how much fun Tinsel would have on a farm and that it would be fun to visit in the summer. With great sadness and tears, the young boy says, "Good-bye" to his dog and thinks that he'll never love anything again. The blue and white illustrations help set the mood. All children would benefit from this sensitively written story. It would be a good choice for any child who has to give up his or her pet for whatever reason.

Themes or Units: Feelings; Health; Pet Animals.

Derby, Janice. *Are You My Friend?* **illus. by Joy Dunn Keenan. Herald Press, 1993. ISBN 0-8361-3609-8 [32 p]. Fiction, Gr. K-3. Disability: Physical (****) (Cat C).**

Throughout the story, a child meets many different people. The child mentions the differences but then also lists some of the things each person likes, just like him. The people he meets have differences because of age, size, disability, and culture. The text is very positive as it points out what people like and what they can do.

<u>Themes or Units</u>: Friendship; We Are Alike, We Are Different.

Dwight, Laura. *We Can Do It!* **Checkerboard Press, 1992. ISBN 1-56288-301-1 [30 p]. Nonfiction, Gr. PS-2. Disabilities: Spina bifida, Down syndrome, cerebral palsy, blind. (****) (Cat A)**

This is a book about five children from diverse cultures with special needs. The children are introduced, their ages and disabilities identified, and then colorful photographs show activities that each child likes to do. For example, Gina who has spina bifida likes to wheel her chair down to the beach and play in the water. This isn't a story about disabilities rather an explanation of what each child can realistically do. It is a very positive book and would help children have a better understanding of what children with disabilities can do.

<u>Themes or Units</u>: Friends at School; We Are Alike, We Are Different.

Dwyer, Kathleen M. *What Do You Mean I Have A Learning Disability?* **photographs by Barbara Beirne. Walker & Co., 1991. ISBN 0-8027-8103-9 [35 p]. Nonfiction, Gr. 1-5. Disability: Learning Disability. (***) (Cat A).**

Jimmy has lots of trouble finding and remembering things. In school, he has a hard time with some of the work. He thinks he is stupid. After an evaluation by Dr. Stone, Jimmy and his parents discover that he has a learning disability. At school he gets help from a tutor. With hard work, his school work improves and Jimmy starts to feel better about himself. A good story to learn what it feels like to have a learning disability.

<u>Themes or Units</u>: Feelings; We Are Alike, We Are Different.

Edwards, Becky. *My Brother Sammy,* illus. by David Armitage. Millbrook Press, 1999. ISBN 0-7613-0439-8 [24 p]. Fiction, Gr. K-3. Disability: Autism. (***) (Cat B).

Sammy's brother tells what it is like to have a brother with autism. He describes what he wishes his brother could do with him, his frustrations, yet his love for his brother. Each time he asks his mom about Sammy, she tell's him Sammy is special. The story would be stronger if this term were not so prevalent throughout the story. At the very end the mom tells the brother that he is a special brother. Well done, soft illustrations help set the mood for the story.

Themes or Units: Brothers & Sisters; We Are Alike, We Are Different.

Edwards, Michelle. *alef-bet—A Hebrew Alphabet Book,* illus. by author. Lothrop, Lee & Shepard Books, 1992. ISBN 0-688-09724-3 [26 p]. Fiction, Gr. K-2. Disability: Physical (wheelchair). (****) (Cat C)

This is a delightful book about the Hebrew alphabet. It is illustrated with bright, colorful pictures. One family is represented throughout and one of their children uses a wheelchair. Each time the child appears, he is depicted as an active, capable member of the family. Using this book would be a fun way to learn about an alphabet in another language.

Themes or Units: Alphabet; Children & Families Around the World; Families.

Elder, Vicci. *Cardiac Kids,* illus. by Annie King. Tenderhearts Publishing, 1994. ISBN 1-886165-11-4 [26 p]. Fiction, Gr. 1-3. Illness: Cardiac Problems. (***) (Cat A).

This little book tells the story of a young girl with cardiac problems. It is told by her older sister and includes her feelings and how sometimes she feels left out when all the attention is given to her little sister. The story describes the young girl's stay in the hospital and all of the tests that are done. A nice books for families who have a child with heart disease.

Themes or Units: Dentists, Doctors, Nurses & Hospitals; Feelings; Health.

Emmert, Michelle. *I'm The Big Sister Now*, illus. Gail Owens. Albert Whitman & Co., 1989. ISBN 0-8075-3458-7 [25 p]. Nonfiction, Gr. K-3. Disability: Cerebral palsy, severe brain damage (multiple disabilities). (****) (Cat A)

This is a story about Amy who has multiple disabilities and is told by her sister. While Amy is unable to do many things, the story emphasizes that she is a person with feelings and describes how Amy is included by her family. As the sister grows older and can help Amy, she feels like she has become the big sister. This story is very sensitively written with soft colored illustrations. The story promotes a positive image by showing how Amy is loved by her family. Children would clearly gain an understanding of what it is like to have these multiple disabilities with the information presented in this book.

Themes or Units: Brothers & Sisters; Families; We Are Alike, We Are Different.

Fain, Kathleen. *Handsigns: A Sign Language Alphabet*, illus. by author. Chronicle Books, 1993. ISBN 0-8118-1196-4 [26 p]. Fiction, Gr. PS-3. Disability: Deaf (sign language). (****) (Cat A).

This book presents an animal for each letter of the alphabet. Each animal is accompanied by the illustration of a hand demonstrating the corresponding sign in American Sign Language. The illustrations are outstanding. Children could learn the letters of the alphabet in sign from this book.

Themes or Units: Alphabet; Sign Language; Wild Birds & Animals; Zoo Animals.

Fleming, Virginia. *Be Good to Eddie Lee*, illus. by Floyd Cooper. Philomel Books, 1993. ISBN 0-399-21993-5 [29 p]. Fiction, Gr. 2-5. Disability: Down syndrome. (**) (Cat B).

This is a story about a young boy with Down syndrome and points out his interactions with children in his neighborhood that are not always positive. One girl plays with him because her mother tells her to play. At the end of the story, he is accepted by this girl because he finds the frog eggs. This book has beautiful illustrations but the story may perpetuate stereotypes of persons with Down syndrome. This story could be used with older children to stress kindness to others and point out what it feels like to be rejected and called names.

Themes or Units: Feelings; Friendship.

Foreman, Michael. *Seal Surfer,* illus. by author. Harcourt Brace, 1996. ISBN 0-15-201399-7 [27 p]. Fiction, Gr. K-3. Disability: Physical (wheelchair, walking sticks). (****) (Cat C).

A young boy goes to the beach with his grandfather where they see a seal being born. They continue going to the beach throughout the four seasons and the boy develops a special bond with the seal. In many of the photographs you see the boy's wheelchair or walking sticks, but his disability doesn't slow him down and he hopes one day he can go to the cliff tops with his own grandchildren. A wonderfully inclusive story that shows the special relationship between a boy and his grandfather.

<u>Themes or Units</u>: **Grandmothers & Grandfathers; Oceans, Lakes & Sea Animals; Seasons.**

Foss, Karen Sue. *The Problem With Hair: A Story for Children Who are Learning About Cancer,* illus. by Steve Wilda. Centering Corp., (1996). ISBN 1-56123-009-5 [14 p]. Fiction, Gr. PS-3. Illness: Cancer. (****) (Cat A).

A short story about four children who are all unhappy with their hair for various reasons. Meanwhile a friend who has cancer loses all her hair because of radiation treatments. This group of children, share their problems with hair and then give their friend a fun hat which makes her feel welcome even though her head is bare. A very realistic story with lovely pencil sketchings.

<u>Themes or Units</u>: **Feelings; Friendship; Giving & Sharing; Hats; Health.**

Fraustino, Lisa Rowe. *The Hickory Chair,* illus. by Benny Andrews. Arthur A. Levine Books, Scholastic Press, 2001. ISBN 0-590-52248-5 [29 p]. Fiction, Gr. K-4. Disability: Blind. (****) (Cat C).

This book shows a close relationship between a grandmother and her grandson, Louis who is blind. After the grandmother dies, the family members look for notes she has left identifying items she was giving each of them. No note was found for Louis. When Louis is as old as Grandmother when she died, his grandchild finds a note in Grandmother's old rocking chair. She hadn't forgotten him after all. The characters are African American. Full page illustrations by a world famous artist help tell the story.

<u>Themes or Units</u>: **Families; Giving & Sharing; Grandmothers & Grandfathers.**

Gaes, Jason. *My Book For Kids With Cansur*, illus. by Tim & Adam Gaes. Melius & Peterson, 1988. ISBN 0-937603-04-X [32 p]. Nonfiction, Gr. PS-4. Chronic Illness: Cancer. (****) (Cat A)

This story was written by eight-year-old Jason. He wants to tell children what it's like to have cancer and stresses everyone who gets cancer does not die. The text is in Jason's own handwriting (printing) with words spelled the way he wrote them. He explains about his own cancer, the tests, and all of the procedures he has experienced. He also tells all the good things about having cancer as well as the not so good. His two brothers illustrated the book with their own drawings. This book would be helpful when talking to young children about cancer. It is factual yet very positive.

Themes or Units: Dentists, Doctors, Nurses & Hospitals; Health.

Gainer, Cindy. *I'm Like You, You're Like Me*, illus. by author. Free Spirit Publishing, 1998. ISBN 1-57542-039-2 [39 p]. Fiction, Gr. PS-3. Disability: Physical (wheelchair). (***) (Cat C).

Through simple text and illustrations, this book points out ways in which children are alike and ways in which they are different. The story is about understanding and celebrating each other. The children are depicted as multicultural and three of the illustrations include a child in a wheelchair. Even though the inclusion is limited, disability is included.

Themes or Units: We Are Alike, We Are Different.

Gardner, Sonia. *Eagle Feather*, illus. by James Spurlock. Writers Press, 1997. ISBN 1-885101-17-1 [30 p]. Fiction, Gr. 1-4. Disability: Blind. (****) (Cat B).

The story is about the Naming Ceremony that takes place for Little One who is blind. He uses a talking stick to represent the strengths he needs to meet daily challenges. Over time his people grow to respect him and his talents and give him the name of Eagle Feather. A wonderful story that shares this naming tradition and emphasizes that everyone has talents. The book has large, beautiful illustrations.

Themes or Units: Children & Families Around the World.

Gehret, Jeanne. *Eagle Eyes*, illus. by Susan Covert. Verbal Images Press, 1991. ISBN 0-9625136-4-4 [27 p]. Fiction, Gr. 1-5. Disability: Attention deficit disorder (ADD). (****) (Cat B).

On a nature walk, Ben's loudness and carelessness frightens all the birds away. At school Ben has trouble paying attention and remembering his school work. Ben is diagnosed and treated for attention deficit disorder. When he and his family return to the park, Ben is the one who is able to help his dad out in an emergency. A very realistic yet positive story about a family living with a son with ADD.

Themes or Units: Brothers & Sisters; Families; Feelings; We Are Alike, We Are Different.

Gehret, Jeanne. *The Dont't-give-up Kid*, illus. Dandra Ann DePauw. Verbal Images Press, 1996. ISBN 1-884281-10-9 [27 p]. Fiction, Gr. 1-3. Disability: Learning disability. (✝✝✝✝) (Cat B).

Alex has lots of difficulty in school. After visiting the psychologist, Alex realizes he has a different learning style and he is not stupid! He realizes that his hero Thomas Edison also had a learning disability. Alex is willing to get help at school and try lots of different ways to learn and be successful. This is a short, upbeat story that shows a child with a learning disability in a positive way. There is a six page Parent Resource included.

Themes or Units: We Are Alike, We Are Different.

Gifaldi, David. *Ben, King of the River*, illus. by Layne Johnson. Albert Whitman & Company, 2001. ISBN 0-8075-0635-4 [28 p]. Fiction, Gr. 1-4. Disability: Developmentally disability. (****) (Cat B).

This story is about a family going on their first camping trip with a five-year-old brother with developmentally disabilities. The story is excellent in portraying how a sibling feels about having a brother with a disability. The trip is a success. Tips for living with a brother or sister with a disability are included in the back of the book.

Themes or Units: Brothers & Sisters; Families; Feelings.

Gilmore, Rachna. *A Screaming Kind of Day*, illus. by Gordon Sauve. Fitzhenry & Whiteside, 1999. ISBN 1-55041-514-X [38 p]. Fiction, Gr. K-3. Disability: Deaf (hearing aids). (****) (Cat C).

Scully is deaf and is having a hard day with her brother. She gets in trouble for playing in the rain, when all she wants is to hear and feel the sensation of rain falling around her. At the end of the day she sits with her mother and enjoys the stars. A realistic story about a day in the life of a family that includes challenges, frustrations and special moments. This family just happens to have a child who is deaf.

Themes or Units: Brothers & Sisters; Families; Feelings; Sounds in the Environment.

Girard, Linda Walvoord. *Alex, the Kid With AIDS*, **illus. by Blanche Sims. Albert Whitman & Co., 1991. ISBN 0-8075-0247-2 [29 p]. Fiction, Gr. 1-4. Chronic Illness: AIDS. (***) (Cat B)**

The school nurse talks to the first grade class about a new classmate, Alex, who has AIDS. The children learn about the disease and that they cannot catch AIDS just by being near Alex. The story shows how funny Alex is and the fun and "trouble" he gets into. Soon, Alex becomes one of Brian's best friends. This story points out that even though Alex has AIDS, he is a typical child. This would be a good story to help children learn about AIDS.

<u>Themes or Units</u>: **Friends at School; Health.**

Girnis, Meg. *ABC for You and Me*, **photographs by Shirley Leamon Green. Albert Whitman, 2000. ISBN 0-8075-0101-8 [26 p]. Nonfiction, Gr. PS-2. Disability: Down syndrome. (****) (Cat C).**

This is an alphabet book—each page has a letter with a child doing something with an item that begins with that letter. The pictures of the children with Down syndrome are fun and beautiful. It really is just an alphabet book that happens to have children with Down syndrome as the models.

<u>Themes or Units</u>: **Alphabet.**

Golden, Barbara Diamond. *Cakes and Miracles*, **illus. by Erika Weiks. Viking, 1991. ISBN 0-670-63047-X [25 p]. Fiction, Gr. K-4. Disability: Blind. (****) (Cat B)**

Hershal is a young boy who is blind. His mother is busily preparing for the Jewish holiday Purim. Hershal wants to help with the baking but his mother says, "no." In a dream, an angel tells him he should make what he sees in his dreams. Hershel makes beautiful cookies and surprises his mother. They take the cookies to the market and every cookie is sold . Hershal is so happy because he has been a big help to his mother. The last two pages tell about the holiday Purim. This is a wonderful story that combines the beauty of the Jewish culture with the disability of being blind.

<u>Themes or Units</u>: **Children & Families Around the World; Holidays Around the World; Sense of Touch; We Are Alike, We Are Different.**

Goodwall, Jane. *Dr. White,* illus. Julie Litty. North-South Books, 1999. ISBN 0-7358-1063-X [28 p]. Fiction, Gr. PS-3. Illness: Hospitalized children. (****) (C).

This book is based on a real story from London. A small, white dog named Dr. White visits sick children at the hospital and helps them feel better. Then a health inspector no longer allows the dog to visit. Each day, the dog lays next to the hospital door. When the Inspector's daughter gets very ill, the nurse lets Dr. White into the room and he helps her get well. Now Dr. White gets permission to stay! A fun story that shows how therapy dogs help people who are sick.

Themes or Units: Dentists, Doctors, Nurses & Hospitals; Health; Pet Animals.

Greenberg, Judith E. *What Is the Sign for Friend?* photographs by Gayle Rothschild. Franklin Watts, 1985. ISBN 0-531-04939-6 [28 p]. Nonfiction, K-3. Disability: Deaf. (****) (Cat A)

Shane is a young boy who was born deaf. This story tells about his disability and does an excellent job of showing the reader all of the things that Shane can do such as: playing soccer, going out for pizza, sleeping over at a friend's house, plus much more. Shane attends school in an integrated classroom. Black and white photographs help tell about Shane's disability. Inserts show sketches of signing that follow the text and photographs. This is an excellent story for emphasizing ability and promoting a positive image of a person with a disability. Cultural diversity is represented in the photographs.

Themes or Units: Friendship; Sign Language; We Are Alike, We Are Different.

Greenfield, Eloise. *William and the Good Old Days,* illus. by Jan Spivey Gilchrist. Harper Collins Publishers, 1993. IBSN 0-06-021093-1 [29 p]. Fiction, PS-2. Disability: Blind, physical (wheelchair). (****) (Cat C)

The story is about a young boy who is African American and is upset because his grandmother is ill and can no longer run her restaurant. He dreams about the good old days. Grandma can no longer see when she comes to live with her grandson's family. Still, they plan to plant the garden together and in the last illustration he is pushing Grandma in a wheelchair. This is a story that shows genuine love between a grandson and grandmother.

Themes or Units: Grandmothers & Grandfathers.

Gregory, Nan. *How Smudge Came,* **illus. by Ron Lightburn. Red Deer College Press, 1995. ISBN 0-88995-143-8 [32]. Fiction, K-3. Disability: Down syndrome. (***) (Cat B).**

This is a story about a young girl who lives in a group home, works at a nursing home and her quest to keep a puppy she has found. The story is harsh in how they inform the girl that she cannot keep a puppy at the group home. Otherwise, the story is very realistic and touching. In the end, Cindy is surprised to find out she can keep the puppy at work.

Themes or Units: Pet Animals.

Gross, Buth Belov. *You Don't Need Words! A Book About Ways People Talk Without Words,* **illus. by Susannah Ryan. Scholastic, 1991. ISBN 0-590-43897-2 [47 p]. Nonfiction, Gr. K-4. Disability: Deaf (sign language). (****) (Cat A).**

This book illustrates many ways people communicate without words, such as gestures, pantomime, sign language, facial expressions, and various signs and symbols in our environment. The story provids interesting information and is a fun way to learn how people communicate besides talking.

Themes or Units: Sense of Sight; Sign Language.

Haines, Sandra. *Becca and Sue Make Two,* **illus. by Gina Phillips. Writers Press, 1995. ISBN 1-885101-15-5 [32 p]. Fiction, K-3. Disability: Down syndrome. (***) (Cat B).**

Becca learns about differences and understands that people do things in different ways. She makes friends with Sue who had Down syndrome. Becca doesn't care that Sue learns more slowly or has some mannerisms different than her own. They are best friends.

Together they learn to play a song on the piano for the school recital, which is a big success. This story promotes acceptance of persons with Down syndrome and uses the theme throughout that differences don't matter. In addition, the reader gains some information about Down syndrome.

Themes or Units: Friendships; We Are Alike, We Are Different.

Haldane, Suzanne. *Helping Hands: How Monkeys Assist People Who Are Disabled,* photographs by author. Dutton Children's Books, 1991. ISBN 0-525-44723-7 [48 p]. Nonfiction, Gr. 3-7. Disability: Physical (wheelchair). (****) (Cat A)

This book is a photo essay about Greg, a teenage boy with quadriplegia and his affectionate helper, Willie, a capuchin monkey. The story shows how the monkeys are trained to assist in everyday tasks such as opening a book or getting an item from the refrigerator. This assistance allows people with quadriplegia to become more self-sufficient. The story shows what Greg can do with the help of his monkey. Children will enjoy seeing the many jobs Willie can do and how fun, yet tender, he is with Greg. At the same time, they will learn some things about what it's like to live with quadriplegia.

Themes or Units: Pet Animals; We Are Alike, We Are Different; Zoo Animals.

Hallinan, P.K. *Heartprints,* illus. by author. Ideals Childrens Books, 1999. ISBN 1-57102-143-4 [22 p]. Fiction, PS-2. Disability: Physical (wheelchair). (****) (Cat C).

This is a story about Heartprints—the impression left behind by a deliberate act of kindness. Each page shows children in some act of kindness. A boy in a wheelchair is included three times. This story sets the stage to talk to children about being kind to one another. The illustrations are cartoonish and fun.

Themes or Units: Friendship; Peace Education.

Hamm, Diane Johnson. *Grandma Drives a Motor Bed,* illus. by Charles Robinson. Albert Whitman & Co., 1987. ISBN 0-8075-3025-5 [27 p]. Fiction, Gr. 1-3. Disability: Physical (wheelchair). (****) (Cat B)

Josh and his mom visit Grandma who has a physical disability. Grandma is at home in a hospital bed most of the time and is able to sit in a wheelchair occasionally. Josh has many questions about how the bed works and why Grandma must be in it. He gets his questions answered and even has an opportunity to "try out" Grandma's bed. The story is very realistic and would answer many questions that children might have. While Grandma is limited in getting around, the story emphasizes all that she can do from her bed. The story promotes a positive attitude.

Themes or Units: Dentists, Doctors, Nurses and Hospitals; Grandmothers & Grandfathers.

Harshman, Marc. *The Storm*, illus. by Mark Mohr. CobbleHill Books—Dutton, 1995. ISBN 0-525-65150-0 [30 p]. Fiction, Gr. K-5. Disability: Physical (wheelchair). (****) (Cat C).

Jonathan comes home from school while his parents go to town for errands. While his parents are gone, the sky turns black and a tornado passes over the farm. Even though Jonathon is afraid, he faces the terror of the storm and saves the horses in the barn. After the storm, he no longer is afraid and hopes people will see him as Johnathon not as a young boy in a wheelchair. This story points out how capable this boy is even though he has a physical disability.

Themes or Units: Farm & Farm Animals; Feelings; Spring; Weather & Storms.

Harter, Debbie. *The Animal Boogie*, illus. by author. Barefoot Books, 2000. ISBN 1-84148-094-0 [30 p]. Fiction, Gr. PS-2. Disability: Physical (wheelchair). (****) (Cat C).

Children go to the jungle and move with a variety of animals as they shake, swing, stomp, slither and flap. The children are represented as multicultural and one uses a wheelchair. There is fun language throughout with lots of repetition, good for phonological awareness. Illustrations are bright and colorful. This is an entertaining book for young children.

Themes or Units: Colors in My World; Zoo Animals.

Hausman, Gerald. *The Story of Blue Elk*, illus. by Kristina Rodanas. Clarion Books, 1998. ISBN 0-395-84512-2 [32 p]. Fiction, Gr. 1-4. Disability: Blind. (****) (Cat B).

The Story of Blue Elk is an American Indian myth. The author provides a one page explanation of the origin of this tale. This story is about a boy named Blue Elk who cannot speak, who falls in love and lets his red cedar flute speak for him. Older children would enjoy this story. Even though the Indian boy cannot speak, he is clearly an important member of his people.

Themes or Units: Children & Families Around the World.

Heelan, Jamee Riggio. *The Making of My Special Hand: Madison's Story*, illus. by Nicola Simmonds. Peachtree Publishers, 1998. Nonfiction, Gr. K-3. Disability: Physical (prosthesis-hand). (****) (Cat A).

The story begins with a picture of Madison who is about a year old. It is her story that tells how her hand was made, how it operates, how it feels, and how she uses it. There are sketches of the process of making her hand and soft colored illustrations of the people in the story. This is an excellent resource for anyone trying to explain what happens when a child loses a limb or is born without one. Could be used in preschool if the story was told rather than read.

<u>Themes or Units</u>: **We Are Alike, We Are Different.**

Heelan, Jamee Riggio. *Rolling Along: The Story of Taylor and His Wheelchair,* illus. by Nicola Simmonds. Peachtree Publishers, 2000. ISBN 1-56145-219-X [29 p]. Nonfiction, Gr. PS-3. Disability: Physical (cerebral palsy, wheelchair, walker). (****) (Cat C)

Taylor and Tyler are twins. The only difference is that Taylor has cerebral palsy. He uses a walker, but tires easily. While some friends felt sorry for him, Taylor was really excited about getting his own wheelchair. With his chair he can go more places on his own and do more things he wants to do. He says, "Now nothing can stop me!" An excellent book to help children learn that having a wheelchair doesn't need to be confining but liberating as now he can move when he wants to.

<u>Themes or Units</u>: **Feelings; Friendship; We Are Alike, We Are Different.**

Henriod, Lorraine. *Grandma's Wheelchair,* illus. by Christa Chevalier. Albert Whitman and Co., 1982. ISBN 0807530352 [29 p]. Fiction, Gr. PS-2. Disability: Physical (wheelchair). (****) (Cat C)

Each morning when Nate goes to kindergarten, his four-year-old brother Thomas goes to Grandma's house. Thomas's mom is about to have a baby so she has lost her lap, but Grandma always has a lap for him as she sits in her wheelchair. Grandma and Thomas keep very busy and have fun making applesauce, vacuuming, dusting, and reading stories. This story clearly points out that a person with a disability can adapt to everyday life and function without losing independence. The illustrations and story promote a positive image of a person with a disability.

<u>Themes or Units</u>: **Families; Grandmothers & Grandfathers; We Are Alike, We Are Different.**

Hesse, Karen. *Lester's Dog,* illus. by Nancy Carpenter. Crown Publishers, Inc., 1993. ISBN 0-517-58357-7 [29 p]. Fiction, Gr. PS-3. Disability: Deaf. (****) (Cat C)

A young boy sits on his front steps. Corey arrives and wants to show the young boy something up the hill. But, he is afraid of Lester's dog.

Corey can't hear his friend's complaints because he is deaf. Corey and his friend discover a little kitten and on the way back home the boy overcomes his fears and yells at Lester's dog to get away. Then on to Mr. Frank's house where they give him the kitten. The words and beautiful illustrations capture the extraordinary friendship between these two boys and the kindness to their neighbor. This is an excellent story to promote acceptance and the attitude of "one of us."

Themes or Units: Feelings; Friendship; Giving & Sharing; Pet Animals.

Hill, Eric. *Where's Spot*, by author. G.P. Putnam's Sons, 1987. ISBN 0-399-21478-X [20 p]. Fiction, PS-K. Disability: Deaf (sign language). (***) (Cat C).

This is a sign language edition of the book *Where's Spot*. An illustrated sign language translation in "Signed English" is on each page. As the story is signed to a child who is deaf, he or she sees the special sign that corresponds to each printed word. The illustrations of the signs are small; it would be difficult for children to learn how to sign from them.

Themes or Units: Pet Animals; Sign Language.

Hines, Anna Grossnickle. *Gramma's Walk*, illus. by author. Greenwillow Books, 1993. ISBN 0-688-11481-4 [28 p]. Fiction, Gr. PS-2. Disability: Physical (wheelchair). (****) (Cat C)

Donnie visits his Gramma who uses a wheelchair. During their visits they have a favorite activity of going on imaginary walks together. Today, they go to the seashore. During their imaginary outing, they see seagulls, deer tracks, boats, etc. The book is organized with the left page showing Donnie and his Gramma talking and sharing, and the right page showing what they imagine on their outing. This is a story about imagination, not about a disability. The story promotes a positive image of this grandmother who happens to be in a wheelchair.

Themes or Units: Fantasy & Imagination; Grandmothers & Grandfathers; Oceans, Lakes & Sea Animals.

Hodges, Candri. *When I Grow Up*, illus. by Dot Yoder. Jason & Nordic Publishers, 1995. ISBN 0-944727-26-3 [32 p.]. K-2. Disability: Deaf (sign language). (***) (Cat B).

Jimmy, a young boy who is deaf, has lots of questions about what it will be like when he grows up. His mother takes him on a Career Day trip where they meet people who are deaf working at the zoo, an art school, a Lawn Care Center, a factory, an office, a restaurant and delivering papers. This story points out how people who are deaf can choose many different occupations when they become adults.

Themes or Units: Community Workers/Occupations.

Hoffman, Eric. *No Fair to Tigers*, illus. by Janice Lee Porter. Redleaf Press, 1999. ISBN 1-884834-62-0 [26 p]. Fiction, Gr. PS-2. Disability: Physical (wheelchair). (***) (Cat C).

Mandy has a pet stuffed tiger. She does lots of pretending with her tiger and insists that he is hungry. Her sister goes with her to the pet shop to buy food, but Mandy can't go inside the store because there are steps and she is in a wheelchair. A fun fantasy story, yet addresses real issues related to using a wheelchair. The story is written in English and Spanish.

Themes or Units: Fantasy & Imagination; Zoo Animals.

Holcomb, Nan. *Fair and Square*, illus. by Dot Yoder. Jason & Nordic Publishers, 1992. ISBN 0-944727-09-3 [30 p.]. Fiction, Gr. PS-1. Disability: Physical (use of switches). (***) (Cat B)

Kevin is a young boy with a physical disability. He uses a wheelchair and has limited use of his hands. He wants to join in playing games with his family and friends but they keep telling him that it's too hard for him. In therapy, he learns how to use switches to run the computer and toy cars. Now he can play with his friends and be like everybody else. The story helps the reader see the importance of using switches to help persons with physical disabilities be more independent. The story promotes an attitude of "one of us."

Themes or Units: We Are Alike, We Are Different.

Holcomb, Nan. *Patrick and Emma Lou*, illus. by Dot Yoder. Jason & Nordic Publishers, 1989. ISBN 0-944727-03-4 [30 p]. Fiction, Gr. PS-1. Disability: Physical (cerebral palsy, walker). (***) (Cat B)

Patrick uses a wheelchair and Emma uses a walker. They are both at physical therapy on the same day. Patrick works on using a walker and Emma cheers him on. Emma is learning to walk with leg braces at the balance bars and Patrick cheers her on. At the end of the story they go for a walk together both using their walkers. The author indicates that this book was written for children with physical disabilities. However, the story ends with a friendship developing between these two children which would be meaningful to children with or without disabilities.

Themes or Units: Friendship; We Are Alike, We Are Different

Holcomb, Nan. *Sarah's Surprise,* illus. by Dot Yoder. Jason & Nordic Publishers, 1990. ISBN 0-944727-07-7 [32 p]. Fiction, PS-1. Disability: Speech & language. (**) (Cat B)

Sarah is six-years-old and uses a communication board. She wants to be able to sing Happy Birthday on her mom's birthday. The therapist surprises Sarah with a new Touch Talker that can say or sing whatever they program it to do. On her mom's birthday Sarah presses the button and begins to "sing" Happy Birthday with everyone else. The story promotes an attitude of "one of us." One could question why Sarah does not use sign language to communicate since she has good use of her hands. Another concern is that the pencil sketchings have pink accents with only girls wearing pink. Few stories are written about this disability.

Themes or Units: Holidays Around the World; We Are Alike, We Are Different.

Holub, Joan. *My First Book of Sign Language,* illus. by author. Troll Communications, 2001. ISBN 0-8167-4033-X [30 p]. Fiction, Gr. PS-3. Disability: Deaf (sign language). (****) (Cat A).

This alphabet book introduces signs for the alphabet and signs for common words that begin with each letter. Each page has illustrations of children doing a variety of activities that begin with the letter that was introduced. Illustrations are cartoon like.

Themes or Units: Alphabet; Sign Language; We Are Alike, We Are Different.

Jansen, Larry. *My Sister is Special,* illus. by Robert Pepper. Standard Publishing, 1998. ISBN 0-7847-0797-9 [22 p]. Fiction, Gr. PS-3. Disability: Down syndrome. (***) (Cat A).

Rachel has Down syndrome. In this story, her brother points out that God makes everyone special in some way including his sister. This story provides a brief glimpse at what it's like being a brother of a little girl with Down syndrome.

Themes or Units: Brothers & Sisters; We Are Alike, We Are Different.

Jordon, MaryKate. *Losing Uncle Tim,* **illus. by Judith Friedman. Albert Whitman & Co., 1989. ISBN 0-8075-4756-5 [32 p]. Fiction, Gr. K-3. Illness: AIDS. (****) (Cat B)**

Daniel is best friends with his Uncle Tim. Then, he discovers that Tim is very ill with AIDS. Daniel gets scared that he may catch AIDS but learns that you can't catch AIDS by taking care of someone. This makes Daniel very happy and he continues to spend lots of time with Tim until he dies. Daniel is sad but remembers all that he has learned from Uncle Tim. This is a sensitive story that provides children with accurate information about the possibility of catching AIDS and the emotional experience of having a loved one die.

Themes or Units: Feelings; Friendship; Health.

Kadish, Sharona. *Discovering Friendship,* **illus. by Dee deRosa. Raintree Steck-Vaughn, 1995. ISBN 0-8114-4458-9 [31 p]. Fiction, Gr. 1-5. Disability: Deaf (sign language). (****) (Cat B).**

Kim, who is deaf, moved to a new school. Samantha befriends her and is willing to go to her house after school and learn sign language. The girls develop a special friendship. This is a lovely story about being friends with someone with a difference and how valuable that friendship can be. This story promotes an attitude of "one of us."

Themes or Units: Friendship; Friends at School; Sign Language.

Karim, Roberta. *Mandy Sue Day,* **illus. by Karen Ritz. Clarion Books, 1994. ISBN 0-395-66155-2 [28 p]. Fiction, Gr. PS-3. Disability: Blind. (****) (Cat C)**

It is Mandy's birthday so she has a day free of chores to choose what she wants to do. Mandy's choice is to spend her day with Ben, her horse and best friend. At bedtime she asks if she can finish the day by sleeping in the barn with Ben. As she gets ready to sleep in the loft, her brother gives her a flashlight. But, she reminds him she doesn't need it because she can't see. This is a beautiful example of inclusion. The story isn't about blindness rather about Mandy Sue's special day and all the fun activities she does with her horse. The illustrations show the love between this girl and her horse.

Themes or Units: Families; Farm & Farm Animals; Pet Animals; Summer; We Are Alike, We Are Different.

Kastner, Jill. *Naomi knows It's Springtime,* **illus. by author. Boyd Mills Press, 1993. ISBN 1-56397-006-6 [32 p]. Fiction, Gr. PS-2. Disability: Blindness. (****) (Cat C)**

This is a story about Naomi who knows when spring arrives by hearing familiar sounds such as the squeaks of newborn birds. She smells the lilies and lilacs that bloom in her yard and serve as signs that winter is over and spring has arrived. The reader finds out on the last page of the story that Naomi is blind. This is a very positive story showing Naomi enjoying a new season in her own special way. Exquisite, impressionist oil paintings help tell the story.

Themes or Units: Smells in the Environment; Sounds in the Environment; Spring; Sense of Touch; We Are Alike, We Are Different.

Kifer, Kathy, Phillips, Jane, Solar, Dahna, & Bernard, Charla. *Foods,* **illus. & photographs by authors. Garlic Press, 1997. ISBN 0-931993-87-3 [14 p]. Nonfiction, Gr. PS-3. Disability: Deaf (sign language). (****) (Cat A).**

This book has photographs of foods familiar to young children—next to each photo is an illustration of a person showing the sign for each food item. The illustrations are very clear, showing with arrows how the hand or fingers move to make each sign. Teacher or parents could use this book to teach signs about foods.

Themes or Units: Fruits & Vegetables; Sign Language.

Kornfield, Elizabeth J. *Dreams Come True,* **photographs by author. Rocky Mountain Children's Press, 1986. ISBN 0-940611-00-7 [24 p]. Nonfiction, Gr. 1-4. Disability/Illness: Epilepsy. (****) (Cat A)**

This is a delightful story about Katie whose dream is to be a figure skater like Dorothy Hamil. Katie has epilepsy. She explains what it is like to have a seizure, describes the tests, and talks about the medication she takes. Katie stresses that she can keep her dream of skating; having epilepsy doesn't mean she has to limit those dreams. This is a very informative and positive story about epilepsy and is supported by the Epilepsy Foundation of America. The story also helps create an image of "one of us" as Katie skates with her friends.

Themes or Units: Health; Sports; We Are Alike, We Are Different.

Krause, Ute. *Pig Surprise,* illus. by author. **Dial Books, 1989. ISBN 0-8037-0714-2 [27 p]. Fiction, Gr. K-3. Disability: Hearing Loss. (****) (Cat B).**

In this story Aunt Agatha calls to find out what Nina wants for her birthday. Aunt Agatha has a hearing loss, so when Nina asks for a guinea pig her aunt thought she said genuine pig. The rest of the story are the antics that occur when Nina receives a real pig for her birthday. A humorous book with delightful illustrations.

Themes or Units: Farm & Farm Animals; Pet Animals; Sounds in the Environment.

Krisher, Trudy. *Kathy's Hats: A Story of Hope,* illus. by Nadine **Bernard Westcott. Albert Whitman & Co., 1992. ISBN 0-8075-4116-8 [29 p]. Fiction, Gr. PS-2. Illness: Cancer. (****) (Cat B)**

This is a moving story about a little girl who has cancer. For her, the worst time is when her hair falls out. She wears a baseball cap but doesn't like it. One day her mother tells her that the most important hat of all is her thinking cap and how you feel about yourself. This is an excellent story as it shares the feelings that Kathy experiences with her treatments, yet it's a story with a positive ending. The story provides hope by pointing out that all cancer doesn't end in death. This is an excellent story for all young children to help alleviate their fears of cancer. In spite of the topic, it is an entertaining story.

Themes or Units: Feelings; Friends at School; Hats; Health; We Are Alike, We Are Different.

Kroll, Virginia L. *Butterfly Boy,* illus. by Berardo Suzan. **Boyds Mills Press, 1997. ISBN 1-56397-371-5 [27 p]. Fiction, Gr. K-3. Disability: Speech & language. (****) (Cat C).**

Grandfather cannot talk but shows excitement as he and his grandson watch a gathering of butterflies in this story set in Mexico. The butterflies are attracted to the color white. The boy's father finds he has to repaint the garage white so the butterflies will come and entertain the grandfather. The boy sits still and the butterflies come so close that his neighbor calls him Butterfly Boy! The story demonstrates how a person who can't speak is still able to communicate.

Themes or Units: Butterflies; Grandmothers & Grandfathers; Summer.

Kuklin, Susan. *Thinking Big: The Story of a Young Dwarf,* photographs by author. Lothrop, Lee & Shephard Books, 1986. ISBN 0-688-05826-4 [43 p]. Nonfiction, Gr. 2-5. Disability: Physical (dwarf). (****) (Cat B)

Jaime is smaller than her classmates because she is a dwarf. She is aware of her strengths and limitations due to her size. She meets the challenges of everyday life with success because of her positive attitude and the support of her family. The story is written in a sensitive and caring style, however, "person first" language is not utilized. This is a well presented factual account of a child with a physical disability and demonstrates her competence in everyday activities.

<u>Themes or Units</u>: **Shapes, Sizes & Weight; We Are Alike, We Are Different.**

Lakin, Patricia. *Dad and Me In The Morning,* illus. by Robert G. Steele. Albert Whitman & Co., 1994. ISBN 0-8075-1419-5 [27 p]. Fiction, Gr. PS-2. Disability: Deaf. (****) (Cat C)

This is a story about young Jacob and his father. Jacob gets up early, wakes his dad, and just the two of them hike to a special place to watch the morning sunrise. The illustrations capture the beautiful colors that appear during the spectacular sunrise. This is not a story about Jacob's deafness rather a story about a relationship between a father and a son. An excellent story that any child would enjoy.

<u>Themes or Units</u>: **Day & Night; Families; Sense of Sight.**

Lasker, Joe. *Nick Joins In,* illus. by author. Albert Whitman & Company, 1980. ISBN 0-8075-5612-2 [29 p]. Fiction, Gr. 2-3. Disability: Physical (leg braces and wheelchair). (***) (Cat B)

Nick is going to a new school and he's scared. He wonders what the kids will think when he can't walk or run. A teacher's aide meets him at the door and pushes him in his wheelchair to his new classroom. The children ask lots of questions and then have fun working and playing with Nick. The story points out things that Nick can do as well as his limitations because of his need to use a wheelchair. The story ends with Nick helping his new classmates retrieve a ball. He is accepted by his peers in this integrated setting. It would have strengthened the story if Nick had been allowed to maneuver his own wheelchair to the classroom demonstrating respect for what he can do.

<u>Themes or Units</u>: **Feelings; Friends at School; Friendship; Transportation; We Are Alike, We Are Different.**

Lears, Laurie. *Becky the Brave: A Story About Epilepsy*, illus. by Gail Piazza. Albert Whitman, 2002. ISBN 0-8075-0601-X [28 p]. Fiction, Gr. K-3. Disability: Physical (epilepsy). (****) (Cat B)

This is a touching story of the relationship between two sisters. The oldest sister is helpful and kind to her little sister. But when Becky has a seizure at school and is embarrassed, it is the little sister who helps by talking to Becky's class and explaining what happened. Becky's classmates write notes, which helps Becky feel comfortable in returning to school. Beautiful large illustrations capture the many emotions.

Themes or Units: Brothers & Sisters; Feelings; Friends at School; Health.

Lears, Laurie. *Ben Has Something to Say: A Story About Stuttering*, illus. by Karen Ritz. Albert Whitman, 2000. ISBN 0-8075-0633-8 [26 p]. Fiction, Gr. PS-3. Disability: Speech & language (stuttering). (****) (Cat B).

A fun story about a dad and his son and their outing to the junk yard. Ben wants to bring the owner's dog a bone but he doesn't want to get permission because he stutters. His dad gently encourages him to use his language and in the end Ben does speak to the owner and ends up playing with the dog. This is a sensitively written story giving the reader insight into the feelings of a person who stutters with soft, realistic illustrations.

Themes or Units: Feelings; Pet Animals.

Lears, Laurie. *Ian's Walk*, illus. by Karen Ritz. Albert Whitman, 1998. ISBN 0-8075-3480-3 [28 p]. Fiction, Gr. K-3. Disability: Autism. (****) (Cat B)

Tara goes to the park with her brother Ian who has autism. She finds some of his behaviors really annoying until he becomes lost. Then she is worried and when she finally finds him Tara walks Ian home and when the behaviors occur again, she patiently waits and is more accepting. This is a sensitive story about a difficult topic. This story would be helpful for siblings or other children to gain a clearer understanding of children with autism.

Themes or Units: Brothers & Sisters; We Are Alike, We Are Different.

Lears, Laurie. *Waiting for Mr. Goose,* **illus. by Karen Ritz. Albert Whitman, 1999. ISBN 0-8075-8628-5 [29 p]. Fiction, Gr. PS-3. Disability: Attention deficit hyperactivity disorder (ADHD). (****) (Cat C).**

It is difficult for Stephen to sit still or pay attention. His quest is to help an injured goose. In order to catch the goose he needs to have lots of patience. Stephen surprises himself and his mom when he is successful in helping the goose. A wonderful story that shows Stephen having success. The story is realistic, very sensitively written with beautiful illustrations.

<u>Themes or Units</u>: Wild Birds & Animals.

Lee, Jeanne M. *Silent Lotus,* **illus. by author. Farrar, Straus & Giroux, 1991. ISBN 0-374-36911-9 [28 p]. Fiction, Gr. K-3. Disability: Deaf. (****) (Cat B).**

Lotus is a beautiful child who isn't able to speak. She is sad, often by herself and very lonely. Her parents see her unhappiness. They take her to the temple for a sign from the gods. Lotus sees the dancers and copies their movements. She moves with grace and wants to learn to dance. The king and queen agree this is a sign. Lotus makes many friends among the dancers, is no longer lonely and becomes a famous dancer. This is a beautiful story from the Vietnamese culture and promotes a positive image of a person who is deaf. Full page, illustrations add to the story.

<u>Themes or Units</u>: **Children & Families Around the World; Feelings; Sports (dancing).**

Lester, Helen. *Hooway for Wodney Wat,* **illus. by Lynn Munsinger. Houghton Mifflin, 1999. ISBN 0-395-92392-1 [32 p]. Fiction, Gr. K-3. Disability: Speech & language. (**) (Cat B).**

Rodney is unable to say his Rs so the children in his class tease him. Later he becomes a hero when he gets rid of the class bully by saying to everyone "take a west." The class bully walks west and doesn't come back while the rest of the children take a rest! Might this book promote teasing a child with a speech problem? The story ends with Rodney being a hero which perpetuates old stereotypes of liking someone for what he or she is able to do. Perhaps this book could be used to introduce a discussion on being kind to your classmates and not being a bully.

<u>Themes or Units</u>: **Friends at School.**

Levi, Dorothy Hoffman. *A Very Special Friend*, **illus. by Ethel Gold. Kendall Green Publications, Gallaudet University Press, 1989. ISBN 0-930325-55-6 [28 p]. Fiction, Gr. K-3. Disability: Deafness. (****) (Cat B)**

One day Frannie gets excited as she sees a moving van at a house nearby. A family is moving in with a little girl her same age named Laura who is deaf and uses sign language. Frannie tells her mom that she cannot be friends because she can't understand Laura. Her mother explains that friends can talk to each other in many ways and often without words. Laura's mom helps Frannie understand some sign language and Frannie and Laura become special friends. This story promotes a positive image and the philosophy of "one of us" as Laura is accepted into her new neighborhood.

Themes or Units: Feelings; Friendship; Homes & Neighborhoods; Sign Language; Summer; We Are Alike, We Are Different.

Levi, Dorothy Hoffman. *A Very Special Sister*, **illus. by Ethel Gold. Kendall Green Publications, 1992. ISBN 0-930323-96-3 [24 p]. Fiction, Gr. PS-2. Disability: Deaf. (****) (Cat B).**

Laura, who is deaf, is excited about becoming a sister. She shares the good news with her friends. Then, Laura begins to worry that the new baby will be able to hear and will be loved more than she. Laura goes on an outing with her mother who notices Laura's sadness. Suddenly, Laura cries and tells her mom of her worry. Her mother helps Laura understand her love and that she will never go away. This is a sensitive story that promotes a positive image of a child who is deaf while recognizing her feelings.

Themes or Units: Brothers & Sisters; Feelings; Friendship; We Are Alike, We Are Different.

Levine, Edna S. *Lisa and Her Soundless World*, **illus. by Gloria Kamen. Human Sciences Press, 1974. ISBN 0-87705-104-6 [40 p]. Fiction, Gr. K-3. Disability: Hearing loss. (****) (Cat B)**

This book does an outstanding job of discussing all of the senses and then explaining what it means to be deaf or have a hearing impairment. When it looks like Lisa isn't hearing anything, her parents take her to the doctor. Lisa needs a hearing aid and while she can't hear everything, she can hear some sounds for the first time. In addition, Lisa works on saying words, is learning how to lip read, and how to use

sign language. This book contains accurate information, is very positive and would be an excellent book to explain deafness to young children. On the final pages, "person first" language is not used.

**Themes or Units: Senses; Sign Language; We Are Alike, We Are
Different.**

Litchfield, Ada B. *A Button In Her Ear,* illus. by Eleanor Mill.
Albert Whitman & Co., 1976. ISBN 0-8075-0987-6 [32 p]. Fiction,
Gr. K-3. Disability: Hearing Loss. (****) (Cat B)

Angela has a mild hearing loss. She has her hearing checked by an audiologist and is fitted for a hearing aid. The next day, she can hear what
everyone is saying. The teacher explains that just as she and several students wear glasses to see better, Angela wears an aid to hear better.
The children hold the button close so they can hear. It is a magic button! The information is accurately and sensitively presented with
Angela making humorous misinterpretations of what people are saying to her. The illustrations are a combination of pencil sketchings and
colored pictures. This story promotes a "one of us" philosophy.

**Themes or Units: Dentists, Doctors, Nurses & Hospitals;
Friends at School; Sounds in the Environment; We Are Alike, We
Are Different.**

Litchfield, Ada B. *A Cane in Her Hand,* illus. by Eleanor Mill.
Albert Whitman & Co. 1977. ISBN 0-8075-1056-4 Fiction, Gr. K-
3. Disability: Partially sighted. (****) (Cat B).

Valerie is not blind but has a visual impairment; even with glasses, she
can't see what other children see. Her mother takes her to the doctor
who tries to figure out why she is losing her vision. To help her get
around without stumbling, she learns how to cane travel. At first she
doesn't want to use the cane because she is not blind but later decides
that it does help her a lot. Her friends try the cane too. The story is
very positive as it shows all of the things Valerie can do including positive interactions with her friends.

Themes or Units: Sense of Sight, Friends at School.

Litchfield, Ada B. *Making Room for Uncle Joe,* illus. by Gail
Owens. Albert Whitman & Co., 1984. ISBN 0-8075-4952-5 [26 p].
Fiction, Gr. 1-4. Disability: Down syndrome. (**) (Cat B)

This story describes the reactions and adjustments of a family when
their uncle with Down syndrome comes to live with them. Dan, a

nephew, tells the story and explains how he worked through his own mixed feelings, how his little sister had almost immediate acceptance of Joe and how his older sister was angry and embarrassed. The story may promote some stereotypic behavior by persons with Down syndrome and does not utilize "person first" language. The author also refers to Down syndrome as Down's syndrome which is incorrect. Overall, this is a loving story of a family's acceptance of Uncle Joe.

Themes or Units: Families; Feelings; Giving & Sharing; We Are Alike, We Are Different.

Litchfield, Ada. *Words in Our Hands*, illus. by Helen Cogancherry. Albert Whitman & Co., 1980. ISBN 0-8075-9212-9 [29 p]. Fiction, Gr. K-3. Disability: Deaf. (***) (Cat A)

Michael, who is nine tells what it's like to live in a family when the mom and dad are both deaf. He explains how they communicate with sign language, lip reading and finger spelling. Examples of signing and finger spelling are included. He also shares how he feels when people stare or children make fun of his parents. It's a very helpful book for explaining deafness to young children. He points out the many things his parents can do which promotes a positive image.

Themes or Units: Families; Sign Language; Sounds in the Environment; We Are Alike, We Are Different.

London, Jonathan. *The Lion Who Has Asthma*, illus. by Nadine Bernard Westcott. Albert Whitman & Co., 1992. ISBN 0-8075-4559-7 [24 p]. Gr. PS-2. Illness: Asthma (nebulizer). (****) (Cat B)

This is an outstanding story about a young boy with asthma. He pretends he's a lion but when it becomes difficult for him to breathe he doesn't feel like a lion anymore. His mom hooks him up to the nebulizer. During this time, he pretends the mask is there because he's piloting a plane. When he breathes easily again, he becomes the king of the jungle, the lion. This is an entertaining story with neat illustrations of the many animals in the jungle. All children would enjoy this story and learn about asthma too.

Themes or Units: Fantasy & Imagination; Health; Tools & Machines; Zoo Animals.

Loski, Diana. *The Boy On The Bus,* **illus. by Gina Phillips. Writer's Press Service, 1994. ISBN 1-885101-02-3 [30 p]. Fiction, Gr. 1-3. Disability: Attention deficit disorder (ADD). (****) (Cat B).**

This story tells about all of the troubles at school for Cory, who has ADD. One day he falls down and Margo, a classmate, walks him to the nurse's office. The nurse explains to Margo about ADD, the medication Cory takes and why he behaves like he does. The nurse tells Margo what Corey really needs is a friend. That day Margo saves a seat for him on the bus next to her. The explanation of ADD is very clear and appropriate for primary aged children. This is a well written story about a topic that is difficult for children to understand.

<u>Themes or Units</u>: **Feelings; Friends at School; We Are Alike, We Are Different.**

Lowell, Gloria Roth. *Elana's Ears or How I Became the Best Big Sister in the World,* **illus. by Karen Stormer Brooks. Magination Press, 2000. ISBN 1-55798-598-7 [29 p]. Fiction, PS-3. Disability: Deaf (hearing loss). (****) (Cat B).**

This story is told by Lacey, the family dog. A new baby comes to this family and Lacey realizes that Elana can't hear. Lacey becomes a hearing dog and helps the baby in many ways. Elana gets hearing aids so now she can hear some sounds. This is a fun story that all young children would enjoy. The story will help children have a better understanding of someone who can't hear.

<u>Themes or Units</u>: **Brothers & Sisters; Pet Animals; Sounds in the Environment.**

Lyon, George Ella. *Cecil's Story,* **illus. by Peter Catalanotto. Orchard Books, 1991. ISBN 0-531-05012-X [29 p]. Fiction, Gr. K-4. Disability: Physical (loss of limb). (****) (Cat B).**

This story is about a boy whose father was in the Civil War. One day the boy's mother leaves to bring his father home. The boy imagines what it would be like if his father didn't return and he'd have to take care of the animals and the plowing. He imagines what it would be like if his father was hurt in the fighting. His father returns with only one arm yet is able to lift the boy into an embrace. This is a very tender story with exquisite soft colored paintings that capture the emotions.

<u>Themes or Units</u>: **Families; Feelings; Peace Education.**

Mackinnon, Christy. *Silent Observer,* illus. by author. Kendall Green Publications, 1993. [42 p]. Nonfiction, Gr. 2-5. Disability: Deaf. (****) (Cat B).

Christy lost her hearing from a bout of whooping cough at the age of two. This story is her biography, how she coped with being deaf when she was living at home and her education at a residential school for the deaf and her agony of homesickness. The story takes place in Canada at an earlier time in history. The story gives the reader wonderful insight into the life of a child who is deaf.

Themes or Units: **We Are Alike, We Are Different.**

MacLachlan, Patricia. *Through Grandpa's Eyes,* pictures by Deborah Kogan Ray. Harper Trophy, 1980. ISBN 0-06-443041-3 [37 p]. Fiction, Gr. K-3. Disability: Blind. (****) (Cat B)

John stays with his grandparents and does everything with his Grandpa who is blind. They exercise together, play the cello, go for walks and read books under the tree. John learns to see the world through his Grandpa's eyes including the smile in Grandmother's voice as she tells him to go to sleep at the end of a busy day. This story provides a positive image of a person who is blind by pointing out the many things that Grandpa can do and the loving relationship he has with his grandson. This is a sensitively written story with warm illustrations.

Themes or Units: **Families; Grandmothers & Grandfathers; Sounds in the Environment; Smells in the Environment; We Are Alike, We Are Different.**

Maguire, Arlene. *Special People, Special Ways,* illus. by Sheila Bailey. Portunus Publishing, 1999. ISBN 1-886440-00-X [28 p]. Fiction, Gr. PS-K. Disability: Variety of disabilities. (***) (Cat B).

The story is in rhyme and stresses that even though people may look or do things differently, they all share the same hopes and fears. It points out we should help people and be thoughtful of others. The book has cartoon illustrations.

Themes or Units: **Friendship; We Are Alike, We Are Different.**

Martin, Bill J.R. *Knots on a Counting Rope*, illus. by Ted Rand. H. Holt, 1987. ISBN 0-0850-0571-4 [32 p]. Fiction, Gr. K-3. Disability: Blind. (***)(Cat B)

This is a story about a Native American boy and his grandfather. Using the story telling tradition, the grandfather tells the boy the story of his birth and how it left the child blind. The counting rope is a metaphor for the passage of time and the boy's growing confidence. The illustrations add to this very sensitive and heartwarming story. There has been some controversy about this book questioning its accuracy in depicting the American Indian.

Themes or Units: Children & Families Around the World; Grandmothers & Grandfathers; We Are Alike, We Are Different.

Mayer, Gina and Mercer. *A Very Special Critter*, illus. by authors. Western Publishers, 1992. ISBN 0-307-12763-X [23 p]. Fiction, Gr. PS-3. Disability: Physical (wheelchair). (****) (Cat B)

Alex is the new boy in class. The other children are curious because Alex is in a wheelchair. They have many questions and find out that Alex can do lots of things. He carries books in his pouches, plays volleyball and dresses up like a car for the Halloween party. What the children discover is that once in a while Alex needs help but so does everyone else. The book is an excellent example of inclusion and acceptance. The author emphasizes everything that Alex can do and being one of the gang is part of it.

Themes or Units: Friends at School; Holidays Around the World; We Are Alike, We Are Different.

McMahon, Patricia. *Listen for the Bus: David's Story*, photographs by John Godt. Boyds Mills Press, 1995. ISBN 1-56397-368-5 [45 p]. Nonfiction, Gr. K-3. Disability: Blind. (***) (Cat A).

This is a photo essay of David's first day at Kindergarten, showing the many things he does at school in an integrated setting. The story continues after school showing all that David does at home and in his community with his parents. The story is positive in that it stresses all that David can do as well as his limitations.

Themes or Units: Friends at School; Homes & Neighborhoods.

McMahon, Patricia. *Summer Tunes: A Martha's Vineyard Vacation,* photographs by Peter Simon. Boyds Mills, 1996. ISBN 1-56397-572-6 [47 p]. Nonfiction, Gr. 1-5. Disability: Physical (cerebral palsy, wheelchair). (***) (Cat B).

This is a photo essay of Conor's vacation on Martha's Vineyard. Conor uses a wheelchair and faces some unique challenges throughout the story. He participates in everything with his family, even the bike rides by being in a trailer behind his father's bike. This is a story of a family vacation and provides insight into how a child in a wheelchair can be a part of his family's adventure.

<u>Themes or Units</u>: Families; Summer.

Merrifield, Margaret. *Come Sit By Me,* illus. by Heather Collins. Women's Press, 1990. ISBN 0-88961-141-6 [26 p]. Fiction, Gr. PS-3. Chronic Illness: HIV—AIDS. (****) (Cat B)

This is an educational storybook for small children and their caregivers about AIDS and HIV infection. Karen asks her mom, "What is AIDS?" Her mother explains and tells her that it is okay to play with Nicholas. Now, other children won't play with Karen because she is playing with the boy with AIDS. Karen's parents organize a parent meeting where they talk about HIV and AIDS. Eventually all of the children play with Nicholas and call to him, "Come sit by me." At the end of the book, information is provided regarding ways you cannot get AIDS plus additional information for parents, teachers, & caregivers.

<u>Themes or Units</u>: Friends at School; Friendship; Health; We Are Alike, We Are Different.

Meyers, Cindy. *Rolling Along With Goldilocks and the Three Bears,* illus. by Carol Morgan. Woodbine, 1999. ISBN 1-890627-12-7 [26 p]. Fiction, Gr. PS-3. Disability: Physical (wheelchair & walker). (****) (Cat C).

This is the traditional story of Goldilocks except in this story baby bear uses a wheelchair. When Goldilocks visits their cottage, the bears are taking baby bear to the physical therapist. Goldilocks falls asleep in baby bear's special bed. When she awakens, she becomes friends with baby bear and tries out his wheelchair. An outstanding inclusionary book that helps children learn about someone who uses a wheelchair.

<u>Themes or Units</u>: Friendship; We Are Alike, We Are Different.

Millman, Isaac. *Moses Goes to a Concert,* **illus. by author. Farrar, Straus & Giroux, 1998. ISBN 0-374453-66-7 [28 p]. Fiction, Gr. PS-3. Disability: Deaf. (****) (Cat B).**

Moses goes to the concert with his classmates who are all deaf. One of the musicians, a percussionist, is also deaf. She doesn't wear shoes so she can follow the orchestra by feeling the vibrations of the music through her stocking feet. After the program, she lets the children play her percussion instruments. The story is told in illustrations, written English and American Sign Language. An interesting story that points out even though a person is deaf, he or she can enjoy lots of things even the orchestra playing music.

Themes or Units: **Friends at School; Music; Sounds in the Environment.**

Millman, Isaac. *Moses Goes to School,* **illus. by author. Farrar, Straus & Giroux, 2000. ISBN 0-374-35069-8 [19 p]. Fiction, Gr. PS-3. Disability: Deaf. (****) (Cat B).**

Moses goes to a special school for the deaf. The story shows a typical day at school where the children play together, talk with friends, do school work, write pen pal letters and work on the computers. The reader begins to realize that these children do lots of things other children do only they communicate using sign. The story is told in pictures, written English and American Sign Language.

Themes or Units: **Friends at School; Sense of Sight.**

Mills, Joyce C. *Little Tree: A Story for Children with Serious Medical Problems,* **illus. by Michael Chesworth. Magination Press, 1992. ISBN 0-945354-52-5 [28 p]. Fiction, Gr. K-3. Health: Serious medical problems. (***) (Cat B).**

Little Tree is sad because the storm caused her to lose some of her branches, but she knows that she will be okay because she still has a strong trunk and roots and a beautiful heart. It is the author's hope that this story will help children who experience life threatening illnesses or accidents find comfort, inspiration and an inner sense of well-being. The story's illustrations are black and white sketches.

Themes or Units: **Feelings; Health.**

Milne, A.A. *Winnie-the-Pooh's ABC: Sign Language Edition,* illus. by Ernest H. Shepard. Dutton Children's Books, 2001. ISBN 0-525-46714-9 [26 p]. Fiction, Gr. PS-2. Disability: Deaf (sign language). (****) (Cat A).

This is a typical ABC book with one letter of the alphabet on each page with wonderful illustrations from Winnie the Pooh. Each page has a letter, a sketch of the finger spelling for the letter, an illustration with a one word description of the illustration and a sketch of a person providing the sign for the one word description. The Winnie the Pooh illustrations makes this book very special.

Themes or Units: Alphabet; Sense of Sight; Sign Language.

Mitchell, Lori. *Different Just Like Me,* illus. by author. Charlesbridge Publishing, 1999. ISBN 0-88106-975-2 [28 p]. Fiction, Gr. K-3. Disability: Blind, Physical (wheelchair), deaf (sign language). (****) (Cat B).

April is anxious to go to her Grandmother's on Friday. The story describes what April does each day of the week including people she meets who are like her but also have some differences. An excellent book that could be used for talking about likenesses and differences in a positive way.

Themes or Units: We Are Alike, We Are Different.

Mitchell, Phillips, Rita. *Hue Boy,* illus. by Caroline Binch. Puffin Pied Piper, 1993. ISBN 0-14-055995-7 [24 p]. Fiction, Gr. K-3. Disability: Physical (small stature). (***) (Cat B).

This is a story about Hue Boy who is black and very small for his age. Everyone tries to help him. His mama feeds him more food, his neighbor has him doing exercises, they had him visit the doctor and found he was healthy, just small. He sits at the harbor and when his father gets off the ship, he runs to him; walking beside his father Hue Boy no longer feels small. This story shows children that people come in different sizes and that is okay.

Themes or Units: Shapes, Sizes & Weights; We Are Alike, We Are Different.

Montoussamy-Ashe, Jeanne. *Daddy & Me,* photographs by author. Alfred A. Knopf, 1993. ISBN 0-679-85096-1 [34 p]. Nonfiction, Gr. PS-3. Chronic

Illness: AIDS. (****) (Cat A)

This is a collection of black and white photographs with limited text that show the loving relationship between a father who has AIDS and his young daughter. The photos show the many things they do together including going to the park, singing and praying. She helps her daddy with his breathing machine much like he has helped her when she was sick. While the reader knows the father has AIDS, the emphasis of this photo essay is on this father-daughter relationship that can still exist even when one is sick with a disease like AIDS.

Themes or Units: Families; Health.

Moon, Nicola. **Lucy's Picture, illus. by Alex Ayliffe. Dial Books, 1994. ISBN 0-8037-1833-0]24 p]. Fiction, Gr. PS-3. Disability: Blind (guide dog). (****) (Cat C)**

Lucy's grandfather is coming to school and she wants to surprise him. The older children are painting pictures, but Lucy wants to make a collage. She collects many items even a clipping of her own hair. Grandpa who is blind is overwhelmed with her picture because he can feel the tree, bird and hair, which is Honey his guide dog. The illustrations are extremely colorful and entertaining. All children would enjoy this story including the loving relationship between Lucy and her Grandpa.

Themes or Units: Colors in My World; Giving & Sharing; Grandmothers & Grandfathers; Sense of Touch.

Moran, George. *Imagine Me On A Sit-Ski!* illus. by Nadine Bernard Westcott. Albert Whitman & Co., 1995. ISBN 0-8075-3618-0 [30 p]. Fiction, Gr. PS-3. Disability: Physical (cerebral palsy); Speech & Language (wordboard). (****) (Cat B)

Billy has cerebral palsy, uses a wheelchair and communicates using a word board. His class goes to the ski lodge to learn to ski! He uses a sit-ski while other students use a variety of other adapted ski equipment. It's an entertaining story showing persons with physical disabilities participating in a sport and having fun. The story is realistic and provides a positive image of persons with physical disabilities.

Themes or Units: Sports; We Are Alike, We Are Different.

Moss, Deborah M. *Lee, the Rabbit with Epilepsy,* illus. by Carol Schwartz. Woodbine House, 1989. ISBN 0-933149-32-8 [32 p]. Fiction, Gr. K-4. Disability & Illness: Epilepsy. (****) (Cat B)

This book uses animal characters to tell the story of Lee who has epilepsy. Lee's parents take her to the doctor who in simple terms describes the condition of epilepsy. The doctor prescribes some medication which will make the seizures go away. Lee is still worried about going places and doing things in case she has a seizure. Grandpa won't take "no" for an answer and takes Lee fishing where she catches a fish. "I knew you could do it," Grandpa says. The book provides accurate information about epilepsy through a story that is realistic and reassuring.

Themes or Units: Dentists, Doctors, Nurses & Hospitals; Families; Fish or Fishing; Grandmothers & Grandfathers; Health; Summer; We Are Alike, We Are Different.

Moss, Deborah M. *Shelley The Hyperactive Turtle,* illus. by Carol Schwartz. Woodbine House, 1989. ISBN 0-933149-31-X [19 p]. Fiction, Gr. K-3. Disability/Illness: Attention deficit hyperactivity disorder (ADHD). (**) (Cat B)

Animal characters are used to tell the story of a turtle who doesn't have friends and feels sad because everyone thinks he is bad. The doctor diagnoses his problem as ADHD. Shelley goes to a therapist each week and takes a pill every morning to help him calm down. The story emphasizes all of the troubles Shelley experiences then ends quickly which limits the opportunity of providing a positive image of Shelley. The story provides inaccurate information about tests that are used to diagnose ADHD. The story doesn't stress that the child is responsible for his or her behavior and not the medication.

Themes or Units: Dentist, Doctor, Nurses, and Hospitals; Health; We Are Alike, We Are Different.

Muldoon, Kathleen M. *Princess Pooh,* illus. by Linda Shute. Albert Whitman & Co., 1989. ISBN 0-8075-6627-6 [29 p]. Fiction, Gr. 2-5. Disability: Physical (crutches, wheelchair). (****) (Cat B)

Patty calls her sister Princess Pooh because she sits on her throne on wheels. When Penny is sleeping, Patty takes off in her wheelchair. Patty falls out of the chair cutting her knee. She crosses a street but only makes it to the middle when the light changes. Patty is sure she is going to get hit. Many other things happen like people looking at her and turning away. Finally she gets off the chair and pushes it home. Patty has a new understanding of her sister. This is an excellent story to help children understand the challenges of having a disability and using a wheelchair.

Themes or Units: Brothers & Sisters; Feelings; Transportation.

Muller, Gerda. *The Garden In The City*, illus. by author. Dutton Children's Books, 1992. ISBN 0-525-44697-4 [36 p]. Fiction, Gr. 1-4. Disability: Physical (wheel chair). (****) (Cat C)

Ben and Caroline, children who live in the city in the same apartment building, decide to have a garden. This story goes through their planning and making the garden. Other friends join in, including one friend who is in a wheelchair. The children come up with innovations that make it possible for him to participate in planting and harvesting. Throughout the story readers learn facts about identifying, growing and caring for a variety of plants. The illustrations are outstanding. Children would have hours of fun looking at the pictures.

Themes or Units: Homes & Neighborhoods; Planting & Gardening; Spring.

Okimoto, Jean Davies. *A Place For Grace*, illus. by Doug Keith. Sasquatch Books, 1993. ISBN 0-912365-73-0 [29 p]. Fiction, Gr. PS-4. Disability: Deaf (hearing dog). (****) (Cat C).

Grace is a small, cute dog who wants to be a guide dog. After she is kicked out of Dog Guide School for being too small, Grace is selected to train to be a hearing dog. The story shows all of the training and the adaptations that are needed because of Grace's size. In the end she receives a diploma. A delightful story that all ages would enjoy, but for young preschoolers the story may need to be told rather than read because of its length.

Themes or Units: Pet Animals.

Orr, Wendy. *Arabella*, illus. by Kim Gamble. Angus & Robertson, 1998. ISBN 0-207-19164-6 [30 p]. Fiction, Gr. K-3. Disability: Physical (wheelchair). (****) (Cat C).

Matthew sails on his grandfather's sailboat to his island and stays with him for a few days while they sail, enjoy nature, and play games. Grandfather shares with him a small replica of a beautiful ship, the Arabella, that is very special to him. One night a storm hits the island, the window blows open and Arabella lands in the sea. Matthew takes the boat and tries to get Arabella. He is caught in the storm and has to work very hard to pull the ropes and return to Grandfather who was very worried. Grandfather thought he had lost what is most special to him—not Arabella, but his grandson whom he rolls down the dock in his wheelchair. This is an excellent example of inclusive literature.

Themes or Units: Grandmothers & Grandfathers; Summer.

O'Shaughnessy, Ellen. *Somebody Called Me A Retard Today . . . and My Heart Felt Sad*, illus. by David Garner. Walker & Co., 1992. ISBN 0-8027-8196-9 [18 p]. Fiction, Gr. PS-K. Disability: Mental retardation, learning disability. (****) (Cat A)

This is a short story that describes how a child feels when called a "retard." The father talks to the child stressing the child's positive characteristics including all of the things the child can do. This is a good story to promote discussion about name calling because the story points out how the recipient feels. The story could be used for any name calling whether or not it's related to having a disability. The child in the illustrations could be a girl or a boy which may increase the story's use.

Themes or Units: Feelings; We Are Alike, We Are Different.

Osofsky, Audrey. *My Buddy*, illus. by Ted Rand. Henry Hold & Co., 1992. ISBN 0-8050-1747-X [28 p]. Fiction, Gr. PS-3. Disability: Physical (muscular dystrophy, wheelchair). (****) (Cat A)

This is a heartwarming story about a young boy with muscular dystrophy and his dog. Buddy has been trained to do things that the boy can not do for himself such as turning on light switches and picking up items. Once trained, Buddy helps at the pet store, at school, at a friend's house and even when the boy is playing T-ball. Children will be amazed at all the things Buddy can do for his master. The story stresses the independence the young boy has because of Buddy. The colorful illustrations capture the acceptance of this boy and his dog and the love between them.

Themes or Units: Pet Animals; We Are Alike, We Are Different.

Pearson, Susan. *Happy Birthday, Grampie,* pictures by Ronald Himler. Dial Books, 1987. ISBN 0-8037-3458-1 [27 p]. Fiction, Gr. PS-3. Disability: Blind. (****) (Cat C)

Martha makes a special birthday card for her Grampa who is blind. At the nursing home, they give a birthday party for Grampa. After Martha gives him her card, Grandpa concentrates on feeling the raised letters on the card which say "I love you." Suddenly, Grandpa's face lights up, he gives Martha a big hug and says, "Martha, I love you too." This story is very sensitively written. The story is realistic considering that Grandpa is 89 years old. The feelings of love and respect exist for young and old, with or without a disability.

Themes or Units: Dentist, Doctors, Nurses & Hospitals (nursing home); Families; Feelings; Giving & Sharing; Grandmothers & Grandfathers; Sense of Touch.

Peckinpah, Sandra Lee. *Rosey . . . the Imperfect Angel*, illus. by Trisha Moore. Scholars Press, 1991. ISBN 0-9627806-0-X [25 p]. Fiction, Gr. 1-3. Disability: Speech & language (cleft lip). (***) (Cat B)

This is a fairy tale about Rosey, a young angel with a cleft lip. In the Land Above, Rosey's peer angels taunt her. With the support of the Boss Angel, Rosie is given the Garden of January where she works and ultimately grows the most beautiful flowers. Rosey is then sent to the Land Below where a new baby was born with a cleft lip. Rosey is to teach the family about the beauty of imperfection. The author has written a delightful fairy tale about a difficult topic. The illustrations are realistic, yet pleasing.

Themes or Units: Fantasy & Imagination; Feelings; Planting & Gardening; We Are Alike, We Are Different.

Peterson, Jeanne Whitehouse. *I Have A Sister My Sister Is Deaf*, pictures by Deborah Kogan Ray. Harper Trophy, 1984. ISBN 0-06-443059-6 [32 p]. Fiction, Gr. PS-3. Disability: Deaf. (****) (Cat A)

A young girl describes what life is like for her little sister who is deaf. She explains that being deaf doesn't hurt, although her sister's feelings are hurt when people don't understand. While her sister may be limited with the words she can speak, she can say more with her facial expressions than most people can with words. The information presented is realistic and emphasizes abilities as well as limitations. The story and the pencil sketched illustrations portray a sister's loving relationship with her little sister. The story is written with simplicity and sensitivity which helps the reader enter the world of a person who has total deafness.

Themes or Units: Brothers & Sisters; Families; We Are Alike, We Are different.

Phillips, Jane, Kifer, Kathy, & Krasnik, Marina. *Pets, Animals & Creatures,* illus. & photographs by authors. Garlic Press, 1994. ISBN 0-931993-89-X [29 p]. Fiction, Gr. PS-3. Disability: Deaf (signing). (****) (Cat A).

This book has photographs of pets and animals and creatures from the farm, forest, arctic, grassland, desert, and water—next to each photo is an illustration of a person demonstrating the sign. The illustrations are very clear, showing with arrows how the hand or fingers move to make the sign. Teachers could use this manual to teach these signs.

Themes or Units: Farm & Farm Animals; Pet Animals; Sign Language; Wild Birds & Animals; Zoo Animals

Pirner, Connie White. *Even Little Kids Get Diabetes,* illus. by Nadine Bernard Wescott. Albert Whitman & Co., 1991. ISBN 0-8075-2158-2 [21 p]. Fiction, Gr. PS-2. Illness: Diabetes. (****) (Cat A)

The story is about a little girl who gets diabetes when she is two years old. The story is very positive with the emphasis on eating the right foods at the right times and having finger pokes and shots so she doesn't get sick. The story also addresses the feelings that other members of the family have as they worry about the disease. This story would help young children understand the illness of diabetes and why the person isn't allowed to eat sweets and needs to have insulin shots in order to be healthy. The illustrations are very colorful.

Themes or Units: Dentists, Doctors, Nurses & Hospitals; Health; We Are Alike, We Are Different.

Porte, Barbara Ann. *Harry's Dog,* illus. by Yossi Abolafia. Greenwillow Books, 1984. ISBN 0-6880-02555-2 [47 p]. Fiction, Gr. K-3. Illness: Allergies. (****) (Cat B)

Harry wants a dog so badly but he can't have one because his Dad is allergic to dogs. So, Harry sneaks a dog into his room. When he is found out, Harry proceeds to tell three far-fetched stories as to how he got the dog and why it can't be returned. His Dad understands because when he was growing up he wanted a dog too, but couldn't because of his allergies. An aunt comes to the rescue agreeing to keep Harry's dog. This is an entertaining story that would help children have a better understanding about allergies. This book is like an early reader with an illustration and 4 to 6 sentences on each page.

Themes or Units: Health; Pet Animals.

Powers, Mary Ellen. *Our Teacher's in a Wheelchair*, pictures by author. Albert Whitman & Company, 1986. ISBN 0-8075-6240-8 [20 p]. Non-fiction, Gr. PS-3. Disability: Physical (wheelchair). (****) (Cat A)

Brian is a teacher in a child-care center. When he was in college he had an accident playing lacrosse which paralyzed his legs and necessitates his using a wheelchair. Black and white photographs show Brian at home as well as working with the children. The story points out all that Brian can do as well as some of the difficulties he encounters. Children need to realize that some of the difficulties are due to the environment (i.e. curbs). The story illustrates that while Brian may need help at times, everyone does. The story is very realistic and sensitively written.

Theme or Units: Community Workers/Occupations; Feelings; Safety; We Are Alike, We Are Different.

Prall, Jo. *My Sister's Special*, photographs by Linda Gray. Children's Press, 1986. ISBN 0-516-03862-1 [31 p]. Nonfiction, Gr. PS-3. Disability: Mental retardation, multiple disabilities (brain damage). (****) (Cat A)

A young brother tells about his sister, Angie, who has brain damage and multiple disabilities as a result of her brain not getting enough oxygen when she was very sick as a young child. Black and white photographs show how he plays with Angie, how they get ready for the day, the communication board that Angie uses, and the outings with their family. While Angie is limited in what she can do, the story remains positive and is a very realistic.

Themes or Units: Brothers & Sisters; We Are Alike, We Are Different.

Pulber, Robin. *Way To Go Alex!* illus. by Elizabeth Wolf. Albert Whitman, 1999. ISBN 0-8075-1583-3 [29 p]. Fiction, Gr. K-4. Disability: Down syndrome. (****) (Cat B).

A sister learns a great deal about her brother who has Down syndrome as she helps him train for the Special Olympics. Through this experience she realizes that there is more than winning first place. This is a respectful account of this boy's experiences in Special Olympics.

Themes or Units: Brothers & Sisters; Sports.

Quinlan, Patricia. *Tiger Flowers*, illus. by Janet Wilson. Dial Books, 1994. ISBN 0-8037-1407-6 [29 p]. Fiction, Gr. K-3. Illness: AIDS. (****) (Cat B)

Joel has a special uncle, Michael. Together they go to baseball games and build a tree house. Joel becomes even closer to his uncle when he comes to live with Joel's family because he is sick with AIDS. When his uncle dies, Joel finds comfort in his many happy memories of his uncle. At the end of the story, Joel gives his sister a Tiger Flower, which was his uncle's favorite flower and now has become Joel's favorite flower too. This is an outstanding story to help children learn about AIDS because it is realistic yet so caring. Vibrant illustrations highlight this story.

Themes or Units: Families; Health

Quinn, Patricia O., & Stern, Judith M. *Putting on the Brakes: Young People's Guide to Understanding Attention Deficit Hyperactivity Disorder*. Magination Press, 2001. ISBN1-55798-795-5 [80 p]. Nonfiction, Gr. 3-8. Disability: Attention deficit hyperactivity disorder (ADHD). (****) Cat A)

This book is for older children. It is very comprehensive with information about every aspect of ADHD including what is ADHD, symptoms, treatments, medication, behavior and making friends. There is a lot of text with small black and white photographs. This would be a good book for older children who want to know more about ADHD.

Themes or Units: We Are Alike, We Are Different.

Rabe, Berniece. *The Balancing Girl*, illus. by Lillian Hoban. E.P. Dutton, 1981. ISBN 0-525-44364-9 [32 p]. Fiction, Gr. K-3. Disability: Physical (wheelchair, leg braces, crutches). (****) (Cat C)

At school, Margaret is so good at balancing things that she is called "The Balancing Girl." Tommy gives Margaret a hard time about all of her balancing activities by belittling and trying to destroy her efforts. Then, the principal asks the children to come up with ideas for booths at the school carnival. Margaret's idea brings in the most money. The story promotes a positive image of a person with a disability and clearly shows Margaret participating in the activities that take place. It promotes a "one of us" attitude.

Themes or Units: Friends at School; We Are Alike, We Are Different.

Rabe, Berniece. *Where's Chimpy?* photographs by Diane Schmidt. Albert Whitman & Co., 1988. ISBN 0-8075-8928-4 [26 p]. Nonfiction, Gr. PS-2. Disability: Down syndrome. (****) (Cat C)

Misty is in bed with dad ready to read a story when she realizes she doesn't have Chimpy, her bedtime monkey. They go back through her day looking for the monkey. At each place, they find something that Misty left behind. When Chimpy is found, Dad reads a story but before going to sleep, they count the newly found toys. The colored photographs capture the warm relationship between Misty and her Daddy. The re-creation of the day's activities points out that Misty goes places, plays with toys and likes things similar to any other young children. Any child would enjoy this outstanding book.

Themes or Units: Families; Naptime & Bedtime; Numbers & Counting; Zoo

Raffi. *One Light, One Sun*, illus. by Eugenie Fernandes. Crown Publishers, Inc., 1988. ISBN 0-517-56785-7 [29 p]. Fiction, Gr. PS-2. Disability: Physical (wheelchair). (****) (Cat C)

This story points out how one sun lights everyone's day. The sun shines on families from three houses as they play and picnic by the stream. As the sun goes down all of the families go home to eat dinner, do activities, and then go to bed. As the sun comes up, the families begin to awaken for another day. One of the families has a child in a wheelchair. He goes outside by the stream and plays with the other children. When he goes home, he eats dinner, and is read a story by his father before bed. The story shows that his routines are similar to the children in the other houses, which promotes a "one of us" attitude.

Themes or Units: Colors in my World; Day & Night; Families; Homes & Neighborhoods; Naptime & Bedtime; Summer.

Rankin, Laura. *The Handmade Alphabet*, illus. by author. Dial Books, 1991. ISBN 0-8037-0975-7 [27 p]. Nonfiction, All ages. Disability: Deaf. (****) (Cat A)

This book introduces the visual world of signing utilizing American Sign Language. Each page illustrates a handshape for the manual alphabet and a corresponding letter of the written alphabet. A picture of an item that begins with that letter is shown with the signing hand. For example, the hand that signs "V" holds a valentine; the hand signing "R" is entwined with a ribbon. The illustrations are very realistic depicting hands of male and female as well as the young and old. Children would need some understanding of signing before this book would be of interest.

<u>Themes or Units</u>: **Alphabet; Sense of Sight; We Are Alike, We Are Different.**

Rheingrover, Jean Sasso. *Veronica's First Year,* illus. by Kay Life. Albert Whitman, 1996. ISBN o-8075-8474-6 [21 p]. Fiction, Gr. PS-3. Disability: Down syndrome. (****) (Cat B).

This is a wonderfully written story about a young boy, and his newly born sister who has Down syndrome. The book focuses on all the things that Veronica can do during her first year. This is a very realistic and respectful story.

<u>Themes or Units</u>: **Brothers & Sisters; We Are Alike, We Are Different.**

Rickert, Janet Elizabeth. *Russ and the Firehouse,* photographs by Pete McGahan. Woodbine, 2000. ISBN 1-890627-17-8 [24 p]. Disability: Down syndrome. (****) (Cat C).

This book is a picture essay of a young child's day visiting the firehouse. It has limited text and large full-page photographs. The young boy has Down syndrome. The story is very inclusive as you see the many things this child is able to do.

<u>Themes or Units</u>: **Community Workers/Occupations (firefighter).**

Rickert, Janet Elizabeth. *Russ and the Almost Perfect Day,* photographs by Pete McGahan. Woodbine, 2000. ISBN 1-890627-18-6 [16 p]. Disability: Down syndrome. (****) (Cat C).

On the way to school, Russ finds a five-dollar bill. He and his friend plan to buy ice cream at lunch with the money. The story continues and points out many good things that happen to Russ at school that day. At lunch, just as he and his friend are about to buy ice cream, they see a girl crying because she lost her lunch money. As much as the boys wanted their ice cream, they gave the girl the money they had found. This is a wonderful story to show the inclusion of a child with Down syndrome in the events that happen at the neighborhood school.

<u>Themes or Units</u>: **Feelings; Friends at School; Giving & Sharing.**

Richert, Janet Elizabeth. *Russ and the Apple Tree Surprise,* photographs by Pete McGrahan. Woodbine, 1999. ISBN 1-890627-16-X [26 p]. Disability: Down syndrome. (****) (Cat C).

With the help of his parents and grandparents, Russ learns about the fruit that is harvested from the apple trees in his back yard. He helps his mom and grandmother make an apple pie which everyone enjoys eating. This young boy has Down syndrome and is included in all of the family activities.

Themes or Units: Apples; Families at Work; Grandmothers & Grandfathers; Planting & Gardening.

Riggio, Anita. *Secret Signs: Along the Underground Railroad,* illus. by author. Boyds Mills Press, 1997. ISBN 1-56397-555-6 [28 p]. Fiction, Gr. K-4. Disability: Deaf (sign language). (****) (Cat C).

Luke and his mother make sugar eggs to sell at the general store—a bad man comes to their house and accuses his mother of hiding slaves. So, this time Luke has to go to the general store alone where he passes on a secret message through one of the sugar eggs. This story shares an important part of history with young children. In addition, it points out how people who are deaf also participated in historical events.

Themes or Units: Feelings.

Riggs, Stephanie. *Never Sell Yourself Short,* photographs by Bill Youmans. Albert Whitman & Co, 2001. ISBN 0-8075-5563-0 [27 p]. Nonfiction, Gr. 1-5. Disability: Dwarfism (achondroplasia). (****) (Cat A).

This story is about a fifteen-year-old boy with dwarfism. The story answers many questions such as why Josh is short and how he copes with the many challenges in his life including school and friendships. Beautiful colored photographs add to the story, which would help children understand what it is like to be a dwarf. This is an excellent book that describes what life is like as a dwarf in a very positive and interesting way. The last page of the book provides additional information about dwarfism.

Themes or Units: Feelings; Friendship; We Are Alike, We Are Different.

Roberts, Karon. *Bright . . . and Behind: A Book for Children and Parents Learning to Cope with Reading and Attention Problems,* **photographs by Wendy Roberts. Edgeworth Communication, 1998. ISBN 0-9663817-3-4 [51 p]. Nonfiction, Gr. K-3. Disability: Learning disability. (***) (Cat B).**

This is a small book 3 1/2 by 5 1/2 inches. Pictures are on the left page with two to three sentences on each right page. It is a story about Wes. He shares with the readers his feelings and frustrations of having a learning disability. Wes also shares what he likes and what is difficult. It is realistic, yet positively written and would help children gain some understanding of what it is like to have a learning disability.

<u>Themes or Units</u>: **Feelings; We Are Alike, We Are Different.**

Roby, Cynthis. *When is Learning Tough: Kids Talk About Their Learning Disabilities,* **photographs by Elena Dorfman. Albert Whiteman, 1994. ISBN 0-8075-8892-X [55 p]. Nonfiction, Gr. 2-6. Disability: Learning disability. (***) (Cat A).**

This is a book that tells the stories of eight children, elementary and middle school, with learning disabilities. Each child tells his or her own story including their challenges, talents and learning techniques. Misconceptions associated with learning disabilities are also explained. The photographs represent children of various cultures. This book provides lots of information that children who have LD would enjoy as well as others who want to know more about this disability.

<u>Themes or Units</u>: **We Are Alike, We Are Different.**

Rogers, Alison. *Luke Has Asthma, Too,* **illus. by Michael Middleton. Waterfront Books, 1987. ISBN 0-914525-06-9 [31 p]. Fiction, Gr. PS-2. Illness: Asthma. (****) (Cat B)**

This is a story about a little boy who has asthma. He looks up to Luke because he has asthma too, yet plays baseball and rides his bike. The story explains what it feels like to have asthma and shows the machines and inhalers that are used. When his asthma gets really bad he has to go to the hospital. He and his dad learn new exercises to do when he has trouble breathing. When he returns home, Luke brings him a baseball cap just like his and they ride their bikes. This story demonstrates respect for the child with asthma and stresses what he can do. It provides accurate information and promotes a positive image.

<u>Themes or Units</u>: **Friendship; Giving & Sharing; Hats; Health; Tools & Machines.**

Rogers, Fred. *Let's Talk About It: Extraordinary Friends,* photographs by Jim Judkis. Puffin Books, 2000. ISBN 0-698-11861-8 [28 p]. Nonfiction, Gr.PS-3. Disabilities: Variety of disabilities. (****) (Cat A).

Six children of various ages, with a variety of disabilities, are introduced in this book through beautiful photographs. The children are busy doing a variety of activities in home, school and community settings. The story stresses that while some children have disabilities and are different in some ways, they are like other children in many other ways such as their likes and needs. This book has limited text with very descriptive photographs of children that would promote discussion. This book is written very respectfully and includes photographs representing various cultures.

Themes or Units: Friends at School: We Are Alike, We Are Different.

Root, Ann, & Gladden, Linda. *Charlie's Challenge,* illus. by Anne Nelson Sweat. U.S.A. Printmaster Press, 1995. ISBN 0-9647186-0-X [31 p]. Fiction, Gr. 1-4. Disability: Learning disability. (***) (Cat B).

This is a story about Charlie who has a difficult time learning at school. With the help of a neuropsychologist, Charlie realizes he isn't stupid. The story describes Charlie's challenges and feelings, and what he is good at. A very sensitively written story that would help children understand what it is like to have a learning disability. Soft pencil sketchings accompany the story.

Themes or Units: Feelings; We Are Alike, We Are Different.

Rosenberg, Maxine B. *Finding A Way: Living with Exceptional Brothers and Sisters,* photographs by George Ancone. Lothrop, Lee & Shepard Books, 1988. ISBN 0-688-06874-X [45 p]. Nonfiction, Gr. K-3. Disability/Illness: Diabetes, asthma, & spina bifida. (***) (Cat B)

This story explores the feelings of siblings from three different families who have a child with a disability or chronic illness. The siblings feelings are openly discussed as are the many good times they have with their brother or sister. The story is honest and realistic and describes many of the daily routines which occur in families. This story promotes a positive image by emphasizing what these children can do as well as the challenges they encounter. This book may help brothers and sister understand and work through the feelings they experience. The author does not use "person first" language.

Themes or Units: Brothers & Sisters; Families; Feelings; Health; We Are Alike, We Are Different.

Rosenberg, Maxine B. My Friend Leslie: The Story of a Handicapped Child, photographs by George Ancona. Lothrop, Lee & Shephard Books, 1983. ISBN 0-688-01690-1 [43 p]. Nonfiction, Gr. K-3. Disability: Multiple Disabilities: Visual, hearing loss, cleft palate and muscular imperfection. (****) (Cat A)

Karin describes her friendship with Leslie who was born with multiple disabilities. The story realistically describes Leslie's disabilities and the resulting frustrations. However, the fun times, the joy of friendship, and Leslie's delightful personality are equally portrayed. Black and white photographs represent cultural diversity and make the book even more outstanding. This story promotes a positive image of a child with a disability by emphasizing her independence, success in the mainstream, and her exuberant friendship. Except for the title, the story does use "person first" language.

Themes or Units: Friends at School; We Are Alike, We Are Different.

Rotner, Shelly & Kelly, Sheila. *A.D.D. Book for Kids*, photographs by Shelley Rotner. Millbrook Press, 2000. ISBN 0-7613-1436-9 [25 p]. Nonfiction, Gr. K-5. Disability: Attention deficit disorder (ADD). (****) (Cat A).

Beautiful photographs of children of various ages are on each page. One or two statements per page describe what it is like to have ADD, i.e. it is hard to keep track of your things, it is difficult to stop and think. It stresses the need for friends to understand their challenges. The story has very realistic information and is sensitively written.

Themes or Units: Feelings; Friends at School; We Are Alike, We Are Different.

Rudner, Barry. *The Handstand*, illus. by Peggy Trabalka. Art-Print, 1990. ISBN 0-925928-05-4 [26 p]. Fiction, Gr. K-3. Disability: Physical (wheelchair). (***) (Cat C).

To join the club all of the children had to prove that they could walk on their hands. One little boy could not do it. His friend who uses a wheelchair figured out a special way. On the day everyone had to walk on their hands this boy and his friend put their hands under their feet and "walked on their hands!" The story ends with the boy making brief comments about individuals with other disabilities and says, " . . . they are nothing less than you and I." A short, fun story that children would enjoy.

Themes or Units: Friendship; We Are Alike, We Are Different.

Russo, Marisabina. *Alex Is My Friend*, illus. by author. Greenwillow Books, 1992. ISBN 0-688-10419-5 [30 p]. Fiction, Gr. PS-2. Disability: Physical (inhibited growth in stature). (****) (Cat B)

Alex and Ben are friends. As they grow older, Ben wonders why Alex isn't bigger because he's a year older. His mom explains that Alex will always remain small. Ben soon realizes that Alex's size doesn't really matter and their friendship continues to grow. A delightful story which emphasizes, that differences don't really matter. Colorful illustrations similar to folk art accompany the story.

Themes or Units: Friendship; Giving and Sharing; Shapes, Sizes & Weights; We Are Alike, We Are Different.

Sanford, Doris. *David Has AIDS*, illus. by Graci Evans. Multnomah Press, 1989. ISBN 0-88070-299-0 [26 p]. Fiction, Gr. K-2. Illness: AIDS. (***) (Cat B)

This story is about David, a young boy who has AIDS and eventually dies. Throughout the story David says prayers to God to help him. The story teaches children about AIDS and about death. It has a limited text with soft, tender illustrations. This is a very sensitive and loving story.

Themes or Units: Friendship; Health.

Sanford, Doris. *Don't Look at Me*, illus. by Graci Evans. Multnomah Press, 1986. ISBN 0-88070-150-1 [24 p]. Fiction, Gr. 1-3. Disability: Mental retardation or learning disability. (****) (Cat A)

This is a story about Patrick who has a difficult time learning and thinks he is dumb. The story is an effort to help Patrick see that it's his attitude and how he thinks about himself that is important. His pet lamb and his grandfather help him understand his feelings and learn what he can do to feel better about himself. This is a heartwarming story that would help children understand their own or others feelings when learning is difficult. The illustrations do an exceptional job of portraying the mood and feelings of the characters.

Themes or Units: Feelings; Friends at School; We Are Alike, We Are Different.

Sanford, Doris. *Help! Fire!* **illus. by Graci Evans. Multnomah Press, 1992. ISBN 0-88070-520-5 [30 p]. Fiction, Gr. K-3. Disability: Physical (legs below the knee are missing). (****) (Cat B)**

Daniel is a young boy who doesn't have legs below his knees. One day, Daniel is home because he doesn't feel well. A neighborhood youngster falls outside their home so his mom and brother take him home. While they are gone, a fire starts. Daniel is frightened and calls 911. Daniel and his two dogs make it to the patio but can't go any further. The firesquad rescues them. The story does an excellent job of showing all the things Daniel can do even with his physical disability. It's an exciting story that all children would love with colorful illustrations.

Themes or Units: Community Workers/Occupations (firefighters); Pet Animals; Safety; We Are Alike, We Are Different.

Sandford, Doris. *No Longer Afraid,* **illus. Graci Evans. Multnomah Press, 1992. ISBN 0-88070-519-1 [30 p]. Fiction, Gr. 1-5. Illness: Cancer. (****) (Cat A).**

A very sensitive story about Jaime who has cancer. The story describes her treatments, hospital stays, her get-togethers with friends, her relapse and her dream that the Make A Wish Foundation makes happen. An excellent book to help children understand what it feels like to be a child with cancer.

Themes or Units: Dentists, Doctors, Nurses & Hospitals; Friendship; Health.

Sargent, Susan & Wirt, Donna Aaron. *My Favorite Place,* **illus. by Allan Eitzen. Abingdon Press, 1983. ISBN 0-687-27538-5 [27 p]. Fiction, Gr. PS-3. Disability: Blind. (****) (Cat C)**

A little girl went to the ocean with her mom and dad. She helped lay out the blanket, swims in the ocean, goes for a walk, and takes a nap on the beach. Throughout the story she comments on things she smells, hears or feels. It isn't until the end of the story that the reader finds out that she is blind. The story promotes a positive image as this little girl fully participates in the day's activities and enjoys the outing. The beach is her favorite place.

Themes or Units: Oceans, Lakes & Sea Animals; Senses; Summer.

Schar, Brigitte. *The Blind Fairy,* **illus. by Julia Gukova. North South Books, 1998. ISBN 1-55858-973-2 [24 p]. Fiction, Gr. K-3. Disability: Blind. (**) (Cat C).**

A fairy who is blind lives in a palace high on top a dark, gloomy mountain. She waits for people to come visit, but no one comes. A group of wicked dwarves have tricked the fairy into believing they are her faithful servants. One day the fairy leaves the mountain and meets an old lady who tells her about the dwarves and how they keep the mountain gloomy. The fairy's eyes are finally opened and with her special powers, she takes action against the dwarves in this fantasy story.

Themes or Units: Fantasy & Imagination.

Schulman, Arlene. *Carmine's Story: A Book About a Boy Living with AIDS,* **photographs by author. Lerner Publications, 1997. ISBN 0-8225-2582-8 [33 p]. Nonfiction, Gr. 2-4. Illness: AIDS. (****) (Cat A).**

Carmine is ten years old and was born with AIDS. This story provides information about AIDS, what it is, how it is acquired, how it spreads and the medical interventions needed to sustain life. Carmine talks about what it is like to have AIDS, live with a grandmother, not be able to go to school, and have friends. Quality information is provided in this book in a way that children would understand.

Themes or Units: Health.

Seuling, Barbara. *I'm Not So Different,* **illus. Pat Schories. Western Publishing Co., 1986. ISBN 0-307-62486-2 [22 p]. Fiction, Gr. K-3. Disability: Physical (wheelchair). (****) (Cat B)**

Kit is a young girl who uses a wheelchair. When she complains about being different, her dad points out how everyone has differences, which don't have to stop a person from being really good at lots of things. At the end of a concert, the rock star talks to Kit. She is excited as she says to her dad, "You're right. I'm not so different." The story promotes a positive image of a person using a wheelchair. The story takes place in integrated settings, i.e. school and community. "Person first" language is not always used.

Themes or Units: Families; Giving & Sharing; We Are Alike, We Are Different.

Shannon, David. *David Goes to School,* illus. by author. The Blue Sky Press, 1999. ISBN 0-590-48087-1 [30 p]. Fiction, Gr. K-2. Disability: Attention deficit hyperactivity disorder. (**) (Cat B).

This is the second book by David Shannon. The story does not mention ADHD but the behaviors David displays at school suggest that may be the problem. David gets in trouble throughout the school day, i.e. he doesn't sit down, he chews gum, he doesn't raise his hand. The story is full of behaviors David should not be doing. At the end of the story David must wash the desks. When he gets done, his teacher finally says "Good job, David." And gives him a star. The behaviors in the book may be realistic but the story emphasizes what David does wrong with little mention of anything positive. The illustrations have the same geometric lines of Shannon's Caldecott winner.

Themes or Units: We Are Alike, We Are Different.

Shannon, David. *No, David!* illus. by author. Scholastic, 1998. ISBN 0-590-93002-8-0 [29 p]. Fiction, Gr. K-2. Disability: Attention deficit hyperactivitiy disorder. (**) (Cat B).

This story does not mention ADHD but the behaviors of David suggest that may be the problem. David gets into trouble throughout the story. On each page it shows him in trouble such as tracking mud across the room or filling the bath tub to overflowing. His mother tells him, "NO, David" or "No, No, No." So, the book is full of nos and at the end after David sits in the corner, his mother calls to him and says, "Yes, David. I love you." While the text may be realistic for some children, it is filled with Nos with little that is positive. The book is a Caldecott Honor book for the interesting illustrations using geometric lines.

Themes or Units: We Are Alike, We Are Different.

Shriver, Maria. *What's Wrong with Timmy?* illus. by Sandra Speidel. Warner Books, 2001. ISBN 0-316-23337-4 [40 p]. Fiction, Gr. 2-6. Disability: No specific disability. (****) (Cat B).

Kate notices a boy who acts a bit differently and asks her mom, "What is wrong with him?" In this story, the mother explains about differences and disabilities to her daughter. She also points out similarities and how everyone wants to be included and loved. The story is very sensitively written. An excellent resource for parents who need a little help in explaining differences to their children.

Themes or Units: Friendship; We Are Alike, We Are Different.

Simpson-Smith. Elizabeth. *A Guide Dog Goes to School*, illus. by Bert Dobson. William Morrow & Co., 1987. ISBN 0-688-06844-8 [47 p]. Nonfiction, Gr. 1-3. Disability: Blind. (****) (Cat A)

A golden retriever called Cinderella is selected to go to guide school. The story takes the reader through the entire training process plus a month's training with the person who is blind and will become its master. While the story is very informative, it is also very entertaining. The reader grows to love Cinderella. Pencil sketches capture the feelings of joy between Cinderella and her new master. This story would interest young children and provide important information about people who are blind, how they use dogs to guide them and, how the dog becomes the master's pet when it isn't working.

Themes or Units: Pet Animals.

Silverstein, Alvin, Silverstein, Virginia, & Nunn, Laura Silverstein. *Dyslexia*, photographs by a variety of photographers. Franklin Watts, A Division of Scholastic, 2001. ISBN 0-531-16560-4 [48 p]. Nonfiction, Gr. 2-6. Disability: Learning disability. (****) (Cat A)

This is a comprehensive book about the learning disability, dyslexia. It discusses what is dyslexia, how to diagnose it, how to get help, and what you can do to help yourself. Some resources are provided in the back. There is a lot of text with colored photographs throughout the book.

Themes or Units: We Are Alike, We Are Different.

Slate, Joseph. *Miss Bindergarten Celebrates the 100th Day of Kindergarten*, illus. by Ashley Wolff. Dutton, 1998. ISBN 0-525-46000-4 [38 p]. Fiction, Gr. PS-K. Disability: Physical (wheelchair). (****) (Cat C)

Miss Bindergarten gets ready to celebrate; she and her class have been together 100 days. Each student must bring 100 of something wonderful. One student uses a wheelchair and is fully included in the class activities. The characters are animals depicted in bright, fun illustrations. The first letter of each student's name is highlighted throughout the story and ends up representing the alphabet. This is an entertaining story.

Themes or Units: Alphabet; Friends at School.

Slate, Joseph. *Miss Bindergarten Gets Ready for Kindergarten*, illus. by Ashley Wolff. Dutton, 1996. ISBN 0-525-45446-2 [35 p]. Fiction, Gr. PS-K. Disability: Physical (wheelchair). (****) (Cat C).

The story shows Miss Bindergarten getting her classroom ready for the first day of kindergarten. The children also get ready and arrive at school. The characters are animals represented in vibrant illustrations. One child uses a wheelchair and is fully included. The first letter of the children's names is highlighted and represents the letters of the alphabet. This is a fun story that young children will enjoy.

Themes or Units: Alphabet; Friends at School.

Slate, Joseph. *Miss Bindergarten Plans a Circus with Kindergarten*, illus. by Ashley Wolff. Dutton, 2002. ISBN 0-525-46884-6 [38 p]. Fiction, Gr. PS-K. Disability: Physical (wheelchair). (****) (Cat C).

Miss Bindergarten and her class plan a circus day. One of the children is in a wheelchair and fully included in the class activities. All of the characters are animals. The first letter of each student's name is highlighted which represents the letters of the alphabet. At the end of the story, the class talks about "circus colors." Vibrant colorful illustrations help tell the story.

Themes or Units: Alphabet; Colors in My World; Friends at School.

Slate, Joseph. *Miss Bindergarten Stays Home*, illus. by Ashley Wolff. Dutton, 2000. ISBN 0-525-46396-8 [38 p]. Fiction, Gr. PS-1. Disability: Physical (wheelchair). (****) (Cat C).

Miss Bindergarten gets sick so a substitute teacher comes for the day. He is a bit rusty and asks the children to help him. One of the children is in a wheelchair and fully included in the activities. All of the characters are animals depicted in colorful, fun illustrations. The first letter of the children's names is highlighted and represents the letters of the alphabet. An entertaining story all young children will enjoy.

Themes or Units: Alphabet; Friends at School; Health.

Slate, Joseph. *Miss Bindergarten Takes a Field Trip*, illus. by Ashley Wolff. Dutton, 2001. ISBN 0-525-46710-6 [35 p]. Fiction, Gr. PS-1. Disability: Physical (wheelchair). (****) (Cat C).

The kindergarten children have a field trip day where they visit the bakery, fire station, post office, library and the park. At the end of the day, they talk about the many shapes they saw throughout the day. The characters are animals depicted in brightly colored illustrations. The first letter in each child's name is highlighted and represents the letters of the alphabet.

Themes or Units: Alphabet; Community Workers/Occupations; Friends at School; Shapes, Sizes & Weights.

Slier, Debby. *Animal Signs: A First Book of Sign Language*, photographs by author. Checkerboard Press, 1993. ISBN 1-56288-385-2 [14 p]. Fiction, PS-K. Disability: Hearing loss, deaf (signing). (****) (Cat A)

This book contains 14 colored photographs of common animals. Each page contains one photograph with a small inset of a child demonstrating the appropriate sign. The insets are black and white sketches of boys and girls from diverse cultures using American Sign Language. Signing is usually used by persons who are deaf or have a hearing loss; this book emphasizes that any child can benefit from using sign language and can have fun using it. This is an excellent book for beginning signing. The pages are made of hardboard which makes the book durable for younger children and may make turning pages easier for some children.

Themes or Units: Farm & Farm Animals; Sense of Sight; Sign Language.

Slier, Debby. *Word Signs: A First Book of Sign Language*, photographs by author. Checkerboard Press, 1993. ISBN 1-56288-386-0 [14 p]. Fiction, PS-K. Disability: Hearing loss, deaf (signing). (****) (Cat A)

Each page contains a colored photograph of a common object (e.g. socks, crayons, baby). Each photograph has a small inset of a child demonstrating the appropriate sign for the object. The insets are sketches of boys and girls from diverse cultures using American Sign Language. The book emphasizes that any child can benefit from using sign language and can have fun using it. This is an excellent book for beginning signing for young children. The pages are made of hardboard, which makes them durable for younger children and may make it easier for some children to turn the pages.

Themes or Units: The Sense of Sight; Sign Language.

Stuve-Bodeen, Stephanie. *We'll Paint the Octopus Red*, illus. by Pam DeVito. Woodbine, 1998. ISBN 1-890627-06-2 [20 p]. Fiction, Gr. PS-3. Disability: Down syndrome. (****) (Cat B).

Emma is about to have a new baby at her house. She talks with her dad about all the things she wants to do with the baby and all the fun she will have. When the baby is born, Dad tells Emma that he was born with Down syndrome, Emma didn't understand. She repeats all of the things she wants to do with the baby. Dad tells her that with patience the baby will be able to do all of those things. This is a very positive story about Down syndrome. It is a great story for siblings, but also for any young child.

Themes or Units: Brothers & Sisters.

Sullivan, Tom. *That Nelson!* illus. by Anne Kennedy. American Editions, 1995. ISBN 1-56189-392-7 [32 p]. Fiction, Gr.PS-3. Disability: Blind (Guide Dog) (****) (Cat B).

This is a story about Nelson, a big black friendly dog who becomes a guide dog. The story is told from the dog's perspective about his time being socialized with a special family, being trained as a guide dog and finally getting a new master who is blind. Nelson expresses his feelings throughout the story. All children would love this fun story.

Themes or Units: Feelings; Pet Animals

Swanson, Susanne M. *My Friend Emily,* illus. by Paul Hart. Writer's Press Service, 1994. ISBN 1-885101-04-X [35 p]. Fiction, Gr. 1-3. Disability/Illness: Epilepsy. (****) (Cat B)

This story is about two young girls who are best friends. Emily has epilepsy. The story does an outstanding job of explaining about epilepsy, describing seizures. The story emphasizes that Emily is like any other child except for the seizures. The story also promotes cultural diversity as the best friends represent two different cultures.

Themes or Units: Friendship; Health; We Are Alike, We Are Different.

Swenson, Judy Harris, & Kunz, Roxane Brown. *Learning My Way: I'm a Winner,* illus. by L. J. Kratoska. Dillon Press, 1986. ISBN 0-87518-351-4 [29 p]. Nonfiction, Gr. 2-5. Disability: Learning disability. (****) (Cat A)

This is a story about a young boy with a learning disability. Because of his difficulties in school, his mother takes him to a doctor who tells Dan that he is smart, he just learns in a different way. A clear description of a learning disability is provided with an emphasis on what Dan can do and how he can compensate for his disability. The story provides accurate information and promotes a positive image of a person with a learning disability.

Themes or Units: We Are Alike, We Are Different.

Taylor, Ron. *All by Self,* **illus. by Jay Jacoby. Light On Books & Videotapes, 1991. ISBN 0-938991-75-2 [64 p]. Nonfiction, Gr. K-6. Disability: Cerebral palsy (wheelchair). (****) (Cat A)**

A father speaks with simplicity and sensitivity about his son who has cerebral palsy. The story describes how a family deals with the questions that can never be answered and the grieving for what will never be. It also portrays the powerful, loving relationship between this father and his child. Through the use of beautiful pencil sketchings and poetic language, Micah's father emphasizes the mutual teaching and learning he experiences with his son and the wonder and joy of discovery. This is a well written story about Micah's journey that is filled with love.

Themes or Units: Families; Feelings; We Are Alike, We Are Different.

Thompson, Mary. *Andy and the Yellow Frisbee,* **illus. by author. Woodbine, 1996. ISBN 0-933149-83-2 [18 p]. Fiction, Gr. K-2. Disability: Autism. (***) (Cat B).**

Rosie, a new girl at school is very intrigued with a little boy with autism who spins his yellow Frisbee every day at recess. Sarah, the sister is worried that the new girl won't understand her brother until she notices that Rosie has brought her own pink Frisbee.

The story shows some behaviors that some children with autism have and the concern of a sibling. Some information about autism is provided and would be particularly helpful to siblings and classmates.

Themes or Units: Brothers & Sisters; Friends at School; We Are Alike, We Are Different.

Thompson, Mary. *My Brother Matthew,* **illus. by author. Woodbine House, 1992. ISBN 0-933149-47-6 [25 p]. Fiction, Gr. K-3. Disability: Physical, speech & language delay (brain injury). (****) (Cat B)**

David tells what it is like to be the older brother of Matthew who was born with a brain injury. When Matthew comes home from the hospital, David interacts and has fun playing with him. As Matthew grows older, David realizes how much they are alike even if Matthew talks and moves differently. David describes some of his feelings as he lives with his brother. The story includes many things Matthew can do and the fun the two boys have together.

Themes or Units: Brothers & Sisters; Families; Feelings; We Are Alike, We Are Different.

Turk, Ruth. *The Doll on the Top of the Shelf*, illus. by Per Volquartz. Owl's Hours Press, 1998. ISBN 1-891992-02-3 [26 p]. Fiction, Gr. K-3. Disability: Blind. (****) (Cat C).

This is a story about a shopping trip with a little girl who is blind and her grandmother. At the toy store, Natalie buys a soft little doll that she loves and when she gets home there are other surprises in the box. A delightful story whose main character is blind. The story also provides a lesson that the newest toys aren't always the best. The book is larger than most (13 1/2 by 11 1/4 inches) and on each page the text is in the upper part of the page with the lower part written in Braille.

Themes or Units: Sense of Touch; Toys.

Turner, Deborah, & Mohler, Diana. *How Willy Got His Wheels*, illus. by Rhonda McHugh. Doral Publishing, 1998. ISBN 0-944875-54-8 [28 p]. Fiction, Gr. PS-3. Disability: Physical. (****) (Cat B).

This is a story about a little dog who has a spinal injury and can't use his hind legs. He is adopted from the veterinary hospital and the master tries many ways to help the dog get around. Finally, they get wheels to hold up his hind legs and now Willy is able to be independent. A fun story about a dog that helps children understand what it's like to have a disability.

Themes or Units: Pet Animals; Transportation.

Verniero, Joan C. *You Can Call Me Willy*, illus. by Verdon Flory. Magination Press, 1995. ISBN 0-945354-60-6 [27 p]. Fiction, Gr. 1-4. Illness: HIV infection and AIDS. (****) (Cat B).

Willy has the HIV virus. She got it from her mother when she was born. Her grandmother had to attend meetings before Willy could begin school because other parents had concerns that their children would get the infection, too. Some parents were worried about her playing on the baseball team, but all of the problems were worked out. From this story children would learn the facts about getting HIV. They would also find out how it feels to have this disease. The illustrations show diverse cultures; Willy is African American.

Themes or Units: Feelings; Friends at School; Health: We Are Alike, We Are Different.

Vigna, Judith. *When Eric's Mom Fought Cancer,* illus. by author. Albert Whitman, 1993. ISBN 0-8075-8883-0 [28 p]. Fiction, Gr. PS-3. Illness: Cancer. (****) (Cat B).

Eric finds out that his mother has breast cancer; he is afraid and angry. He and his dad go skiing, then Eric has a chance to talk to his dad about the cancer. He buys his mom a new hat and surprises her. This story would open up discussion of the feelings we have when someone we care about is sick. Realistic and sensitively written.

Themes or Units: Feelings; Giving & Sharing; Health.

Wahl, Jan. *Jamie's Tiger,* illus. by Tomie de Paola. Harcourt Brace Jovanovich, 1978. ISBN 0-15-239500-8 [40 p]. Fiction, Gr. PS-3. Disability: Hearing loss. (****) (Cat B)

Jamie develops a hearing loss and is frightened about what is happening to him until the doctor explains about his hearing loss. Someone from school teaches him to lip read, hand talk and finger spell. Jamie grows lonely until old friends begin to learn how to finger spell and discover it isn't so hard to learn and it can be their secret code. The illustrations show the emotions of sadness changing to happiness as he interacts with his friends. This story promotes an attitude of "one of us" as it shows that a hearing loss can happen to anyone and you can still be friends.

Themes or Units: Friendship; Sign Language; We Are Alike, We Are Different.

Walker, Dava. *Puzzles,* illus. by Cornelius Van Wright & Ying-Hwa Hu. Carolina Wren Press, 1996. ISBN 0-914996-29-0 [30 p]. Fiction, Gr. 1-4. Illness: Sickle cell disease. (****) (Cat B).

Cassie is a school age child with sickle cell disease. This is a story about how it feels to have this disease and how it effects your daily life at school and at home. In school she ends up giving a report on this disease and then the children have a better understanding of her. Beautiful, soft illustrations help set the tone for the story.

Themes or Units: Friends at School; Health.

Walker, John C. *In Other Words,* illus. by Connie Steiner. Firefly Books, 1993. ISBN 1-55037-309-9 [29 p]. Fiction, Gr. 1-3. Disability: Physical (cerebral palsy). (***) (Cat B).

John is unable to communicate by speaking but he clearly has thoughts of what he would like to say. A new girl comes to his school and the two of them find they can communicate by just knowing what the other wants to say. They imagine they go into outer space and are able to talk to others and don't need wheelchairs! In this story John goes to a special school for children with disabilities; this is a segregated setting.

Themes or Units: Fantasy & Imagination.

Wanous, Suzanne. *Sara's Secret,* illus. by Shelly O. Haas. Carolrhoda Books, 1995. ISBN 0-87614-856-9 [39 p]. Fiction, Gr. 1-5. Disability: Physical (cerebral palsy), mental disability. (****) (Cat B).

Sara is going to a new school. She doesn't tell anyone about her brother who has cerebral palsy and mental disabilities because she is afraid they will tease her. Then one day, the teacher talks about disabilities and asks each student to bring something to school the next day that relates to disabilities. After much thought and discussion with her mother, Sara decides to bring her brother Justin. An excellent story to show the fears that siblings of children with disabilities may have. Very sensitively written with soft illustrations.

Themes or Units: Brothers & Sisters; Feelings; Friends at School; We Are Alike, We Are Different.

Watson, Esther. *Talking to Angels,* illus. by author. Harcourt Brace & Co., 1996. ISBN 0-15-201077-7 [26 p]. Fiction, Gr. K-3. Disability: Autism. (***) (Cat A).

Christa has autism. Her older sister wrote and drew the illustrations for this book to help others understand how Christa sees the world in a way different from most people. The illustrations look as though a child drew them. Limited text accompanies the illustrations. Very sensitively written.

Themes or Units: Brothers & Sisters; Fantasy & Imagination; We Are Alike, We Are Different.

Wellbrook Collection. *Bear Spot Learns a Lot: Growing Up with Diabetes.* **Tim Peters & Co., 1997. ISBN 1-879874-67-0 [20 p]. Fiction, Gr. PS-3. Illness: Diabetes. (***) (Cat A).**

The Ranger finds a sick cub bear. The veterinarian discovers the bear has diabetes. The cub learns all about diabetes and how to take care of himself. He grows up to be a big strong bear because he took care of his diabetes. An entertaining story to help children understand this chronic illness. (12 by 10 1/4 inches).

<u>Themes or Units</u>: **Health; Zoo Animals.**

Wellbrook Collection. *Dotty the Dalmatian Has Epilepsy.* **Tim Peters & Co., 1996. ISBN 1-879874-35-0 [17 p]. Fiction, Gr. PS-3. Illness: Epilepsy. (****) (Cat A.**

Dotty has a seizure so her mother takes her to a veterinarian. He put Dotty on medication to prevent seizures but Dotty was worried whether or not she can be a mascot and help the firefighters. The siren blows and they are off to a fire where Dotty is able to locate a baby in the burning house. Dotty earns a medal for her work and knows she will be okay. Good information about epilepsy including seizures. Beautiful, large illustrations in a 12 by 10 1/4 inch book.

<u>Themes or Units</u>: **Health; Pet Animals.**

Wellbrook Collection. *Hip-Hop The Hyperactive Hippo.* **Tim Peters & Co., 1996. ISBN 1-87987-55-5 [18 p]. Fiction, Gr. PS-3. Disability: Attention deficit with hyperactivity disorder (ADHD). (****) (Cat B).**

Hippo has trouble slowing down and following directions so his parents take him to the doctor. Hippo is healthy but just needs a little extra help. The challenges of not listening and being very active are treated in a very sensitive and respectful manner. The illustrations of the various animals are soft and realistic. Size of book is 12 by 10 1/4 inches.

<u>Themes or Units</u>: **We Are Alike, We Are Different; Zoo Animals.**

Well brook Collection. *Hooray for Harold: Dealing with Hearing Loss.* **Tim Peters & Co., 1997. ISBN 1-879874-68-7 [15 p]. Fiction, Gr. PS-3. Disability: Hearing loss (hearing aids). (****) (Cat B).**

Harold, a mouse, has trouble hearing so his mom takes him to the doctor. An audiologist tests his hearing and finds he has a hearing loss in both ears but it can be corrected with hearing aids. Harold likes to hear but the children at school tease him about his aids. During a storm he hears Chipmonk calling for help and Harold is able to help him to safety. Chip apologies for teasing Harold about his aids because if he didn't have them he wouldn't have heard Chip calling for help. Fun, large illustrations in a book 12 by 10 1/4 inches.

Themes or Units: **Sounds in the Environment; Wild Birds & Animals.**

Wellbrook Collection. *I'm Still Me: Coping with Leukemia.* Tim Peters & Co., 1997. ISBN 1-879874-54-7 [20 p]. Fiction, Gr. PS-3. Illness: Leukemia. (****) (Cat A).

The story is about Herbie, a chick who doesn't feel good and is diagnosed with leukemia. After mother hen answers all of the farm animals' questions about leukemia, the animals welcome Herbie back from the hospital. Good information about leukemia including why Herbie loses some of his hair. Beautiful, large illustrations in a book 12 by 10 1/4 inches.

Themes or Units: **Farm & Farm Animals; Health.**

Wellbrook Collection. *Way to go Bravo: Learning to Live with Asthma.* Tim Peters & Co., 1996. ISBN -1-879874-60-1 [16 p]. Fiction, Gr. PS-3. Illness: Asthma. (***) (Cat A).

Bravo, a horse, is not feeling well. After going to the veterinarian, he finds out what he has to do to be healthy. Now he feels so good that he races and evens wins one of the races. A little confusing to children when the veterinarian is a horse, yet when Bravo races, he interacts with people. Good information about asthma, great illustrations, book is 12 by 10 1/4 inches.

Themes or Units: **Farm & Farm Animals; Health; Pet Animals.**

Wheeler, Cindy. *Simple Signs,* illus. by author. Viking, 1995. ISBN 0-670-86282-7 [28 p]. Fiction, Gr. PS-6. Disability: Deaf (sign language). (****) (Cat A).

This book introduces young children to twenty-eight signs for common words in their everyday environment. Each page has an illustration of an item and then a sketch of a child signing. The signs are very clear with arrows showing which way the hand moves. This is an excellent selection of common, yet important words.

Themes or Units: **Pet Animals; Sign Language.**

Whinston, Joan Lenett. *I'm Joshua & Yes I Can,* **illus. by Wally Littman. Vantage Press, 1989. ISBN 0-533-07959-4 [34 p]. Fiction, Gr. 3-6. Disability: Cerebral palsy (leg braces). (****) (Cat B)**

This story centers around Joshua's first day in first grade and his fears about children who might make fun of him because he has cerebral palsy. He realizes that although there are things he cannot do, he does have special talents. With courage and determination he deals with his limitations and the awkward moments and regains confidence in himself and his abilities. This book promotes acceptance and an attitude of "one of us" as it addresses both Joshua's challenges and his abilities. Cartoon like characters accompany the story.

Themes or Units: Feelings; Friends at School; We Are Alike, We Are Different.

White, Paul. *Janet at School,* **photographs by Jeremy Finlay. Thomas Y. Crowell, Co., 1978. ISBN 0-381-99556-9 [23 p]. Nonfiction, Gr. PS-2. Disability: Physical, spina bifida (leg braces & wheelchair). (****) (Cat B)**

Janet is a five-year-old with spina bifida who attends school in a mainstream classroom. The story provides an account of her daily routines and the adaptations that are utilized so that Janet can be independent. The story also provides a clear explanation of spina bifida that young children would be able to understand. This story emphasizes many things that Janet can do as well as her limitations and describes how she is included in her family's outings. The color photographs add to the story.

Themes or Units: Families; We Are Alike, We Are Different.

White, Peter. *Think About Being Blind,* **photographs from many resources. Smart Apple Media, 2000. ISBN 1-887068-84-8 [32 p]. Nonfiction, Gr. K-6. Disability: Blind. (****) (Cat A).**

Through many pictures and text, this book provides a summary of what it is like to be blind, some of the challenges faced by people who are blind, and the ways they cope with everyday life. The author is blind. This book provides brief information about many issues and would be an excellent resource to answer the many questions children have about people who are blind.

Themes or Units: Sense of Sight; We Are Alike, We Are Different.

Wiener, Lori, Best, Aprille, & Pizzo, Phillip (Eds.). *Be A Friend: Children Who Live with HIV Speak,* **illus. by children with HIV. Albert Whitman, 1994. ISBN 0-8075-0590-0 [40 p]. Nonfiction, Gr. All Ages. Illness: HIV and AIDS. (****) (Cat A).**

Children from five to fifteen years of age tell what it is like to live with HIV infection and AIDS. The children's writings and art work are included in this collection. They talk about being scared, how people treat them, about dying and many other emotions. This book would help children learn about the facts of this disease, but in addition, the children's letters would help them learn about the emotional aspects that are so difficult to live with. This book promotes understanding and empathy regarding AIDS.

Themes or Units: Feelings; Health.

Willis, Jeanne. *Susan Laughs,* **illus. by Tony Ross. Henry Holt, 1999. ISBN 0-8050-6501-6 [26 p]. Fiction, Gr. PS-1. Disability: Physical (wheelchair). (***) (Cat B).**

Susan is a little girl with a physical disability which makes it necessary for her to use a wheelchair. The story is short with one or two words per page telling all of the things that Susan can do—such as: swim, wave, grin, paint, hear, hug, and feel. On the last page you see Susan in a wheelchair for the first time with the words, "That is Susan through and through—just like me, just like you." A fun book that stresses all that Susan can do.

Themes or Units: Friendship; We Are Alike, We Are Different.

Wolf, Bernard. *HIV Positive,* **photographs by author. Dutton Children's Books, 1997. ISBN 0-525-45459-4 [45 p]. Nonfiction, Gr. 1-5. Illness: AIDS. (****) (Cat A).**

This is a story of a young mother who has AIDS. It chronicles how her life with her two young chldren is effected by this disease. The sad times and the happy times are shown from a family perspective. The book provides straightforward information about AIDS and its causes.

Themes or Units: Health.

Woolley, Maggie. *Think About Being Deaf,* **photographs from many resources. Smart Apple Media, 2000. ISBN 1-887068-85-6 [32 p]. Nonfiction, Gr. K-6. Disability: Deaf. (****) (Cat A).**

This book follows the same format as *Think About Being Blind.* Many pictures and text are used to provide a summary of what it is like to be deaf, the many challenges faced by individuals who are deaf, and the ways they cope. The author is deaf. Important information is provided about many issues. This book would be a good resource to answer questions children have about people who are deaf.

Themes or Units: Sounds in the Environment; We Are Alike, We Are Different.

Wright, Betty Ren. *My Sister Is Different*, illus. by Helen Cogancherry. Raintree Steck-Vaughn, 1992. ISBN 0-8172-1369-4 [28 p]. Fiction, Gr. K-3. Disability: Mental retardation. (****) (Cat B)

Carlo has an older sister who has mental retardation. He tells how difficult it is when he has to watch her. It isn't until he loses her in a department store that he thinks about all the good things she does such as making the baby laugh and happily helping with dishes. When Carlo finds Terry, he begins to appreciate her for who she is and doesn't mind looking after her. The story is very realistic regarding feelings that siblings have toward their brother or sister with a disability. It is sensitively written, respectful and has colorful illustrations that capture the many emotions that are experienced.

Themes or Units: Brothers & Sisters; We Are Alike, We Are Different.

Wright, Christine. *Just Like Emma: How She Has Fun in God's World*, illus. by Biz Hull. Augsburg Fortress Publishers, 1993. ISBN 0-8066-2617-8 [26 p]. Fiction, Gr. K-3. Disability: Physical (spina bifida). (****) (Cat B)

This is a story about Emma who has spina bifida. She lives with her father and younger brother. Throughout the story Emma participates in household tasks such as drying the dishes and making out the grocery list. Humor is incorporated into the story when she and her brother put crushed chips into the cereal box for their dad's breakfast. Emma even goes swimming with her family and out smarts her brother. The emphasis in this story is what Emma can do for herself and with her family. This is a very positive yet realistic story. The illustrations are colorful and very life like.

Themes or Units: Brothers & Sisters; Families; We Are Alike, We Are Different.

Young, Ed. *Seven Blind Mice*, illus. by by author. Philomel Books, 1992. ISBN 0-399-22261-8 [36 p]. Fiction, Gr. PS-2. Disability: Blind. (****) (Cat B).

Seven blind mice are surprised to find a strange "something" by their pond. Each mouse, a different bright color, goes out to investigate. Each comes back and describes what they think they "see." The seventh mouse discovers that it is an elephant. This story retells in verse the Indian fable of *The Blind Men and the Elephant*. The story will help children understand what it is like to be blind and the challenge to identify something by its feel, size, etc. This book is a Caldecott Honor Book.

Themes or Units: Colors in My World; Senses; Sense of Touch; Zoo Animals.

Zelonsky, Joy. *I Can't Always Hear You*, illus. by Barbara Bejna & Shirlee Jensen. Raintree Steck-Vaughn, 1991. ISBN 0-8172-1355-4 [30 p]. Fiction, Gr. K-3. Disability: Hearing loss (hearing aids). (****) (Cat B)

Kim begins school in an integrated class at a new building where she doesn't know anyone. She has a hearing loss, wears a hearing aid and worries about being different. With the help of her teacher and new classmates she soon realizes that everyone has individual differences (i.e. one student wears braces, one is adopted, another is very tall). This is a very realistic story about differences that promotes a positive image of a person with a hearing loss. The story also promotes cultural diversity; a teacher and student are African American and Kim is Asian.

Themes or Units: Friends at School; Sounds in the Environment; We Are Alike, We Are Different.

CHAPTER SIX

Children's Books Cross-Referenced by Disability and Chronic Illness

INTRODUCTION

In this chapter, the children's books in this collection have been cross-referenced by disability and chronic illness. In the event that a story contains information about more than one disability or illness, it is cross-referenced for all that are present. This list includes books for eleven disability areas: attention deficit hyperactivity disorder (ADHD), autism or pervasive developmental disorder (PDD), blind, low vision or partially sighted, blind and deaf, chronic illnesses (includes allergies, asthma, diabetes, cancer, cardiac, HIV/AIDS, juvenile rheumatoid arthritis, muscular dystrophy, and sickle cell anemia), deaf or hearing loss, learning disability, mental retardation/developmental disability (includes Down syndrome), multiple disability, physical disability (includes cerebral palsy, epilepsy, size/dwarf, spina bifida), and speech & language.

BOOKS LISTED BY DISABILITY AND CHRONIC ILLNESS

Attention Deficit Hyperactivity Disorder (ADHD)

Carlson, Nancy. *Sit Still!*

Corman, Clifford L., & Trevino, Esther. *Eukee The Jumpy Jumpy Elephant*

Gehret, Jeanne. *Eagle Eyes*

Lears, Laurie. *Waiting for Mr. Goose*

Loski, Diana. *The Boy On The Bus*

Moss, Deborah M. *Shelley, the Hyperactive Turtle*

Quinn, Patricia O., & Stern, Judith M. *Putting on the Breaks: Young People's Guide to Understanding Attention Deficit Hyperactivity Disorder*

Rotner, Shelly & Kelly, Sheila. *A.D.D. Book for Kids*

Shannon, David. *David Goes to School*

Shannon, David. *No, David!*

Wellbrook Collection. *Hip-Hop The Hyperactive Hippo*

Autism or Pervasive Developmental Disorder (PDD)

Amenta, Charles A. *Russell is Extra Special: A Book for About Autism for Children*

Edwards, Becky. *My Brother Sammy*

Lears, Laurie. *Ian's Walk*

Thompson, Mary. *Andy and the Yellow Frisbee*

Watson, Esther. *Talking to Angels*

Blind, Low Vision, or Partially Sighted

Alexander, Sally Hobart. *Mom Can't See Me*

Alexander, Sally Hobart. *Mom's Best Friend*

Allen, Anne. *Sports for the Handicapped*

Arnold, Caroline. *A Guide Puppy Grows Up*

Barrett, Mary Brigid. *Sing to the Stars*

Brown, Tricia. *Someone Special, Just Like You*

Carter, Alden R. *Seeing Things My Way*

Cohen, Miriam. *See You Tomorrow, Charles*

Condra, Estelle. *See The Ocean*

Davis, Patricia. *Brian's Bird*

Fraustino, Lisa Rowe. *The Hickory Chair*

Gardner, Sonia. *Eagle Feather*
Golden, Barbara Diamond. *Cakes and Miracles*
Greenfield, Eloise. *William and the Good Old Days*
Hausman, Gerald. *The Story of Blue Elk*
Karim, Roberta. *Mandy Sue Day*
Kroll, Virginia L. *Naomi Knows It's Springtime*
Litchfield, Ada B. *A Cane in Her Hand*
MacLachlan, Patricia. *Through Grandpa's Eyes*
Martin, Bill & Archambault, John. *Knots on a Counting Rope*
McMahon Patricia. *Listen for the Bus: David's Story*
Mitchell, Lori. *Different Just Like Me*
Moon, Nicola. *Lucy's Pictures*
Newth, Phillip. *Roly Goes Exploring*
Pearson, Susan. *Happy Birthday, Grampie*
Sargent, Susan & Wirt, Donna Aaron. *My Favorite Place*
Schar, Brigitte. *The Blind Fairy*
Simpson-Smith, Elizabeth. *A Guide Dog Goes to School*
Sullivan, Tom. *That's Nelson*
Turk, Ruth. *The Doll on the Top of the Shelf*
White, Peter. *Think About Being Blind*
Young, Ed. *Seven Blind Mice*

Blind/Deaf
Addabbo, Carole. *Dina the Deaf Dinosaur*
Adler, David A. *A Picture Book of Helen Keller*

Chronic Illness
Goodwall, Jane. *Dr. White*
Mills, Joyce C. *Little Tree: A Story for Children with Serious Medical Problems*

Allergies
Delton, Judy. *I'll Never Love Anything Ever Again*
Porte, Barbara Ann. *Harry's Dog*

Asthma

Alden, Joan. *A Boy's Best Friend*

Carter, Alden R., & Carter, Siri M. *I'm Tougher Than Asthma*

London, Jonathan. *The Lion Who Has Asthma*

Rogers, Alison. *Luke Has Asthma*

Rosenberg, Maxine B. *Finding a Way: Living with Exceptional Brothers and Sisters*

Wellbrook Collection. *Way to go Bravo: Learning to Live with Asthma*

Diabetes

Althea. *I Have Diabetes*

Beatty, Monica Driscoll. *My Sister Rose Has Diabetes*

Pirner, Connie White. *Even Little Kids Get Diabetes*

Rosenberg, Maxine B. *Finding a Way: Living with Exceptional Brothers and Sisters*

Silverstein, Ivin A., & Silverstein, Virginia B. *Runaway Sugar: All About Diabetes*

Wellbrook Collection. *Bear Spot Learns a Lot: Growing Up with Diabetes*

Cancer

Borden, Louise. *Good Luck, Mrs. K.!*

Coerr, Eleanor. *Sadako*

Foss, Karen Sue. *The Problem With Hair*

Gaes, Jason. *My Book for Kids with Cansur*

Krisher, Trudy. *Kathy's Hats: A Story of Hope*

Sanford, Doris. *No Longer Afraid*

Vigna, Judith. *When Eric's Mom Fought Cancer*

Wellbrook Collection. *I'm Still Me: Coping with Leukemia*

Cardiac

Elder, Vicci. *Cardiac Kids*

HIV/AIDS

Girard, Linda Walvoord. *Alex, the Kid with AIDS*

Jordon, MaryKate. *Losing Uncle Tim*

Merifield, Margaret. *Come Sit By Me*

Montoussamy-Ashe, Jeaanne. *Daddy and Me*

Quinlan, Patricia. *Tiger Flowers*

Sanford, Doris. *David has AIDS*

Schulman, Arlene. *Carmine's Story: A Book About a Boy Living with AIDS*

Verniero, Joan C. *You Can Call Me Willy*

Wiener, Lori, Best, Aprille, & Pizzo, Philllip. *Be a Friend: Children Who Live with HIV Speak*

Wolf, Bernard. *HIV Positive*

Juvenile Rheumatoid Arthritis

Aldape, Virginia Totorica. *Nicole's Story*

Sickle Cell Anemia

Walker, Dava. *Puzzles*

Muscular Dystrophy

Osofsky, Audrey. *My Buddy*

Deaf or Hearing Loss

Allen, Anne. *Sports for the Handicapped*

Ancona, George & Ancona, Mary Beth. *Handtalk Zoo*

Aseltine, Lorraine, Mueller, Evelyn, & Tait, Nancy. *I'm Deaf and It's Okay*

Bahan, Ben & Dannis, Joe. *My ABC Signs of Animal Friends*

Baker, Pamela J. *My First Book of Sign*

Booth, Barbara. *Mandy*

Bove, Linda. *Sesame Street Sign Language ABC*

Brown, Tricia. *Someone Special, Just Like You*

Chaplin, Susan Gibbons. *I Can Sign My ABCs*

Charlip, Remy. *Handtalk Birthday*

Collins, S. Harold. *The Beginning Sign Language Series*

Fain, Kathleen. *Handsigns: A Sign Language Alphabet*

Gilmore, Rachna. *A Screaming Kind of Day*

Greenberg, Judith D. *What Is the Sign for Friend?*

Gross, Ruth Belov. *You Don't Need Words! A Book About Ways People Talk*

Hesse, Karen. *Lester's Dog*

Hill, Eric. *Where's Spot*

Hodges, Candri. *When I Grow Up*

Kadish, Sharona. *Discovering Friendship*

Krause, Ute. *Pig Surprise*

Lakin, Patricia. *Dad and Me in the Morning*

Lee, Jeanne M. *Silent Lotus*

Levi, Dorothy Hoffman. *A Very Special Friend*

Levi, Dorothy Hoffman. *A Very Special Sister*

Levine, Edna S. *Lisa and Her Soundless World*

Litchfield, Ada B. *A Button in Her Ear*

Litchfield, Ada B. *Words in Our Hands*

Lowell, Gloria Roth. *Elana's Ears or How I Became the Best Big Sister in the World*

Mackinnon, Christy. *Silent Observer*

Millman, Isaac. *Moses Goes to a Concert*

Millman, Isaac. *Moses Goes to School*

Milne, A.A. *Winnie-the-Pooh's ABC: Sign Language Edition*

Mitchell, Lori. *Different Just Like Me*

Okimoto, Jean Davies. *A Place for Grace*

Peterson, Jeanne Whitehouse. *I Have a Sister My Sister is Deaf*

Rankin, Laura. *The Handmade Alphabet*

Riggio, Anita. *Secret Signs: Along the Underground Railroad*

Slier, Debby. *Animal Signs: A First Book of Sign Language*

Slier, Debby, *Word signs: A First Book of Sign Language*

Wahl, Jan. *Jamie's Tiger*

Wellbrook Collection. *Hooray for Harold: Dealing with Hearing Loss*

Wheeler, Cindy. *Simple Signs*

Woolley Maggie. *Think About Being Deaf*

Zelonsky, Joy. *I Can't Always Hear You*

Learning Disability

Cohen, Miriam. *It's George*

Dwyer, Kathleen M. *What Do You Mean I Have a Learning Disability*

O'Shaughnessy, Ellen. *Somebody Called Me A Retard Today . . . and My Heart Felt Sad*

Roberts, Karon. *Bright . . . and Behind: A Book for Children and Parents Learning to Cope with Reading and Attention Problems*

Roby, Cynthia. *When is Learning Tough: Kids Talk About Their Learning Disabilities*

Root, Ann, & Gladden, Linda. *Charlie's Challenge*

Sanford, Doris. *Don't Look at Me*

Silverstein, Alvin, Silverstein, Virginia, & Nunn, Laura Silverstein. *Dyslexia.*

Swenson, Judy Harris, & Kunz, Roxane Brown. *Learning My Way: I'm a Winner*

Mental Retardation/Developmental Disability

Allen, Anne. *Sports for the Handicapped*

Bergman, Thomas. *We Laugh, We Love, We Cry: Children Living with Mental Retardation*

Cohen, Miriam. *It's George*

Gifaldi, David. *Ben, King of the River*

O'Shaughnessy, Ellen. *Someone Called Me A Retard Today . . . and My Heart Felt Sad*

Prall, Jo. *My Sister's Special*

Sanford, Doris. *Don't Look at Me*

Wanous, Suzanne. *Sara's Secret*

Wright, Betty Ren. *My Sister is Different*

Down Syndrome

Bouwkamp, Julie A. *Hi, I'm Ben! And I've Got a Secret*

Brown, Tricia. *Someone Special, Just Like You*

Cairo, Shelley. *Our Brother Has Down's Syndrome*

Carter, Alden R. *Big Brother Dustin*

Carter, Alden R. *Dustin's Big School Day*

DeBear, Kirsten. *Be Quiet, Marina!*

Fleming, Virginia. *Be Good to Eddy Lee*

Girnis, Meg. *ABC for You and Me*

Gregory, Nan. *How Smudge Came*

Haines, Sandra. *Becca and Sue Make Two*

Jansen, Larry. *My Sister is Special*

Litchfield, Ada B. *Making Room for Uncle Joe*
Pulber, Robin. *Way to Go Alex!*
Rabe, Berniece. *Where's Chimpy?*
Rheingrover, Jean Sasso. *Veronica's First Year*
Rickert, Janet Elizabeth. *Russ and the Firehouse*
Richert, Janet Elizabeth. *Russ and the Almost Perfect Day*
Richert, Janet Elizabeth. *Russ and the Apple Tree Surprise*
Stuve-Bodeen, Stephanie. *We'll Paint the Octopus Red*

Multiple Disabilities
Emmert, Michelle. *I'm The Big Sister Now*
Prall, Jo. *My Sister's Special*
Rosenberg, Maxine B. *My Friend Leslie: The Story of a Handicapped Child*

Physical Disabilities
Allen, Anne. *Sports for the Handicapped*
Borton, Lady. *Junk Pile!*
Brink, David. *David's Story: A Book About Surgery*
Brown, Tricia. *Someone Special, Just Like Me*
Bunting, Eve. *The Sunshine Home*
Bunting, Eve. *The Wall*
Burns, Kay. *Our Mom*
Carlson, Nancy. *Arnie and the New Kid*
Caseley, Judith. *Apple Pie and Onions*
Caseley, Judith. *Harry and Willy and Carrothead*
Cowen-Fletcher, Jane. *Mama Zooms*
Craig, Lori. *One Step at a Time*
Crunk, Tony. *Big Mama*
Damrell, Liz. *With The Wind*
Derby, Janice. *Are You My Friend?*
Edwards, Michelle. *alef-bet—A Hebrew Alphabet Book*
Foreman, Michael. *Seal Surfer*
Gainer, Cindy. *I'm Like You, You're Like Me*
Haldane, Suzanne. *Helping Hands: How Monkeys Assist People Who Are Disabled*
Hallinan, P.K. *Heartprints*

Hamm, Diane Johnson. *Grandma Drives a Motor Bed*

Harshman, Marc. *The Storm*

Harter, Debbie. *The Animal Boogie*

Heelan, Jamee Riggio. *The Making of My Special Hand: Madison's Story*

Henriod, Lorraine. *Grandma's Wheelchair*

Hines, Anna Grossnickle. *Gramma's Walk*

Hoffman, Eric. *No Fair to Tigers*

Lasker, Joe. *Nick Joins In*

Lyon, George Ella. *Cecil's Story*

Mayer, Gina and Mercer. *A Very Special Critter*

Meyers, Cindy. *Rolling Along with Goldilocks and the Three Bears*

Mitchell, Lori. *Different Just Like Me*

Moran, George. *Imagine Me On A Sit-Ski!*

Muldoon, Kathleen. *Princess Pooh*

Muller, Gerda. *The Garden in the City*

Orr, Wendy. *Arabella*

Powers, Mary Ellen. *Our Teacher's in a Wheelchair*

Rabe, Berniece. *The Balancing Girl*

Raffi. *One Light, One Sun*

Rudner, Barry. *The Handstand*

Sanford, Doris. *Help! Fire!*

Seuling, Barbara. *I'm Not So Different*

Slate, Joseph. *Miss Bindergarten Celebrates the100th Day of Kindergarten*

Slate, Joseph. *Miss Bindergarten Gets Ready for Kindergarten*

Slate, Joseph. *Miss Bindergarten Plans a Circus with Kindergarten*

Slate, Joseph. *Miss Bindergarten Stays Home*

Slate, Joseph. *Miss Bingergarten Takes a Field Trip*

Thompson, Mary. *My Brother Matthew*

Turner, Deborah, & Mohler, Diana. *How Willy Got His Wheels*

Willis, Jeanne. *Susan Laughs*

Cerebral Palsy
Bergman, Thomas. *Going Places: Children Living with Cerebral Palsy*

Carter, Alden R. *Stretching Ourselves: Kids with Cerebral Palsy*

DeBear, Kirsten. *Be Quiet, Marina!*

Heelan, Jamee Riggio. *Rolling Along: The Story of Taylor and His Wheelchair*

McMahon, Patricia. *Summer Tunes: A Martha's Vineyard Vacation*

Taylor, Ron. *All by Self*

Walker, John C. *In Other Words*

Wanous, Suzanne. *Sara's Secret*

Whinston, Joan Lenett. *I'm Joshua & Yes I Can*

Epilepsy

Althea. *I Have Epilepsy*

Kornfield, Elizabeth J. *Dreams Come True*

Lears, Laurie. *Becky the Brave: A Story About Epilepsy*

Moss, Deborah M. *Lee, the Rabbit with Epilepsy*

Swanson, Suzanne. *My Friend Emily*

Wellbrook Collection. *Dotty the Dalmatian Has Epilepsy*

Spina Bifida

Rosenberg, Maxine B. *Finding a Way: Living with Exceptional Brothers and Sisters*

Wright, Christine. *Just Like Emma: How She Has Fun in God's World*

Size/Dwarf

Amer, Kim, & Brill, Marlene. *Short Mort and the Big Bully*

Kuklin, Susan. *Thinking Big: The Story of a Young Dwarf*

Mitchell, Lori Phillips. *Hue Boy*

Riggs, Stephanie. *Never Sell Yourself Short*

Russo, Marisabina. *Alex Is My Friend*

Speech and Language

Berry, Steve. *The Boy Who Wouldn't Speak*

Brearley, Sue. *Talk to Me*

Kroll, Virginia L. *Butterfly*

Lears, Laurie. *Ben Has Something to Say: A Story About Stuttering*

Lester, Helen. *Hooway for Wodney Wat*

Peckinpah, Sandra Lee. *Rosey . . . the Imperfect Angel*

Thompson, Mary. *My Brother Matthew*

Variety of disabilities (books with a variety of disabilities included, but no disability emphasized)

Atkinson, Mary. *Why Do Some people Use wheelchairs? Questions Children Ask About Disabled People.*

Bunnett, Rochelle. *Friends at School*

Bunnett, Rochelle. *Friends in the Park*

Maguire, Arlene. *Special People, Special Ways*

Rogers, Fred. *Let's Talk About It: Extraordinary Friends*

Shriver, Maria. *What's Wrong with Timmy?*

CHAPTER SEVEN

Curriculum Planning Using Theme and Literature-Based Approaches

INTRODUCTION

The majority of early childhood professionals use a theme or literature-based approach to plan their curriculum. For each theme or unit, they develop a Text Set of children's books that relate to their chosen theme. Parents also seek books with a particular theme. To assist in the selection of literature by theme, the books in this collection have been analyzed to identify the theme or themes into which the books can appropriate be incorporated.

When professionals make a selection of books for a theme or unit, it's important that some books in their selection incorporate diversity of culture and ability. It seems that efforts to increase the use of literature diverse in culture has steadily progressed over recent years, while the use of literature about disabilities and illness has been left far behind. Chapter Eight, Books Cross-References by Theme, will provide you with children's books that can easily be selected for inclusion into your themes or units, each representing diversity of ability.

DEVELOPING TEXT SETS

A Text Set is a collection of two or more books that are related in some way. The relationship might be by theme, topic, author or any other relationship that can be identified. For example, a teacher may have a collection of books written by a favorite author. This is a Text Set related by author. Another teacher may have a collection of books about dogs. This is a Text Set related by theme. You may have a collection of books of poetry. This is a Text Set related by content, i.e. all books contain poetry.

The reason for grouping books into Text Sets is because books read and considered together are much more powerful than when each is considered alone. Text Sets foster critical thinking as readers look for relationships. They are used to facilitate discussion and learning as readers make connections between stories and their own personal stories (Heine, 1991).

Consider a Text Set of books about families. One book is about an African-American family, one is about a Caucasian dad raising a child alone, and the third is about a family who has a child who is deaf. By reading all three books in this Text Set children are able to make relationships and learn more about families than by merely reading any one of the books.

For discussion purposes, it is best to limit the number of books in the Text Set to three or four (Harste, Short, & Burke, 1988). In early childhood programs it may be necessary to limit Text Sets to only two or three books. While two or three books may be the focus of discussion, teachers will have a larger Text Set for each particular theme from which they select books for discussion. Outlined below are several examples of small Text Sets (eight books), which include books that represent diversity of culture and disability.

Transportation

This Is The Way We Go To School—Baer (culture)

All Aboard ABC—Magee & Newman

Zoomrimes: Poems About Things That Go—Cassedy

Mama Zooms—Cowen-Fletcher (disability)

Here Comes The Monster Truck—Sullivan

Inside A Freight Train—McHenry

The Little Engine That Could—Piper

How Willy Got His Wheels—Turner & Mohler (disability)

Early Counting

Ten, Nine, Eight—Bang (culture)

Aaron and Gayla's Counting Book—Greenfield (culture)

Where's Chimpy?—Rabe (disability)

Shouting Sharon: A Riotous Counting Rhyme—Pace

Feast for 10—Falwell (culture)

Ten Cats Have Hats—Marzollo

Each Orange Had 8 Slices: A Counting Book—Giganti

Twelve Ways to Get to 11—Merriam

Giving and Sharing

The Selfish Crocodile—Faustin

Jared and the Ordinary, Hand-Dandy, Extraordinary, Plain Brown String—Webb

Let's Care About Sharing—Hallinan

Grandpa's Soup—Kadono (culture)

Chubbo's Pool—Lewin

Lester's Dog; Hesse (disability)

The Rainbow Fish—Pfister

Lucy's Pictures—Moon (disability)

Planting and Gardening

Amanda and the Magic Garden—Himmelman

Alison's Zinnia—Lobel

The Garden in the City—Muller (disability)

Seeds—Shannon

Red Flower Goes West—Turner (cultural)

Flower Garden—Bunting

Russ and the Apple Tree Surprise—Richert (disability)

Bertha's Garden—Dyjak

Sounds in the Environment

Clifford's Noisy Day—Bridwell

The Very Quiet Cricket—Carle

The Remarkable Farkle McBride—Lithgow

Who Say a Dog Goes Bow-wow?—Zutter (culture)

Naomi Know It's Springtime—Kroll (disability)
The Cow in the House—Ziefert
Moses Goes to a Concert—Millman (disability)
Splish Splash—Graham

Farm and Farm Animals
What If?—Benjamin
Barnyard Banter—Fleming
Mandy Sue Day—Karim (disability)
Who Says Moo?—Young
On Ramon's Farm—Geeslin (culture)
Zinnia and Dot—Ernst
With the Wind—Damrell (disability)
Kiss the Cow—Root

USING A THEME APPROACH

When using a theme approach an idea or concept is selected and all of the activities for the day or several days are planned around this theme. Themes can be identified in three ways: 1) by the children; you have some children who are really interested in a particular topic so you develop a unit on this theme (e.g. dinosaurs, dogs), 2) by society or your community; you develop a unit around the theme of spring because spring is ready to happen (e.g. after September 11th many teachers did a unit on the theme of peace), and 3) by teachers; the teacher knows important concepts the children should be learning and develops units based on these important themes (e.g. colors, positions in space, shapes). Using the chosen theme, the teacher plans activities for each area of the curriculum. Below is an example of activities for one day. Additional activities could be developed if it seemed appropriate to have the theme or unit run for several days.

Shapes
- Snack—Crackers and cheese cut into various shapes
- Art—Sponge painting using sponges cut in various shapes.
- Gross Motor—Children hop, crawl and jump to various shapes taped on the floor.

- Language/Cognition—The teacher names a shape; the children find something in the environment with that shape and name the object.

- Fine Motor/Manipulatives—Children cut out various shapes of different sizes

- Music—Sing and move to a favorite song about shapes.

- Science/Math—Make pictures of houses, trees, etc. with precut shapes.

- Books/Reading—Read stories that in some way relate to shapes in the story or illustrations such as: *Color Zoo* by Lois Ehlert. All of the zoo animals are made using various shapes. *No, David!* by Shannon. The illustrations use interesting geometric shapes.

USING A LITERATURE-BASED APPROACH

Some early childhood professionals use a literature-based approach to develop their curriculum. This means that one children's book is selected and a unit is developed around a theme from the story. All of the activities for that day or several days will relate in some way to the story. In addition to the primary book from which the theme is taken, a number of other books that relate to the theme would also be read to the children.

In many stories, more than one theme is incorporated into the story. When this happens, the teacher must select the theme that will be stressed and developed into a unit. For example, in the story *Rainbow Fish* three possible themes emerge: 1) fish and fishing 2) friendship, and 3) sharing. Fish could be selected and the children would learn lots of things about a variety of fish and fishing. If friendship is selected, the children would learn about friendship and do many activities that promote friendship in their program. And, finally, if sharing is selected, the children would learn about sharing and have opportunities within the curriculum to practice sharing.

The Cross-Referenced Listing (see Chapter Eight) includes the theme of Friendship, with a number of books identified that stress friendship while including a character in the story who has a disability or chronic illness. For example, *Come Sit By Me* is a delightful story about a friendship at school with a child who has AIDS. In addition to the concept of friendship, the children also have the opportunity to hear about the illness represented in the book. This exposure becomes a time for the children to ask questions and gain valuable information. Integrating learning about disabilities or illnesses throughout the curriculum is a natural way for children to learn much like we integrate culture and ethnicity. Information gained in this manner makes more sense to young children than learning about disabilities only during "Disability Awareness Week."

Examples of Literature-Based Theme/Unit Development

The book, *Corduroy,* is an adventure of a teddy bear who searches for his missing button and finds a friend. The literature-based theme could be Bears and throughout the instruction children learn all sorts of things about bears and have fun activities to help them learn. Or, the theme could be Friendship with activities planned throughout the day that promote learning about friendship. The following examples of themes or units provide activities for one day. Additional activities would be developed if the teacher feels it is appropriate for the unit to run for several days.

Bears

- Snack—serve foods that bears eat (e.g. berries, honey)
- Art—experience painting with brown, black and white paints
- Gross Motor—"Going on a Bear Hunt" activity
- Language/Cognition—the children act out parts of the story of *Corduroy*
- Fine Motor/Manipulatives—Teddy Bear Bingo
- Music—play music and have children move like bears
- Science/Math—read and discuss information on how and why bears hybernate
- Books/Reading—read additional books about teddy bears or bears such as: *Golden Bear* by Ruth Young (culture), *The Best-Loved Bear* by Diana Noonan, *Paddington Bear* by Michael Bond.

Friendship

- Snack—with a classmate (friend) children prepare mini peanut butter jelly sandwiches for snack
- Art—with a friend, paint at the easel; share materials
- Gross Motor—in pairs, help each other move through an obstacle course
- Language/Cognition—two friends work at the flannel board telling each other a story

- Fine Motor/Manipulatives—make beaded necklaces to take home and give to someone special
- Music—share musical instruments with a friend next to you
- Science/Math—work in groups of two at the magnet center; sharing materials
- Books/Reading—read additional books about friendship such as: *The Rainbow Fish* by Pfister, *A Very Special Friend* by Levi (disability), *Friends at the Park* by Bunnett (disability)

USING INCLUSIONARY LITERATURE UNITS/WEBS

Included in this collection of children's books with characters with disabilities and illness, there are a number of books that are appropriate to use as the main story in a literature-based approach. Within this collection, choose a story that has a theme appropriate for the ages of the children with whom you are working.

For example, *Kathy's Hats* is a story about a little girl who has cancer and loses her hair because of the chemotherapy. She hates losing her hair so her mother gives her a baseball cap which she proceeds to fill with a variety of pins that people have given her. Then, the teacher at school has a hat party. This would be an excellent book to use for literacy-based instruction. Using the book *Kathy's Hats* and the theme of Hats, below is an example of a teaching unit or web that could run for several days.

Literature-Based Approach
Book: *Kathy's Hats*   **Theme:** Hats

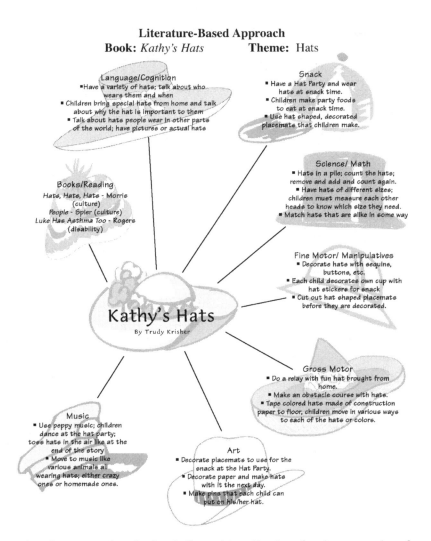

Language/Cognition
▪Have a variety of hats; talk about who wears them and when
▪ Children bring special hats from home and talk about why the hat is important to them
▪ Talk about hats people wear in other parts of the world; have pictures or actual hats

Snack
▪ Have a Hat Party and wear hats at snack time.
▪ Children make party foods to eat at snack time.
▪ Use hat shaped, decorated placemats that children make.

Science/ Math
▪ Hats in a pile; count the hats; remove and add and count again.
▪ Have hats of different sizes; children must measure each other heads to know which size they need.
▪ Match hats that are alike in some way

Books/Reading
Hats, Hats, Hats - Morris (culture)
People - Spier (culture)
Luke Has Asthma Too - Rogers (disability)

Fine Motor/ Manipulatives
▪ Decorate hats with sequins, buttons, etc.
▪ Each child decorates own cup with hat stickers for snack
▪ Cut out hat shaped placemats before they are decorated

Kathy's Hats
By Trudy Krisher

Gross Motor
▪ Do a relay with fun hat brought from home.
▪ Make an obstacle course with hats.
▪ Tape colored hats made of construction paper to floor, children move in various ways to each of the hats or colors.

Music
▪ Use peppy music; children dance at the hat party; toss hats in the air like at the end of the story.
▪ Move to music like various animals all wearing hats; either crazy ones or homemade ones.

Art
▪ Decorate placemats to use for the snack at the Hat Party.
▪ Decorate paper and make hats with it the next day.
▪ Make pins that each child can put on his/her hat.

Another example of a book from this collection that is appropriate for the literature-based approach is *Where's Chimpy?* This is a story about a little girl who is getting ready to go to bed but when her daddy is ready to read her a bedtime story, she can't find her nighttime pal, Chimpy, the monkey. She and her daddy backtrack and go everywhere she was that day, and at each place they find a toy that she has left behind. Finally, she finds Chimpy in the bathroom under a towel. Across the bottom of the bed are the nine items she and her daddy found which makes this story a fun book for a theme or unit on counting. Using the book *Where's Chimpy?* and the theme of Counting, below is an example of a teaching unit or web for several days.

Literature-Based Approach
Book: *Where's Chimpy* **Theme:** Counting

Art
- Children paint pictures at an easel; when finished each counts the number of colors used.
- Make a collage made of shapes; children count the number of shapes each get to use for their pictures.
- Each child gets a certain number of markers to make a picture; children count out the markers.

Snack
- Children get 3 or 4 crackers; each child counts out his or her own crackers.
- Children count out napkins and cups.
- Have finger foods for snacks, e.g. raisins, tiny marshmellows; each counts his or her serving

Gross Motor
- Simon Says: Walk 5 steps, jump 3 times, turn around 2 times; all movements are done a certain number of times.
- Children toss beanbags into a box; each child counts out the number of beanbags for tossing.
- Roll a playground ball into milk cartons; count how many were knocked over.

Books/Reading
Read additional books about numbers and counting such as:
12 Ways to Get to 11 - Merriam
Look Whooo's Coming - MacDonald
Anno's Counting Book - Anno (culture)

Language/Cognition
- Sort colored items into piles. Count number of articles in each pile of colors.
- Do the activity "sink and float" in a water table. Count number of items in the sink pile and in float pile.
- Put a certain number of items in, on, behind, under a box; change numbers and prepositions to challenge each child.

Where's Chimpy
By Berniece Rabe

Science
- Do exploratory activity with magnets. Put items in groups of those that adhere to magnets and those that don't. Count the items in each pile.
- Use food coloring to color water. Children count number of drops needed for each color.

Fine Motor/Manipulatives
- Children string beads to make a necklace; count beads.
- Pounding nails into tree stump; count the number of nails
- Children make shapes or items out of playdough; count the items made.

Math
- Match correct number of objects to numeral. Have dots with numerals so children who can't identify number can count and be successful.

Music
- Each child gets several cards of different colors. Sing color song, each child holds up the number of colors corresponding to the song, i.e. two blue, one yellow
- Children march to the beat of a drum. Together the children count the number of beats as they march.

There are endless activities that you can develop for your students that fit into a particular theme or unit. Many books are available that list themes or units and activities. However, rarely do they include books from the genre of literature included in this annotated bibliography. Choose books from this collection of literature to make your units more inclusive and diverse which also provides your students the opportunity to look at the world with a wider lens.

References

Harste, J. C., Short, K. G., & Burke, C. (1988). *Creating classrooms for authors.* Portsmouth, NH: Heinemann.

Heine, P. (1991). The Power of related books. *The Reading Teacher,* 45(1), 75-77.

CHAPTER EIGHT

Children's Books Cross-Referenced by Theme

INTRODUCTION

When using the cross-referenced listing of books by theme, look up the theme that is of interest to you. If that particular theme is not on the list, look up a related theme. For example if you want to read a book about monkeys or are teaching a unit on monkeys, you would look up the theme, "Monkeys." You would find there is no theme exclusively about monkeys. Next, you would look for a related theme. In this search you would find that there is a theme on "Zoo Animals." This is where you would look to find an appropriate book for your unit. Under "Zoo Animals" you would find two books about monkeys that could be used. There will be times when you will be unable to find books related to a particular theme. This is because the collection of literature for young children that includes characters with disabilities or illness is limited. However, additional books are being published each year that you will want to add to your text sets and lesson plans

BOOKS LISTED BY THEME

Alphabet

Bahan, Ben, & Dannis, Joe. *My ABC Signs of Animal Friends*

Baker, Pamela J. *My First Book of Sign Language*

Bove, Linda. *Sesame Street Sign Language ABC*

Chaplin, Susan Gibbons. *I Can Sign My ABCs*

Collins, S. Harold. *The Beginning Sign Language Series*

Edwards, Michelle. *alef-bet—a Hebrew Alphabet Book*

Fain, Kathleen. *A Sign Language Alphabet*

Girnis, Meg. *ABC for You and Me*

Holub, Joan. *My First Book of Sign Language*

Milne, A.A. *Winnie-the-Pooh's ABC: Sign Language Edition*

Rankin, Laura. *The Handmade Alphabet*

Slate, Joseph. *Miss Bindergarten Celebrates the 100th Day of Kindergarten*

Slate, Joseph. *Miss Bindergarten Gets Ready for Kindergarten*

Slate, Joseph. *Miss Bindergarten Plans a Circus with Kindergarten*

Slate, Joseph. *Miss Bindergarten Stays Home*

Slate, Joseph. *Miss Bindergarten Takes a Field Trip*

Apples

Caseley, Judith. *Apple Pie and Onions*

Rickert, Janet Elizabeth. *Russ and the Apple Tree Surprise*

Brothers & Sisters

Amadeo, Diane M. *There's a Little Bit of Me in Jamey*

Cairo, Shelley. *Our Brother Has Down's Syndrome*

Carter, Alden R. *Big Brother Dustin*

Davis, Patricia. *Brian's Bird*

Edwards, Becky. *My Brother Sammy*

Emmert, Michelle. *I'm the Big Sister Now*

Gehret, Jeanne. *Eagle Eyes*

Gifaldi, David. *Ben, King of the River*

Gilmore, Rachna. *A Screaming Kind of Day*

Jansen, Larry. *My Sister is Special*

Lears, Laurie. *Becky the Brave: A Story About Epilepsy*

Lears, Laurie. *Ian's Walk*

Levi, Dorothy Hoffman. *A Very Special Sister*

Lowell, Gloria Roth. *Elana's Ears or How I Became the Best Big Sister in the World*

Muldoon, Kathleen M. *Princess Pooh*

Peterson, Jeanne Whitehouse. *I Have a Sister My Sister is Deaf*

Prall, Jo. *My Sister's Special*

Pulber, Robin. *Way to Go Alex!*

Rheingrover, Jean Sasso. *Veronica's First Year*

Rosenberg, Maxine B. *Finding a Way: Living with Exceptional Brothers and Sisters*

Stuve-Bodeen, Stephanie. *We'll Paint the Octopus Red*

Thompson, Mary. *Andy and the Yellow Frisbee*

Thompson, Mary. *My Brother Matthew*

Wanous, Suzanne. *Sara's Secret*

Watson, Esther. *Talking to Angels*

Wright, Betty Ren. *My Sister is Different*

Wright, Christine. *Just Like Emma: How She Has Fun in God's World*

Butterflies

Kroll, Virginia L. *Butterfly Boy*

Children & Families Around the World

Edwards, Michelle. *alef-bet—A Hebrew Alphabet Book*

Gardner, Sonia. *Eagle Feather*

Golden, Barbara Diamond. *Cakes and Miracles*

Hausman, Gerald. *The Blue Elk*

Lee, Jeanne M. *Silent Lotus*

Martin, Bill J.R., & Archambault, John. *Knots on a Counting Rope*

Colors in My World

Harter, Debbie. *The Animal Boogie*

Moon, Nicole. *Lucy's Pictures*

Raffi. *One Light, One Sun*

Slate, Joseph. *Miss Bindergarten Plans a Circus with Kindergarten*
Young, Ed. *Seven Blind Mice*

Community Workers/Occupations
Borden, Louise. *Good Luck, Mrs. K.!*
Hodges, Candri. *When I Grow Up*
Powers, Mary Ellen. *Our Teacher's in a Wheelchair*
Rickert, Janet Elizabeth. *Russ and the Firehouse*
Sanford, Doris. *Help! Fire!*
Slate, Joseph. *Miss Bindergarten Takes a Field Trip*

Day and Night
Booth, Barbara. *Mandy*
Lakin, Patricia. *Dad and Me in the Morning*
Raffi. *One Light, One Sun*

Dentist, Doctors, Nurses & Hospitals
Amadeo, Diane M. *There's a Little Bit of Me in Jamey*
Beatty, Monica Driscoll. *My Sister Rose Has Diabetes*
Brink, David. *David's Story: A Book About Surgery*
Bunting, Eve. *The Sunshine Home*
Elder, Vicci. *Cardiac Kids*
Gaes, Jason. *My Book For Kids With Cansur*
Goodwall, Jane. *Dr. White*
Hamm, Diane Johnson. *Grandma Drives a Motor Bed*
Litchfield, Ada B. *A Button in Her Ear*
Moss, Deborah M. *Lee, the Rabbit with Epilepsy*
Moss, Deborah M. *Shelley, the Hyperactive Turtle*
Pearson, Susan. *Happy Birthday, Grampie*
Pirner, Connie White. *Even Little Kids Get Diabetes*
Sanford, Doris. *No Longer Afraid*

Dinosaurs
Addabbo, Carole. *Dina the Deaf Dinosaur*

Families

Addabbo, Carole. *Dina the Deaf Dinosaur*

Alden, Joan. *A Boy's Best Friend*

Alexander, Sally Hobart. *Mom Can't See Me*

Amenta, Charles A. *Russell is Extra Special: A Book About Autism for Children*

Bunting, Eve. *The Sunshine Home*

Burns, Kay. *Our Mom*

Carter, Alden R. *Big Brother Dustin*

Condra, Estelle. *See The Ocean*

Cowen-Fletcher, Jane. *Mama Zooms*

Craig, Lori. *One Step at a Time*

Edwards, Michelle. *alef-bet—A Hebrew Alphabet Book*

Emmert, Michelle. *I'm the Big Sister Now*

Fraustine, Lisa Rowe. *The Hickory Chair*

Gehret, Jeanne. *Eagle Eyes*

Gifaldi, David. *Ben, King of the River*

Gilmore, Rachna. *A Screaming Kind of Day*

Henriod, Lorraine. *Grandma's Wheelchair*

Karim, Roberta. *Mandy Sue Day*

Lakin, Patricia. *Dad and Me in the Morning*

Litchfield, Ada B. *Making Room for Uncle Joe*

Litchfield, Ada B. *Words in Our Hands*

Lyon, George Ella. *Cecil's Story*

MacLachlan, Patricia. *Through Grandpa's Eyes*

McMahon, Patricia. *Summer Tunes: A Martha's Vineyard Vacation*

Montoussamy-Ashe, Jeanne. *Daddy & Me*

Moss, Deborah M. *Lee, the Rabbit with Epilepsy*

Pearson, Susan. *Happy Birthday, Grampie*

Peterson, Jeanne Whitehouse. *I Have a Sister My Sister is Deaf*

Quinlan, Patricia. *Tiger Flowers*

Rabe, Berniece. *Where's Chimpy?*

Raffi. *One Light, One Sun*

Rosenberg, Maxine B. *Finding a Way: Living with Exceptional Brothers and Sisters*

Seuling, Barbara. *I'm Not So Different*

Taylor, Ron. *All By Self*
Thompson, Mary. *My Brother Matthew*
Wright, Christine. *Just Like Emma: How She Has Fun in God's World*

Families at Work
Alexander, Sally Hobart. *Mom Can't See Me*
Rickert, Janet Elizabeth. *Russ and the Apple Tree Surprise*

Fantasy & Imagination
Berry, Steve. *The Boy Who Wouldn't Speak*
Borton, Lady. *Junk Pile*
Collins, Harold S. *The Beginning Sign Language Series*
Cowen-Fletcher, Jane. *Mama Zooms*
Damrell, Liz. *With the Wind*
Henriod, Lorraine. *Grandma's Wheelchair*
Hines, Anna Grossnickle. *Gramma's Walk*
Hoffman, Eric. *No Fair to Tigers*
London, Jonathan. *The Lion Who Has Asthma*
Peckinpah, Sandra Lee. *Rosey . . . the Imperfect Angel*
Schar, Brigitte. *The Blind Fairy*
Walker, John C. *In Other Words*
Watson, Esther. *Talking to Angels*

Farm & Farm Animals
Damrell, Liz. *With the Wind*
Harshman, Marc. *The Storm*
Karim, Roberta. *Mandy Sue Day*
Krause, Ute. *Pig Surprise*
Slier, Debbie. *Animal Signs: A First Book of Sign Language*
Wellbrook Collection. *I'm Still Me: Coping with Leukemia*
Wellbrook Collection. *Way to Go Bravo: Learning to Live with Asthma*

Feelings
Amadeo, Diane M. *There's a Little Bit of Me in Jamey*
Amer, Kim, & Brill, Marlene. *Short Mort and the Big Bully*

Aseltine, Lorraine, Mueller, Evelyn, & Tait, Nancy. *I'm Deaf and It's Okay*

Beatty, Monica Driscoll. *My Sister Rose Has Diabetes*

Bunting, Eve. *The Sunshine Home*

Bunting, Eve. *The Wall*

Calmenson, Stephanie. *Rosie: A Visiting Dog's Story*

Carlson, Nancy. *Arnie and the New Kid*

Caseley, Judith. *Apple Pie and Onions*

Caseley, Judith. *Harry and Willy and Carrothead*

Damrell, Liz. *With the Wind*

DeBear, Kirsten. *Be Quiet, Marina!*

Delton, Judy. *I'll Never Love Anything Ever Again*

Dwyer, Kathleen M. *What Do You Mean I Have a Learning Disability?*

Elder, Vicci. *Cardiac Kids*

Fleming, Virginia. *Be Good to Eddy Lee*

Foss, Karen Sue. *The Problem with Hair: A Story for Children Who are Learning About Cancer*

Gehret, Jeanne. *Eagle Eyes*

Gifaldi, David. *Ben, King of the River*

Gilmore, Rachna. *A Screaming Kind of Day*

Harshman, Marc. *The Storm*

Heelan, James Riggio. *Rolling Along: The Story of Taylor and His Wheelchair*

Hesse, Karen. *Lester's Dog*

Jordon, MaryKate. *Losing Uncle Tim*

Krisher, Trudy. *Kathy's Hats: A Story of Hope*

Lasker, Joe. *Nick Joins In*

Lears, Laurie. *Becky the Brave: A Story About Epilepsy*

Lears, Laurie. *Ben Has Something to Say: A Story About Stuttering*

Lee, Jeanne M. *Silent Lotus*

Levi, Dorothy Hoffman. *A Very Special Friend*

Levi, Dorothy Hoffman. *A Very Special Sister*

Litchfield, Ada B. *Making Room for Uncle Joe*

Loski, Diana. *The Boy On The Bus*

Lyon, George Ella. *Cecil's Story*

Mills, Joyce C. *Little Tree: A Story for Children with Serious Medical Problems*

Muldoon, Kathleen M. *Princess Pooh*

O'Shaughnessy, Ellen. *Somebody Called Me a Retard today . . . and My Heart Felt Sad*

Pearson, Susan. *Happy Birthday, Grampie*

Peckinpah, Sandra Lee. *Rosey . . . the Imperfect Angel*

Powers, Mary Ellen. *Our Teacher's in a Wheelchair*

Rickert, Janet Elizabeth. *Russ and the Almost Perfect Day*

Riggio, Anita. *Secret Signs: Along the Underground Railroad*

Riggs, Stephanie. *Never Sell Yourself Short*

Roberts, Karon. *Brightand Behind: A Book for Children and Parents Learning To Cope with Reading and Attention Problems*

Root, Ann & Gladden, Linda. *Charlie's Challenge*

Rosenberg, Maxine B. *Finding a Way: Living with Exceptional Brothers and Sisters*

Rotner, Shelly, & Kelly, Sheila. *A.D.D. Book for Kids*

Sanford, Doris. *Don't Look at Me*

Sullivan, Tom. *That Nelson!*

Taylor, Ron. *All By Self*

Thompson, Mary. *My Brother Matthew*

Verniero, Joan C. *You Can Call Me Willy*

Vigna, Judith. *When Eric's Mom Fought Cancer*

Wanous, Suzanne. *Sara's Secret*

Whinston, Joan Lenett. *I'm Joshua & Yes I Can*

Wiener, Lori, Best, Aprille, & Pizzo, Phillip. *Be a Friend: Children Who Live With HIV*

Fish or Fishing

Moss, Deborah M. *Lee, the Rabbit with Epilepsy*

Friends at School

Amer, Kim, & Brill, Marlene. *Short Mort and the Big Bully*

Aseltine, Lorraine, Mueller, Evelyn, & Tait, Nancy. *I'm Deaf and It's Okay*

Borden, Louise. *Good Luck, Mrs. K.!*

Brown, Tricia. *Someone Special, Just Like You*

Bunnett, Rochelle. *Friends at School*

Carlson, Nancy. *Arnie and the New Kid*

Carlson, Nancy. *Sit Still!*

Carter, Alden R. *Dustin's Big School Day*

Carter, Alden R., & Carter, Siri M. *I'm Tougher Than Asthma*

Carter, Alden R. *Seeing Things My Way*

Carter, Alden R. *Stretching Ourselves: Kids with Cerebral Palsy*

Caseley, Judith. *Harry and Willy and Carrothead*

Cohen, Miriam. *See You Tomorrow, Charles*

Corman, Clifford L., & Trevino, Esther. *Eukee The Jumpy Jumpy Elephant*

DeBear, Kirsten. *Be Quiet, Marina!*

Dwight, Laura. *We Can Do It!*

Girard, Linda Walvoord. *Alex, the Kid With AIDS*

Kadish, Sharona. *Discovering Friendship*

Krisher, Trudy. *Kathy's Hats: A Story of Hope*

Lasker, Joe. *Nick Joins In*

Lears, Laurie. *Becky the Brave: A Story About Epilepsy*

Lester, Helen. *Hooway for Wodney Wat*

Litchfield, Ada B. *A Button in Her Ear*

Litchfield, Ada B. *A Cane in Her Hand*

Loski, Diana. *The Boy On The Bus*

Mayer, Gina & Mercer. *A Very Special Critter*

McMahon, Patricia. *Listen for the Bus: David's Story*

Merrifield, Margaret. *Come Sit By Me*

Millman, Isaac. *Moses Goes to a Concert*

Millman, Isaac. *Moses Goes to School*

Rabe, Berniece. *The Balancing Girl*

Rickert, Janet Elizabeth. *Russ and the Almost Perfect Day*

Rogers, Fred. *Let's Talk About It: Extraordinary Friends*

Rosenberg, Maxine B. *My Friend Leslie: The Story of a Handicapped Child*

Rotner, Shelly, & Kelly, Sheila. *A.D.D. Book for Kids*

Sanford, Doris. *Don't Look at Me*

Slate, Joseph. *Miss Bindergarten Celebrates the 100th Day of Kindergarten*

Slate, Joseph. *Miss Bindergarten Gets Ready for Kindergarten*

Slate, Joseph. *Miss Bindergarten Plans a Circus with Kindergarten*

Slate, Joseph. *Miss Bindergarten Stays at Home*

Slate, Joseph. *Miss Bindergarten Takes a Field Trip*
Thompson, Mary. *Andy and the Yellow Frisbee*
Verniero, Joan C. *You Can Call Me Willy*
Walker, Dava. *Puzzles*
Wanous, Suzanne. *Sara's Secret*
Whinston, Joan Lenett. *I'm Joshua & Yes I Can*
Zelonsky, Joy. *I Can't Always Hear You*

Friendship
Barrett, Mary Brigid. *Sing to the Stars*
Borton, Lady. *Junk Pile*
Brink, David. *David's Story: A Book About Surgery*
Brown, Tricia. *Someone Special, Just Like You*
Bunnett, Rochelle. *Friends in the Park*
Carlson, Nancy. *Arnie and the New Kid*
Caseley, Judith. *Harry and Willy and Carrothead*
Cohen, Miriam. *It's George*
DeBear, Kirsten. *Be Quiet, Marina!*
Derby, Janice. *Are You My Friend?*
Fleming, Virginia. *Be Good to Eddy Lee*
Foss, Karen Sue. *The Problem with Hair: A Story for Children Who Are Learning About Cancer*
Greenberg, Judith E. *What Is the Sign for Friend?*
Haines, Sandra. *Becca and Sue Make Two*
Hallinan, P.K. *Heartprints*
Heelan, James Riggio. *Rolling Along: The Story of Taylor and His Wheelchair*
Holcomb, Nan. *Patrick and Emma Lou*
Hesse, Karen. *Lester's Dog*
Jordon, MaryKate. *Losing Uncle Tim*
Kadish, Sharona. *Discovering Friendship*
Lasker, Joe. *Nick Joins In*
Levi, Dorothy Hoffman. *A Very Special Friend*
Levi, Dorothy Hoffman. *A Very Special Sister*
Maguire, Arlene. *Special People, Special Ways*

Merrifield, Margaret. *Come Sit By Me*

Meyer, Cindy. *Rolling Along With Goldilocks and the Three Bears*

Riggs, Stephanie. *Never Sell Yourself Short*

Rogers, Alison. *Luke Has Asthma, Too*

Rudner, Barry. *The Handstand*

Russo, Marisabina. *Alex Is My Friend*

Sanford, Doris. *David Has AIDS*

Sanford, Doris. *No Longer Afraid*

Shriver, Maria. *What's Wrong with Timmy?*

Swanson, Susanne M. *My Friend Emily*

Wahl, Jan. *Jamie's Tiger*

Willis, Jeanne. *Susan Laughs*

Fruits & Vegetables

Collins, Harold S. *The Beginning Sign Language Series*

Giving & Sharing

Amadeo, Diane M. *There's a Little Bit of Me in Jamey*

Arnold, Caroline. *The Guide Puppy Grows Up*

Calmenson, Stephanie. *Rosie: A Visiting Dog's Story*

Carlson, Nancy. *Arnie and the New Kid*

Charlep, Remy. *Handtalk Birthday*

Davis, Patricia. *Brian's Bird*

Foss, Karen Sue. *The Problem with Hair: A Story for Children Who Are Learning About Cancer*

Fraustino, Lisa Rowe. *The Hickory Chair*

Hesse, Karen. *Lester's Dog*

Litchfield, Ada B. *Making Room for Uncle Joe*

Moon, Nicole. *Lucy's Pictures*

Pearson, Susan. *Happy Birthday, Grampie*

Rickert, Janet Elizabeth. *Russ and the Almost Perfect Day*

Rogers, Alison. *Luke Has Asthma, Too*

Russo, Marisabina. *Alex Is My Friend*

Seuling, Barbara. *I'm Not So Different*

Vigna, Judith. *When Eric's Mom Fought Cancer*

Grandmothers & Grandfathers

Booth, Barbara. *Mandy*

Bunting, Eve. *The Sunshine Home*

Caseley, Judith. *Apples Pie and Onions*

Crunk, Tony. *Big Mama*

Foreman, Michael. *Seal Surfer*

Fraustino, Lisa Rowe. *The Hickory Chair*

Greenfield, Eloise. *William and the Good Old Days*

Hamm, Diane Johnson. *Grandma Drives a Motor Bed*

Henriod, Lorraine. *Grandma's Wheelchair*

Hines, Anna Grossnickle. *Gramma's Walk*

Kroll, Virginia L. *Butterfly Boy*

MacLachlan, Patricia. *Through Grandpa's Eyes*

Martin, Bill J.R. & Archambault, John. *Knots on a Counting Rope*

Moon, Nicole. *Lucy's Pictures*

Moss, Deborah M. *Lee, the Rabbit with Epilepsy*

Orr, Wendy. *Arabella*

Pearson, Susan. *Happy Birthday, Grampie*

Rickert, Janet Elizabeth. *Russ and the Apple Tree Surprise*

Hats

Krisher, Trudy. *Kathy's Hats: A Story of Hope*

Rogers, Alison. *Luke Has Asthma, Too*

Health

Aldape, Virginia Totorica. *Nicole's Story*

Alden, Joan. *A Boy's Best Friend*

Althea. *I Have Diabetes*

Althea. *I Have Epilepsy*

Amadeo, Diane M. *There's a Little Bit of Me in Jamey*

Beatty, Monica Driscoll. *My Sister Rose Has Diabetes*

Borden, Louise. *Good Luck, Mrs. K.!*

Brink, David. *David's Story: A Book About Surgery*

Bunting, Eve. *The Sunshine Home*

Caarter, Alden R. *I'm Tougher Than Asthma*

Coerr, Eleanor. *Sadako*

Craig, Lori. *One Step at a Time*

Delton, Judy. *I'll Never Love Anything Ever Again*

Elder, Vicci. *Cardiac Kids*

Foss, Karen Sue. *The Problem with Hair: A Story for Children Who Are Learning About Cancer*

Gaes, Jason. *My Book For Kids About Cansur*

Girard, Linda Walvoord. *Alex, the Kid With AIDS*

Goodwall, Jane. *Mr. White*

Jordon, MaryKate. *Losing Uncle Tim*

Kornfield, Elizabeth J. *Dreams Come True*

Krisher, Trudy. *Kathy's Hats: A Story of Hope*

Lears, Laurie. *Becky the Brave: A Story About Epilepsy*

London, Jonathan. *The Lion Who Has Asthma*

Merrifield, Margaret. *Come Sit By Me*

Mills, Joyce C. *Little Tree: A Story for Children with Serious Medical Problems*

Montoussamy-Ashe, Jeanne. *Dabby & Me*

Moss, Deborah M. *Lee, the Rabbit with Epilepsy*

Moss, Deborah M. *Shelley the Hyperactive Turtle*

Pirner, Connie White. *Even Little Kids Get Diabetes*

Porte, Barbara Ann. *Harry's Dog*

Quinlan, Patricia. *Tiger Flowers*

Rogers, Alison. *Luke Has Asthma, Too.*

Rosenberg, Maxine B. *Finding a Way: Living with Exceptions Brothers and Sisters*

Sanford, Doris. *David Has AIDS*

Sanford, Doris. *No Longer Afraid*

Schulman, Arlene. *Carmine's Story: A Book About a Boy Living with AIDS*

Slate, Joseph. *Miss Bindergarten Stays Home*

Swanson, Susanne M. *My Friend Emily*

Verniero, Joan C. *You Can Call Me Willy*

Vigna, Judith. *When Eric's Mom Fought Cancer*

Walker, Dava. *Puzzles*

Wellbrook Collection. *Bear Spot Learns a Lot; Growing Up with Diabetes*

Wellbrook Collection. *Dotty the Dalmatian Has Epilepsy*
Wellbrook Collection. *I'm Still Me: Coping with Leukemia*
Wellbrook Collection. *Way to Go Bravo: Learning to Live with Asthma*
Wiener, Lori, Best, Aprille, & Pizzo, Phillip. *Be a Friend: Children Who Live with Hiv*
Wolf, Bernard. *HIV Positive*

Holidays Around the World
Coerr, Eleanor. *Sadako*
Golden, Barbara Diamond. *Cakes and Miracles*
Holcomb, Nan. *Sarah's Surprise*
Mayer, Gina & Mercer. *A Very Special Critter*

Homes & Neighborhoods
Borton, Lady. *Junk Pile*
Bunnett, Rochelle. *Friends in the Park*
Crunk, Tony. *Big Mama*
Levi, Dorothy Hoffman. *A Very Special Friend*
McMahon, Patricia. *Lister for the Bus: David's Story*
Muller, Gerda. *The Garden in the City*
Raffi. *One Light, One Sun*

Music
Millman, Isaac. *Moses Goes to a Concert*

Naptime & Bedtime
Rabe, Berniece. *Where's Chimpy?*
Raffi. *One Light, One Sun*

Numbers & Counting
Newth, Phillip. *Roly Goes Exploring*
Rabe, Berniece. *Where's Chimpy?*

Oceans, Lakes & Sea Animals
Condra, Estelle. *See The Ocean*
Foreman, Michael. *Seal Surfer*

Hines, Anna Grossnickle. *Gramma's Walk*

Sargent, Susan & Wirt, Donna Aaron. *My Favorite Place*

Peace Education

Bunting, Eve. *The Wall*

Coerr, Eleanor. *Sadako*

Hallinan, P.K. *Heartprints*

Lyon, George Ella. *Cecil's Story*

Pet Animals

Alden, Joan. *A Boy's Best Friend*

Alexander, Sally Hobart. *Mom's Best Friend*

Arnold, Caroline. *A Guide Puppy Grows Up*

Calmenson, Stephanie. *Rosie: A Visiting Dog's Story*

Collins, Harold S. *The Beginning Sign Language Series*

Damrell, Liz. *With the Wind*

Davis, Patricia. *Brian's Bird*

Delton, Judy. *I'll Never Love Anything Ever Again*

Goodwall, Jane. *Mr. White*

Gregory, Nan. *How Smudge Came*

Haldane, Suzanne. *Helping Hands: How Monkeys Assist People Who Are Disabled.*

Hesse, Karen. *Lester's Dog*

Hill, Eric. *Where's Spot*

Karim, Roberta. *Mandy Sue Day*

Krause, Ute. *Pig Surprise*

Lears, Laurie. *Ben Has Something to Say: A Story About Stuttering*

Lowell, Gloria Roth. *Elana's Ears or How I Became the Best Big Sister in the World*

Okimoto, Jean Davies. *A Place for Grace*

Osofsky, Audrey. *My Buddy*

Porte, Barbara Ann. *Harry's Dog*

Sanford, Doris. *Help! Fire!*

Simpson-Smith, Elizabeth. *A Guide Dog Goes to School*

Sullivan, Tom. *That Nelson!*

Turner, Deborah & Mohler Diana. *How Willy Got His Wheels*
Wellbrook Collection. *Dotty the Dalmatian Has Epilepsy*
Wellbrook Collection. *Way to Go Bravo: Learning to Live with Asthma*
Wheeler, Cindy. *Simple Signs*

Planting & Gardening
Muller, Gerda. *The Garden in the City*
Peckinpah, Sandra Lee. *Rosey . . . the Imperfect Angel*
Rickert, Janet Elizabeth. *Russ and the Apple Tree Surprise*

Safety
Brown, Tricia. *Someone Special, Just Like You*
Cohen, Miriam. *It's George*
Powers, Mary Ellen. *Our Teacher's in a Wheelchair*
Sanford, Doris. *Help! Fire!*

Seasons
Foreman, Michael. *Seal Surfer*

Sense of Sight
Alexander, Sally Hobart. *Mom Can't See Me*
Alexander, Sally Hobart. *Mom's Best Friend*
Ancona, George, & Ancona, Mary Beth. *Handtalk Zoo*
Arnold, Caroline. *A Guide Puppy Grows Up*
Carter, Alden R. *Seeing Things My Way*
Chaplin, Susan Gibbons. *I Can Sign My ABCs*
Condra, Estelle. *See The Ocean*
Gross, Ruth Belov. *You Don't Need Words! A Book About Ways people Talk Without Words*
Lakin, Patricia. *Dad and Me in the Morning*
Litchfield, Ada B. *A Cane in Her Hand*
Millman, Isaac. *Moses Goes to School*
Milne, A.A. *Winnie-the-Pooh's ABC: Sign Language Edition*
Newth, Phillip. *Roly Goes Exploring*
Rankin, Laura. *The Handmade Alphabet*

Slier, Debby. *Animal Signs: A First Book of Sign Language*
Slier, Debby. *Word Signs: A First Book of Sign Language*
White, Peter. *Think About Being Blind*

Sense of Touch
Adler, David A. *A Picture Book of Helen Keller*
Alexander, Sally Hobart. *Mom Can't See Me*
Golden, Barbara Diamond. *Cakes and Miracles*
Kroll, Virginia L. *Naomi Knows It's Springtime*
Moon, Nicole. *Lucy's Picture*
Newth, Phillip. *Roly Goes Exploring*
Pearson, Susan. *Happy Birthday, Grampie*
Turk, Ruth. *The Doll at the Top of the Shelf*
Young, Ed. *Seven Blind Mice*

Senses
Adler, David A. *A Picture Book of Helen Keller*
Levine, Edna S. *Lisa and Her Soundless World*
Sargent, Susan, & Wirt, Donna Aaron. *My Favorite Place*
Young, Ed. *Seven Blind Mice*

Shapes, Sizes & Weights
Kuklin, Susan. *Thinking Big: The Story of a Young Dwarf*
Mitchell, Rita Phillips. *Hue Boy*
Newth, Phillip. *Roly Goes Exploring*
Russo, Marisabina. *Alex Is My Friend*
Slate, Joseph. *Miss Bindergarten Takes a Field Trip*

Sign Language
Addabbo, Carole. *Dina the Deaf Dinosaur*
Ancona, George, & Ancona, Mary Beth. *Handtalk Zoo*
Bahan, Ben, & Dannis, Joe. *My ABC Signs of Animal Friends*
Bove, Linda. *Sesame Street Sign Language ABC*
Chaplin, Susan Gibbons. *I Can Sign My ABCs*
Charlip, Remy. *Handtalk Birthday*

Collins, Harold S. *The Beginning Sign Language Series*

Fain, Kathleen. *A Sign Language Alphabet*

Greenberg, Judith E. *What Is the Sign for Friend?*

Gross, Ruth Belov. *You Don't Need Words! A Book About Ways People Talk Without Words*

Holub, Joan. *My First Book of Sign Language*

Hill, Eric. *Where's Spot*

Kadish, Sharona. *Discovering Friendship*

Levi, Dorothy Hoffman. *A Very Special Friend*

Levine, Edna A. *Lisa and Her Soundless World*

Litchfield, Ada B. *Words in Our Hands*

Milne, A.A. *Winnie-the-Pooh's ABC: Sign Language Edition*

Slier, Debby. *Animal Signs: A First Book of Sign Language*

Slier, Debby. *Word Signs: A First Book of Sign Language*

Wahl, Jan. *Jamie's Tiger*

Wheeler, Cindy. *Simple Signs*

Smells in the Environment

Kroll, Virginia L. *Naomi Knows It's Springtime*

MacLachlan, Patricia. *Through Grandpa's Eyes*

Sounds in the Environment

Condra, Estelle. *See The Ocean*

Gilmore, Rachna. *A Screaming Kind of Day*

Kroll, Virginia L. *Naomi Knows It's Springtime*

Krause, Ute. *Pig Surprise*

Litchfield, Ada B. *A Button in Her Ear*

Litchfield, Ada B. *Words in Our Hands*

Lowell, Gloria Roth. *Elana's Ears or How I Became the Best Big Sister in the World*

MacLachlan, Patricia. *Through Grandpa's Eyes*

Millman, Isaac. *Moses Goes to a Concert*

Wellbrook Collection. *Hooray for Harold: Dealing with Hearing Loss*

Woolley, Maggie. *Think About Being Deaf*

Zelonsky, Joy. *I Can't Always Hear You*

Sports
Allen, Anne. *Sports for the Handicapped*
Kornfield, Elizabeth J. *Dreams Come True*
Lee, Jeanne M. *Silent Lotus*
Moran, George. *Imagine Me on a Sit-Ski!*
Prall, Jo. *Way to Go Alex!*

Spring
Harshman, Marc. *The Storm*
Kroll, Virginia L. *Naomi Knows It's Springtime*
Muller, Gerda. *The Garden in the City*

Summer
Bunnett, Rochelle. *Friends in the Park*
Condra, Estelle. *See The Ocean*
Karim, Roberta. *Mandy Sue Day*
Kroll, Virginia L. *Butterfly Boy*
Levi, Dorothy Hoffman. *A Very Special Friend*
McMahon, Patricia. *Summer Tunes: A Martha's Vineyard Vacation*
Moss, Deborah M. *Lee, the Rabbit with Epilepsy*
Orr, Wendy. *A Place for Grace*
Raffi. *One Light, One Sun*
Sargent, Susan & Wirt, Donna Aaron. *My Favorite Place*

Tools & Machines
London, Jonathan. *The Lion Who Has Asthma*

Toys
Turk, Ruth. *The Doll at the Top of the Shelf*

Transportation
Burns, Kay. *Our Mom*
Cowen-Fletcher, Jane. *Mama Zooms*
Lasker, Joe. *Nick Joins In*
Muldoon, Kathleen M. *Princess Pooh*
Turner, Deborah & Mohler, Diana. *How Willy Got His Wheels*

We Are Alike, We Are Different

Adler, David A. *A Picture Book of Helen Keller*

Alexander, Sally Hobart. *Mom Can't See Me*

Amenta, Charles A. *Russell is Extra Special: A Book About Autism for Children*

Amer, Kim, & Brill, Marlene. *Short Mort and the Big Bully*

Arnold, Caroline. *A Guide Puppy Grows Up*

Atkinson, Mary. *Why Do Some People Use Wheelchairs?*

Barrett, Mary Brigid. *Sing to the Stars*

Bergman, Thomas. *Going Places: Children Living with Cerebral Palsy*

Bergman, Thomas. *We Laugh, We Love, We Cry: Children Living with Mental Retardation*

Berry, Steve. *The Boy Who Wouldn't Speak*

Borton, Lady. *Junk Pile*

Bouwkamp, Julie A. *Hi, I'm Ben! . . . And I've Got a Secret*

Brearley, Sue. *Talk To Me*

Brown, Tricia. *Someone Special, Just Like You*

Bunnett, Rochelle. *Friends at School*

Bunnett, Rochelle. *Friends in the Park*

Bunting, Eve. *The Wall*

Burns, Kay. *Our Mom*

Cairo, Shelley. *Our Brother Has Down's Syndrome*

Nancy Carlson. *Arnie and the New Kid*

Nancy Carlson. *Sit Still!*

Carter, Alden R. *Seeing Things My Way*

Carter, Alden R. *Stretching Ourselves: Kids with Cerebral Palsy*

Caseley, Judith. *Harry and Willy and Carrothead*

Charlip, Remy. *Handtalk Birthday*

Cohen, Miriam. *See You Tomorrow, Charles*

Condra, Estelle. *See The Ocean*

Corman, Clifford L., &Trevino, Esther. *Eukee The Jumpy Jumpy Elephant*

Cowen-Fletcher, Jane. *Mama Zooms*

Craig, Lori. *One Step at a Time*

Damrell, Liz. *With the Wind*

DeBear, Kirsten. *Be Quiet, Marina!*

Derby Janice. *Are You My Friend?*

Dwyer, Kathleen M. *What Do You Mean I Have a Learning Disability*

Edwards, Becky. *My Brother Sammy*

Emmert, Michelle. *I'm the Big Sister Now*

Gainer, Cindy. *I'm Like You, You're Like Me*

Gehret, Jeanne. *Eagle Eyes*

Dwight, Laura. *We Can Do It!*

Gehret, Jeanne. *The Don't-give-up Kid*

Golden, Barbara Diamond. *Cakes and Miracles*

Greenberg, Judith E. *What Is the Sign for Friend?*

Haines, Sandra. *Becca and Sue Make Two*

Haldane, Suzanne. *Helping Hands: How Monkeys Assist People Who Are Disabled*

Heelan, James Riggio. *Rolling Along: The Story of Taylor and His Wheelchair*

Henriod, Lorraine. *Grandma's Wheelchair*

Holcomb, Nan. *Fair and Square*

Holcomb, Nan. *Patrick and Emma Lou*

Holcomb, Nan. *Sarah's Surprise*

Holub, Joan. *My First Book of Sign Language*

Jansen, Larry. *My Sister is Special*

Karim, Roberta. *Mandy Sue Day*

Kornfield, Elizabeth J. *Dreams Come True*

Krisher, Trudy. *Kathy's Hats: A Story of Hope*

Kroll, Virginia L. *Naomi Knows It's Springtime*

Kuklin, Susan. *Thinking Big: The Story of a Young Dwarf*

Lasker, Joe. *Nick Joins In*

Lears, Laurie. *Ian's Walk*

Levi, Dorothy Hoffman. *A Very Special Friend*

Levi, Dorothy Hoffman, *A Very Special Sister*

Levine, Edna A. *Lisa and Her Soundless World*

Litchfield, Ada B. *A Button in Her Ear*

Litchfield, Ada B. *Making Room for Uncle Joe*

Litchfield, Ada B. *Words in Our Hands*

Loski, Diana. *The Boy On The Bus*

Mackinnon, Christy. *Silent Observer*

MacLachlan, Patricia. *Through Grandpa's Eyes*

Maguire, Arlene. *Special People, Special Ways*

Martin, Bill J.R. & Archambault, John. *Knots on a Counting Rope*

Mayer, Gina & Mercer. *A Very Special Critter*

Merrifield, Margaret. *Come Sit By Me*

Meyers, Cindy. *Rolling Along with Goldilocks and the Three Bears*

Mitchell, Lori. *Different Just Like Me*

Mitchell, Rita Phillips. *Hue Boy*

Moran, George. *Imagine Me on a Sit-Ski!*

Moss, Deborah M. *Lee, the Rabbit with Epilepsy*

Moss, Deborah M. *Shelley, the Hyperactive Turtle*

Newth, Phillip. *Roly Goes Exploring*

O'Shaughnessy, Ellen. *Somebody Called Me a Retard today . . . and My Heart Felt Sad*

Osofsky, Audrey. *My Buddy*

Peckinpah, Sandra Lee. *Rosey . . . the Imperfect Angel*

Peterson, Jeanne Whitehouse. *I Have a Sister My Sister is Deaf*

Pirner, Connie White. *Even Little Kids Get Diabetes*

Powers, Mary Ellen. *Our Teacher's in a Wheelchair*

Prall, Jo. *My Sister's Special*

Quinn, Patricia O., & Stern, Judith A. *Putting on the Brakes: Young People's Guide to Attention Deficit Hyperactivity Disorder*

Rabe, Berniece. *The Balancing Girl*

Rankin, Laura. *The Handmade Alphabet*

Rheingrover, Jean Sasso. *Veronica's First Year*

Riggs, Stephanie. *Never Sell Yourself Short*

Roberts, Karon. *Bright . . . and Behind: A Book for Children and Parents Learning To Cope with Reading and Attention Problems*

Roby, Cynthia. *When Learning is Tough: Kids Talk About Their Learning Disabilities*

Rogers, Fred. *Let's Talk About It: Extraordinary Friends*

Root, Ann, & Gladdin, Linda. *Charlie's Challenge*

Rosenberg, Maxine B. *Finding a Way: Living with Exceptional Brothers and Sisters*

Rosenberg, Maxine B. *My Friend Leslie: The Story of a Handicapped Child*

Rotner, Shelly, & Kelly, Sheila. *A.D.D. Book for Kids*

Rudner, Barry. *The Handstand*

Russo, Marisabina. *Alex Is My Friend*

Sanford, Doris. *Don't Look at Me*

Sanford, Doris. *Help! Fire!*

Seuling, Barbara. *I'm Not So Different*

Shannon, David. *David Goes to School*

Shannon, David. *No, David!*

Shriver, Maria. *What's Wrong with Timmy?*

Silverstein, Alvin, Silverstein, Virginia, & Nunn, Laura Silverstein. *Dyslexia*

Swanson, Susanne M. *My Friend Emily*

Swenson, Judy Harris, & Junz, Roxane Brown. *Learning My Way: I'm a Winner*

Taylor, Ron. *All By Self*

Thompson, Mary. *Andy and the Yellow Frisbee*

Thompson, Mary. *My Brother Matthew*

Verniero, Joan C. *You Can Call Me Willy*

Wahl, Jan. *Jamie's Tiger*

Wanous, Suzanne. *Sara's Secret*

Watson, Esther. *Talking to Angels*

Wellbrook Collection. *Hip-Hop The Hyperactive Hippo*

Whinston, Joan Lenett. *I'm Joshua & Yes I Can*

White, Peter. *Think About Being Blind*

Willis, Jeanne. *Susan Laughs*

Woolley, Maggie. *Think About Being Deaf*

Wright, Betty Ren *My Sister is Different*

Wright, Christine. *Just Like Emma: How She Has Fun in God's World*

Zelonsky, Joy. *I Can't Always Hear You*

Weather or Storms

Harshman, Marc. *The Storm*

Wild Birds & Animals

Bahan, Ben & Dannis, Joe. *My ABC Signs of Animal Friends*

Collins, Harold S. *The Beginning Sign Language Series*

Fain, Kathleen. *Handsigns: A Sign Language Alphabet*

Heelan, James Riggio. *The Making of My Special Hand: Madison's Story*

Lears, Laurie. *Waiting for Mr. Goose*

Wellbrook Collection. *Hooray for Harold: Dealing with Hearing Loss*

Winter

Moran, George. *Imagine Me on a Sit-Ski!*

Zoo Animals

Ancona, George, & Ancona, Mary Beth. *Handtalk Zoo*

Bahan, Ben & Dannis, Joe. *My ABC Signs of Animal Friends*

Collins, Harold S. *The Beginning Sign Language Series*

Fain, Kathleen. *Handsigns: A Sign Language Alphabet*

Haldane, Suzanne. *Helping Hands: How Monkeys Assist People Who Are Disabled*

Harter, Debbie. *The Animal Boogie*

Henriod, Lorraine. *Grandma's Wheelchair*

Hoffman, Eric. *No Fair to Tigers*

London, Jonathan. *The Lion Who Has Asthma*

Rabe, Berniece. *Where's Chimpy?*

Wellbrook Collection. *Bear Spot Learns a Lot: Growing Up with Diabetes*

Wellbrook Collection. *Hip-Hop the Hyperactive Hippo*

Young, Ed. *Seven Blind Mice*

CHAPTER NINE

Text Set Lesson Plan

INTRODUCTION

A Text Set Lesson Plan has been developed to help you organize the children's literature you choose to use with each of your themes or units. The Lesson Plan has a space at the top to identify the theme. Next, there are three sections for you to list children's books in the Text Set that relate to the theme by incorporating books that represent: 1) disabilities or chronic illness, 2) diverse cultures, and 3) other favorite books.

For the first section of the Text Set Lesson Plan, Books Incorporating Disabilities or Chronic Illness, refer to Chapter Eight where the books in this collection are listed by theme or unit. Simply select books from the theme that are appropriate for the children with whom you are working. Remember, most often children's books can be used effectively outside the recommended grade levels. Next, in section two, add your choice of books that incorporate diverse cultures and in section three, add other favorite books related to the theme.

Once you have developed Text Set Lesson Plans for each theme that you use in your curriculum, it will be an easy task to select children's literature for your units. Merely check your Lesson Plans for the theme you will be teaching and immediately you will know which books are appropriate. Within each Text Set, you select how many books you plan to use.

With this format, you will be able to continually update your Text Set Lesson Plans by adding newly published books and new favorites that you discover. Additional Text Set Lesson Plans can be developed for each new theme you choose to teach.

Sample Text Set Lesson Plans for the themes of Farm & Farm Animals and Fantasy & Imagination are provided. The Text Set Lesson Plan form is also provided which can be reproduced so you are able to develop as many Text Set Lesson Plans as you might need. I suggest you begin with the next unit you will be teaching and develop the Text Set Lesson Plan for that unit. Then each time you teach a new unit, continue developing your Lesson Plans. Over time you will have developed Text Set Lesson Plans for every theme that you teach. This is a realistic approach for developing your Text Set Lesson Plans.

Text Set Lesson Plan

Theme   Farm & Farm Animals

Books Incorporating Disabilities or Illness:

Damrell, Liz. *With the Wind*

Harshman, Marc. *The Storm*

Karim, Roberta. *Mandy Sue Day*

Krause, Ute. *Pig Surprise*

Slier, Debbie. *Animal Signs: A First Book of Sign Language*

Wellbrook Collection. *I'm Still Coping with Leukemia*

Wellbrook collection. *Way to Go Bravo: Learning to Live with Asthma*

Books Incorporating Diverse Cultures:

Other Favorite Books:

Text Set Lesson Plan

Theme   Fantasy & Imagination

Books Incorporating Disabilities or Illness:

Berry, Steve. *The Boy Who Wouldn't Speak*

Borton, Lady. *Junk Pile!*

Collins, Harold S. *The Beginning Sign Language Series*

Cowen-Fletcher, Jane. *Mama Zooms*

Damrell, Liz. *With the Wind*

Henriod, Lorraine. *Grandma's Wheelchdir*

Hines, Anna Grossnickle. *Gramma's Walk*

Hoffman, Eric. *No Fair to Tigers*

London, Jonathan. *The Lion Who Has Asthma*

Peckinpah, Sandra Lee. *Rosey . . . the Imperfect Angel*

Schar, Brigitte. *The Blind Fairy*

Walker, John C. *In Other Words*

Watson, Esther. *Talking to Angels*

Books Incorporating Diverse Cultures:

Other Favorite Books:

Text Set Lesson Plan

Theme _____

Books Incorporating Disabilities or Illness:

_____
_____
_____
_____
_____
_____
_____
_____

Books Incorporating Diverse Cultures:

_____
_____
_____
_____
_____
_____
_____
_____

Other Favorite Books:

_____
_____
_____
_____
_____
_____
_____

APPENDIX A

Images & Encounters Profile
(A checklist to Review Books for Inclusion
and depiction of Persons with Disabilities)

For each item below, indicate whether you believe the criteria are present or not present in the STORYLINE, LANGUAGE, or ILLUSTRATIONS. Check YES if the criterion was addressed positively, check NO if the criterion was addressed negatively, and check NP if the criterion was not present. YES are the preferred responses. The reviewer is cautioned to be aware of the NO responses when reading and/or discussing each book as these responses may influence how you choose to use the book.

YES	NO	NP	
_____	_____	_____	1. Promotes empathy not pity.
_____	_____	_____	2. Depicts acceptance not ridicule.
_____	_____	_____	3. Emphasizes success rather than, or in addition, to failure.
_____	_____	_____	4. Promotes positive images of persons with disabilities.
_____	_____	_____	5. Assists children in gaining accurate understanding of the disability.
_____	_____	_____	6. Demonstrates respect for persons with disabilities.
_____	_____	_____	7. Promotes attitude of "one of us" not "one of them."
_____	_____	_____	8. Uses language which stresses person first, disability second philosophy, i.e. Jody who is blind.
_____	_____	_____	9. Describes the disability or person with disabilities as realistic (i.e., not subhuman or superhuman.)
_____	_____	_____	10. Illustrates characters in a realistic manner.

When in doubt about using a particular book which includes a person with a disability, ask yourself, "Would this story embarrass or humiliate a child with a disability?" If the answer is YES, consider carefully how to best use this book (Blaska & Lynch, 1994).

(Revised by J. Blaska, 2002)

APPENDIX B

Children's Books That Include
Persons With Disabilities or Illness

Alphabetized by Title

ABC for You and Me, Meg Girnis

A.D.D. Book for Kids, Shelly Rotner & Sheila Kelly

alef-bet—A Hebrew Alphabet Book, Michelle Edwards

Alex is My Friend, Marisabina Russo

Alex, The Kid with AIDS, Linda Walvoord Girard

All By Self, Ron Taylor

An Alphabet of Animal Signs, Harold S. Collins

Animal Boogie (The), Debbie Harter

Animal Signs: A First Book of Sign Language, Debby Slier

Andy and the Yellow Frisbee, Mary Thompson

Apple Pie and Onions, Judith Caseley

Arabella, Wendy Orr

Are You My Friend? Janice Derby

Arnie and the New Kid, Nancy Carlson

Balancing Girl (The), Berniece Rabe

Be a Friend: Children Who Live with HIV Speak, Lori Wiener, Aprille Best,
& Phillip Pizzo

Be Good to Eddie Lee, Virginia Fleming

Be Quiet, Marina. Kirsten DeBear

Bear Spot Learns a Lot: Growing Up with Diabetes, Wellbrook Collection

Becca and Sue Make Two, Sandra Haines

Becky the Brave: A Story About Epilepsy, Wellbrook Collection

Ben Has Something to Say, Laurie Lears

Ben, King of the River, David Gifaldi,

Big Brother Dustin, Alden R. Carter

Big Mama, Tony Crunk

Blind Fairy (The), Briggitte Schar

Boy On the Bus (The), Diana Loski

Boy Who Wouldn't Speak (The), Steve Berry

Boy's Best Friend (A), Joan Alden

Brian's Bird, Patricia Davis

Bright . . . and Behind: A Book for Children and Parents Learning to Cope with Reading and Attention Problems, Karon Roberts

Butterfly Boy, Virginia L. Kroll

Button in Her Ear (A), Ada B. Litchfield

Cakes and Miracles, Barbara Diamond Golden

Cane in Her Hand (A), Ada B. Litchfield

Cardiac Kids, Vicci Elder

Carmen's Story: A Book About a Boy Living with AIDS, Arlene Schulman

Cecil's Story, George Ella Lyon

Charlie's Challenge, Ann Root & Linda Gladden

Come Sit By Me, Margaret Merrifield

Dad and Me in the Morning, Patricia Lakin

Daddy & Me, Jeanne Montoussamy-Ashe

David Goes to School, David Shannon

David Has AIDS, Doris Sanford

David's Story: A Book About Surgery, David Brink

Different Just Like Me, Lori Mitchell

Dina the Deaf Dinosaur, Carole Addabbo

Discovering Friendship, Sharona Kadish

Doll on Top of the Shelf (The), Ruth Turk

Don't Look at Me, Doris Sanford

Dotty the Dalmatian Has Epilepsy, Wellbrook Collection

Dr. White, Jane Goodwall

Dreams Come True, Elizabeth J. Kornfield

Dustin's Big School Day, Alden R. Carter

Dyslexia. Alvin Silverstein, Virginia Silverstein, & Laura Silverstein Nunn

Eagle Eyes, Jeanne Gehret

Eagle Feathers, Sonia Gardner

Elana's Ears or How I Became the Best Big Sister in the World, Gloria Roth Lowell

Eukee The Jumpy Jumpy Elephant, Clifford L. Corman

Even Little Kids Get Diabetes, Connie White Pirner

Fair and Square, Nan Holcomb

Finding a Way: Living with Exceptional Brothers & Sisters, Maxine B. Rosenberg

Foods, Harold S. Collins

Friends at School, Rochelle Bunnett

Friends in the Park, Rochelle Bunnett

Fruits and Vegetables, Harold S. Collins

Garden in the City (A), Gerda Muller

Going Places: Children Living with Cerebral Palsy, Thomas Bergman

Good Luck Mrs. K! Louise Borden

Gramma's Walk, Anna Grossnickle Hines

Grandma Drives a Motor Bed, Diane Johnson Hamm

Grandma's Wheelchair, Lorraine Henriod

Guide Dog Goes to School (A), Elizabeth E. Simpson-Smith

Guide Dog Puppy Grows Up (A), Caroline Arnold

Handmade Alphabet (The), Laura Rankin

Handsigns: A Sign Language Alphabet, Kathleen Fain

Handstand (The), Barry Rudner

Handtalk Birthday, Remy Charlip

Handtalk Zoo, George & Mary Beth Ancona

Happy Birthday, Grampie, Susan Pearson

Harry and Willy and Carrothead, Judith Caseley

Harry's Dog, Barbara Ann Porte

Heartprints, P.K. Hallinan

Help! Fire! Doris Sanford

Helping Hands: How Monkeys Assist People Who are Disabled, Suzanne Haldane

He's My Brother, Joe Lasker

Hi, I'm Ben!And I've Got a Secret, Julie Bouwkamp

Hickory Chair (The), Lisa Rowe Fraustino

Hip-Hop the Hyperactive Hippo, Wellbrook Collection

HIV Positive, Bernard Wolf

Hooray for Harold: Dealing with Hearing Loss, Wellbrook Collection

Hooway for Wodney, Helen Lester

How Smudge Came, Nan Gregory

How Willy Got His Wheels, Deborah Turner & Diana Mohler

Hue Boy, Rita Phillips Mitchell

I Can Sign My ABCs, Susan Gibbons Chaplin

I Can't Always Hear You, Joy Zelonsky

I Have a Sister My Sister is Deaf, Jeanne Whitehouse Peterson

I Have Diabetes, Althea

I Have Epilepsy, Althea

Ian's Walk, Lauri Lears

I'll Never Love Anything Ever again, Judy Delton

I'm Deaf And It's Okay, Lorraine Aseltine, Evelyn Mueller, & Nancy Tait

I'm Joshua & Yes I Can, Joan Lenett Whinston

I'm Like You, You're Like Me, Cindy Gainer

I'm Not So Different, Barbara Seuling

I'm Still Me: Coping with Leukemia, Wellbrook Collection

I'm the Big Sister Now, Michelle Emmert

I'm Tougher Than Asthma, Alden R. Carter & Siri M. Carter

Imagine Me on a Sit-Ski! George Moran

In Other Words, John Walker

It's George, Miriam Cohen

Jamie's Tiger, Jan Wahl

Junk Pile! Lady Borton

Just Like Emma: How She Has Fun in God's World, Christine Wright

Kathy's Hats: A Story of Hope, Trudy Krisher

Knots on a Counting Rope, Bill J.R. Martin & John Archambault

Learning My Way: I'm a Winner, Judy Harris Swenson & Roxane Brown Keinz

Lee, the Rabbit with Epilepsy, Deborah M. Moss

Lester's Dog, Karen Hesse

Let's Talk About It: Extraordinary Friends, Fred Rogers

Lion Who Has Asthma (The), Jonathan London

Lisa and Her Soundless World, Edna S. Levine

Listen for the Bus, Particia McMahon

Little Tree: A Story for Children with Serious Medical Problems, Joyce C. Mills

Losing Uncle Tim, MaryKate Jordon

Lucy's Picture, Nicola Moon

Luke Has Asthma, Too, Alison Rogers

Making of My Hand: Madison's Story (The), Jamee Riggio Heelan

Making Room for Uncle Joe, Ada B. Litchfield

Mama Zooms, Jane Cowen-Fletcher

Mandy, Barbara Booth

Mandy Sue Day, Roberta Karim

Miss Bindergarten Celebrates the 100th Day of Kindergarten, Joseph Slate

Miss Bindergarten Gets Ready for Kindergarten, Joseph Slate

Miss Bindergarten Plans a Circus with Kindergarten, Joseph Slate

Miss Bindergarten Stays Home, Joseph Slate

Miss Bindergarten Takes a Field Trip, Joseph Slate

Mom Can't See Me, Sally Hobart Alexander

Mom's Best Friend, Sally Hobart Alexander

Moses Goes to a Concert, Issac Millman

Moses Goes to School, Issac Millman

Mother Goose in Sign, Harold S. Collins

My ABC Signs of Animal Friends, Ben Bahan & Joe Dannis

My Book for Kids with Cansur, Jason Gaes

My Brother Matthew, Mary Thompson

My Brother Sammy, Becky Edwards

My Buddy, Audrey Osofsky

My Favorite Place, Susan Sargant & Donna Aaron Wirt

My First Book of Sign, Pamela J. Baker

My First Book of Sign Language, Joan Holub

My Friend Emily, Susannne M. Swanson

My Friend Leslie: The Story of a Handicapped Child, Maxine B. Rosenberg

My Sister Is Different, Betty Ren Wright

My Sister is Special, Lary Jansen

My Sister Rose has Diabetes, Monica Driscoll Beatty

My Sister's Special, Jo Prall

Naomi Knows Its Springtime, Virginia L. Kroll

Never Sell Yourself Short, Stephanie Rigg

Nick Joins In, Joe Lasker

Nicole's Story, Virginia Totorica Aldape

No, David! David Shannon

No Longer Afraid, Doris Sandford

One Light, One Sun, Raffi

One Step at a Time, Lori Craig

Our Brother Has Down's Syndrome, Shelley Cairo

Our Mom, Kay Burns

Our Teacher's In a Wheelchair, Mary Ellen Powers

Patrick and Emma Lou, Nan Holcomb

Pets, Animals & Creatures, Harold S. Collins

Picture Book of Helen Keller (A), David A. Adler

Pig Surprise, Ute Krause

Place for Grace (A), Jean Davis Okimoto

Princess Pooh, Kathleen M. Muldoon

Problem with Hair (The), Karen Sue Foss

Putting on the Brakes, Patricia O. Quinn & Judith M. Stern

Puzzles, Dava Walker

Rolling Along: The Story of Taylor and His Wheelchair, Jamee Riggio Heelan

Rolling Along with Goldilocks and the Three Bears, Cindy Meyers

Roly Goes Exploring, Philip Newth

Rosey: A Visiting Dog's Story, Stephanie Calmenson

Rosey . . . The Imperfect Angel, Sandra Lee Peckinpah

Runaway Sugar: All About Diabetes, A. Ivin Silverstein

Russ and the Almost Perfect Day, Jane Elizabeth Rickert

Russ and the Apple Tree Surprise, Jane Elizabeth Rickert

Russ and the Firehouse, Jane Elizabeth rickert

Russell is Extra Special: A Book About Autism for Children, Charles A. Amenta

Sadako, Eleanor Coerr

Sarah's Surprise, Nan Holcomb

Sara's Secret, Suzanne Wanous

Screaming Kind of Day (A), Rachna Gilmore

Seal Surfer, Michael Foreman

Secret Signs: Along the Underground Railroad, Anita Riggio

See the Ocean, Estelle Condra

See You Tomorow, Charles, Miriam Cohen

Seeing Things My Way, Alden R. Carter

Sesame Street Sign Language ABC, Linda Bove

Seven Blind Mice, Ed Young

Shelley, the Hyperactive Turtle, Deborah M. Moss

Short Mort and the Big Bully, Kim Amer & Marlene Brill

Signing at School, Harold S. Collins

Silent Lotus, Jeanne M. Lee

Silent Observer, Christy Mackinnon

Simple Signs, Cindy Wheeler

Sing to the Stars, Mary Brigid Barrett

Sit Still, Nancy Carlson

Somebody Called Me A Retard Today . . . and My Heart Felt Sad, Ellen
  O'Shaughnessy

Someone Special, Just Like You, Tricia Brown

Songs in Sign, Harold S. Collins

Special People, Special Ways, Arlene Maguire

Sports for the Handicapped, Anne Allen

Storm (The), Marc Harshman

Story of Blue Elk (The), Gerald Hausman

Stretching Ourselves: Kids with Cerebral Palsy, Alden R. Carter

Summer Tunes: A Martha's Vineyard Vacation, Patricia McMahon

Sunshine Home (The), Eve Bunting

Susan Laughs, Jeanne Willis

Talk to Me, Sue Brearley

Talking to Angels, Esther Watson

That's Nelson, Tom Sullivan

There's a Little Bit of Me in Jamey, Diane M. Amadeo

Think About Being Blind, Peter White

Think About Being Deaf, Maggie Woolley

Thinking Big: The Story of a Young Dwarf, Susan Kuklin

Through Grandpa's Eyes, Patricia MacLachlan

Tiger Flowers, Patricia Quinlan

Veronica's First Year, Jean Sasso Rheingrover

Very Special Critter (A), Gina & Mercer Mayer

Very Special Friend (A), Dorothy Hoffman Levi

Very Special Sister (A), Dorothy Hoffman Levi

Waiting for Mr. Goose, Laurie Lears

Wall (The), Eve Bunting

Way to Go Alex!, Robin Pulber

Way to Go Bravo: Learning to Live with Asthma, Wellbrook Collection

We Can Do It! Laura Dwight

We Laugh, We Love, We Cry: Children Living with Mental Retardation, Thomas Bergman

We'll Paint the Octopus Red, Stephanie Stuve Bodeen

What Do You Mean I Have a Learning Disability? Kathleen M. Dwyer

What is the Sign for Friend? Judith E. Greenberg

What's Wrong with Timmy? Maria Shriver

When Eric's Mom Fought Cancer, Judith Vigna

When I Grow Up, Candri Hodges

When is Learning Tough: Kids Talk About Their Learning Disabilities, Cynthia Roby

Where's Chimpy? Berniece Rabe

Where's Spot, Eric Hill

Why do People Use Wheelchairs? Questions Children Ask About Disabled People, Mary Atkinson

William and the Good Old Days, Eloise Greenfield

Winnie-the-Pooh's ABC: Sign Language Edition, A.A. Milne

With the Wind, Liz Damrell

Word Signs: A First Book of Sign Language, Debby Slier

Words in Our Hands, Ada Litchfield

You Can Call Me Willy, Joan Verniero

You Don't Need Words! A Book About Ways People Talk Without Words, Ruth Belov Gross

APPENDIX C

Children's Books Cross-Referenced by Categories
(According to How the Disability
or Illness Was Treated in the Story)

INTRODUCTION

The books in the annotated bibliography were analyzed to determine how the authors present the disability or illness and how it is incorporated into the story. This information will be helpful when selecting literature for young children. Additional information on the Categories can be found in Chapter Five.

Category A: Books provide factual information about a disability or illness.

Category B: Books provide information about disability or illness in a story format.

Category C: Books provides stories with character/s with disability or illness. There may be little or no information about a disability or illness. Books in Category C are inclusionary literature.

Each Category has its place in the disability literature for young children. Books in Category A provide information about a disability or illness and are especially effective when you want children to learn about a specific disability or illness. Books in Category B provide information in a story format which will hold a young child's interest longer, and generally the information does not have as much depth as books in Category A. Books in Category C are very important as they allow children to see characters of varying abilities in the storyline. These stories integrate persons with disabilities or illness in a natural way much like what children see in their schools or communities. In addition, children with disabilities and illness are able to see people like themselves in some of the stories they read. Children without disabilities begin to learn about people who are different from themselves, but find they also have many similarities.

Books Listed by Categories

Category A

Books Provide Factual Information About Disability or Chronic Illness

Aldape, Virginia Totorica. *Nicole's Story*

Alexander, Sally Hobert. *Mom Can't See Me*

Alexander, Sally Hobert. *Mom's Best Friend*

Allen, Anne. *Sports for the Handicapped*

Althea. *I Have Diabetes*

Althea. *I Have Epilepsy*

Amenta, Charles A. *Russell is Extra Special: A Book About Autism for Children*

Atkinson, Mary. *Why Do Some People Use Wheelchairs? Questions Children Ask About Disabled People*

Bahan, Ben & Dannis, Joe. *My ABC Signs of Animal Friends*

Baker, Pamela J. *My first Book of Sign*

Bergman, Thomas. *Going Places: Children Living with Cerebral Palsy*

Bergman, Thomas. *We Laugh, We Love, We Cry: Children Living with Mental Retardation*

Bove, Linda. *Sesame Street Sign Language ABC*

Brearley, Sue. *Talk To Me*

Brink, David. *David's Story: A Book About Surgery*

Brown, Tricia. *Someone Special, Just Like You*

Burns, Kay. *Our Mom*

Cairo, Shelley. *Our Brother Has Down's Syndrome*

Calmenson, Stephanie. *Rosie: A Visiting Dog's Story*

Carter, Alden R. *Seeing Things My Way*

Carter, Alden R. *Stretching Ourselves: Kids with Cerebral Palsy*

Chaplin, Susan Gibbons. *I Can Sign My ABCs*

Collins, Harold S. *The Beginning Sign Language Series*

Dwight, Laura. *We Can Do It!*

Dwyer, Kathleen M. *What Do You Mean I Have a Learning Disability?*

Elder, Vicci. *Cardiac Kids*

Emmert, Michelle. *I'm The Big Sister Now*

Fain, Kathleen. *Handsigns: A Sign Language Alphabet*

Foss, Karen Sue. *The Problem With Hair*

Gaes, Jason. *My Book For Kids With Cansur*

Greenberg, Judith E. *What Is the Sign for Friend?*

Gross, Ruth Belov. *You Don't Need Words! A Book About Ways People Talk Without Words*

Haldane, Suzanne. *Helping Hands: How Monkeys Assist People Who Are Disabled*

Heelan, Jamee Riggio. *The Making of My Special Hand: Madison's Story*

Holub, Joan. *My First Book of Sign Language*

Jansen, Larry. *My Sister is Special*

Kornfield, Elizabeth J. *Dreams Come True*

Litchfield, Ada B. *Words In Our Hands*

McMahon, Patricia. *Listen for the Bus: David's Story*

Milne, A.A. *Winnie-the-Pooh's ABC: Sign Language Edition*

Montoussamy-Ashe, Jeanne. *Daddy and Me*

O'Shaughnessy, Ellen. *Somebody Called Me A Retard Today . . . and My Heart Felt Sad*

Osofsky, Audrey. *My Buddy*

Peterson, Jeanne Whitehouse. *I Have A Sister My Sister is Deaf*

Pirner, Connie White. *Even Little Kids Get Diabetes*

Powers, Mary Ellen. *Our Teacher's in a Wheelchair*

Prall, Jo. *My Sister's Special*

Quinn, Patricia O., & Stern, Judith M. *Putting on the Brakes*

Rankin, Laura. *The Handmade Alphabet*

Riggs, Stephanie. *Never Sell Yourself Short*

Roby, Cynthia. *When is Learning Tough: Kids Talk About Their Learning Disabilities*

Rogers, Fred. *Let's Talk About It: Extraordinary Friends*

Rosenberg, Maxine B. *My Friend Leslie: The Story of a Handicapped Child*

Rotner, Shelly & Kelly, Sheila. *A.D.D. Book for Kids*

Sanford, Doris. *Don't Look at Me*

Sanford, Doris. *No Longer Afraid*

Schulman, Arlene. *Carmin's Story: A Book About a Boy Living with AIDS*

Silverstein, Ivan A., & Silverstein, Virginia B. *Runaway Sugar: All About Diabetes*

Silverstein, Ivan, Silverstein, Virginia, & Nunn, Laura Silverstein. *Dyslexia*

Simpson-Smith, Elizabeth. *A Guide Dog Goes to School*

Slier, Debby. *Animal Signs: A First Book of Sign Language*

Slier, Debby. *Word Signs: A First Book of Sign Language*

Swenson, Judy Harris, & Kunz, Rosane Brown. *Learning My Way: I'm a Winner*

Taylor, Ron. *All By Self*

Watson, Esther. *Talking to Angels*

Wellbrook Collection. *Bear Spot Learns a Lot: Growing Up With Diabetes*

Wellbrook Collection. *Dotty the Dalmatian Has Epilepsy*

Wellbrook Collection. *I'm Still Me: Coping with Leukemia*

Wellbrook Collection. *Way to go Bravo: Learning to Live with Asthma*

Wheeler, Cindy. *Simple Signs*

White, Peter. *Think About Being Blind*

Weiner, Lori, Best, Aprille, & Pizzo, Phillip. *Be A Friend: Children Who Live with HIV Speak*

Wolf, Bernard. *HIV Positive*

Woolley, Maggie. *Think About Being Deaf*

Category B

Books Provide Information About Disability or Illness in Story Format

Addabbo, Carole. *Dina the Deaf Dinosaur*

Adler, David. *A Picture Book of Helen Keller*

Alden, Joan. *A Boy's Best Friend*

Amadeo, Diane M. *There's a Little Bit of Me In Jamey*

Amer, Kim, & Brill, Marlene. *Short Mort and the Big Bully*

Ancona, George, & Ancona, Mary Beth. *Handtalk Zoo*

Arnold, Caroline. *A Guide Dog Puppy Grows Up*

Aseltine, Lorraine, Mueller, Evelyn, & Tait, Nancy. *I'm Deaf and It's Okay*

Beatty, Monica Driscoll. *My Sister Rose Has Diabetes*

Berry, Steve. *The Boy Who Wouldn't Speak*

Bouwkamp, Julie A. *Hi, I'm Ben…And I've Got a Secret*

Bunnett, Rochelle. *Friends at School*

Bunnett, Rochelle. *Friends in the Park*

Bunting, Eve. *The Sunshine Home*

Carlson, Nancy. *Arnie and the New Kid*

Carlson, Nancy. *Sit Still!*

Carter, Alden R., & Siri M. *I'm Tougher Than Asthma*

Carter, Alden R. *Seeing Thing My Way*

Carter, Alden R. *Stretching Ourselves: Kids with Cerebral Palsy*

Caseley, Judith. *Harry and Willy and Carrothead*

Charlip, Remy. *Handtalk Birthday*

Coerr, Eleanor. *Sadako*

Cohen, Miriam. *It's George*

Cohen, Miriam. *See You Tommorrow, Charles*

Corman, Clifford L., & Trevino, Esther. *Eukee The Jumpy Jumpy Elelphant*

Craig, Lori. *One Step at a Time*

DeBear, Kirsten. *Be Quiet, Marina!*

Delton, Judy. *I'll Never Love Anything Ever Again*

Edwards, Becky. *My Brother Sammy*

Fleming, Virginia. *Be Good to Eddy Lee*

Gardner, Sonia. *Eagle Feather*

Gehret, Jeanne. *Eagle Eyes*

Gehret, Jeanne. *The Don't-Give-Up Kid*

Gifaldi, David. *Ben, King of the River*

Girard, Linda Walvoord. *Alex, the Kid With Aids*

Golden, Barbara Diamond. *Cakes and Miracles*

Gregory, Nan. *How Smudge Came*

Haines, Sandra. *Becca and Sue Make Two*

Hamm, Diane Johnson. *Gramma Drives a Motor Bed*

Hausman, Gerald. *The Story of Blue Elk*

Hodges, Candri. *When I Grow Up*

Holcomb, Nan. *Fair and Square*

Holcomb, Nan. *Patrick and Emma Lou*

Holcomb, Nan. *Sarah's Surprise*

Jordon, MaryKate. *Losing Uncle Tim*

Kadish, Sharona. *Discovering Friendship*

Krause, Ute. *Pig Surprise*

Krisher, Trudy. *Kathy's Hats: A Story of Hope*

Kuklin, Susan. *Think Big: The Story of a Young Dwarf*

Lasker, Joe. *Nick Joins In*

Lears, Laurie. *Becky the Brave: A Story About Epilepsy*

Lears, Laurie. *Ben Has Something to Say: A Story About Stuttering*

Lears, Laurie. *Ian's Walk*

Lee, Jeanne M. *Silent Lotus*

Lester, Helen. *Hooway for Wodney Wat*

Levi, Dorothy Hoffman. *A Very Special Friend*

Levi, Dorothy Hoffman, *A Very Special Sister*

Levine, Edna S. *Lisa and Her Soundless World*

Litchfield, Ada B. *A Button in Her Ear*

Litchfield, Ada B. *A Cane in Her Hand*

Litchfield, Ada B. *Making Room for Uncle Joe*

London, Jonathan. *The Lion Who Has Asthma*

Loski, Diana. *The Boy on the Bus*

Lowell, Gloria Roth. *Elana's Ears or How I Became the Best Big Sister in the World*

Lyon, George Ella. *Cecil's Story*

Mackinnon, Christy. *Silent Observer*

MacLachlan, Patricia. *Through Grandpa's Eyes*

Maguire, Arlene. *Special People, Special Ways*

Martin, Bill J.R., & Archambault, John. *Knots on a Counting Rope*

Mayer, Gina & Mercer. *A Very Special Critter*

McMahon, Patricia. *Summer Tunes: A Martha's Vineyard Vacation*

Merrifield, Margaret. *Come Sit By Me*

Millman, Isaac. *Moses Goes to a Concert*

Millman, Isaac. *Moses Goes to School*

Mills, Joyce C. *Little Tree: A Story for Children with Serious Medical Problems*

Mitchell, Lori. *Different Just Like Me*

Mitchell, Rita Phillips. *Hue Boy*

Moran, George. *Imagine Me on a Sit-Ski!*

Moss, Deb Root, Ann, & Gladden, Linda. *Charlie's Challenge*

Moss, Deborah M. *Lee, the Rabbit with Epilepsy*

Moss, Deborah M. *Shelley, the Hyperactive Turtle*

Muldoon, Kathleen M. *Princess Pooh*

Peckinpah, Sandra Lee. *Rosey . . . the Imperfect Angel*

Porte, Barbara Ann. *Harry's Dog*

Pulber, Robin. *Way To Go Alex!*

Quinlan, Patricia. *Tiger Flower*

Rheingrover, Jean Sasso. *Veronica's First Year*

Roberts, Karon. *Bright . . . and Behind: A Book for Children and Parents Learning to Cope with Reading and Attention Problems*

Rogers, Alison. *Luke Has Asthma, Too*

Root, Ann, & Gladden, Linda. *Charlie's Challenge*

Rosenberg, Maxine B. *Finding a Way: Living with Exceptional Brothers and Sisters*

Russo, Marisabina. *Alex Is My Friend*

Sanford, Doris. *David Has AIDS*

Sanford, Doris. *Help! Fire!*

Sueling, Barbara. *I'm Not So Different*

Shannon, David. *David Goes to School*

Shannon, David. *No, David!*

Shriver, Maria. *What's Wrong with Timmy?*

Stuve-Bodeen, Stephanie. *We'll Paint the Octopus Red*

Sullivan, Tom. *That Nelson!*

Swanson, Susanne M. *My Friend Emily*

Thompson, Mary. *Andy and the Yellow Frisbee*

Thompson, Mary. *My Brother Matthew*

Turner, Deborah, & Mohler, Diana. *How Willy Got His Wheels*

Verniero, Joan C. *You Can Call Me Willy*

Vigna, Judith. *When Eric's Mom Fought Cancer*

Wahl, Jan. *Jamie's Tiger*

Walker, Dava. *Puzzles*

Walker, John C. *In Other Words*

Wanous, Suzanne. *Sara's Secret*

Wellbrook Collection. *Hip-Hop the Hyperactive Hippo*

Wellbrook Collection. *Hooray for Harold: Dealing with Hearing Loss*

Whinston, Joan Lenett. *I'm Joshua and Yes I Can*

Willis, Jeanne. *Susan Laughs*
Wright, Betty Ren. *My Sister is Different*
Wright, Christine. *Just Like Emma: How She Has Fun in God's World*
Young, Ed. *Seven Blind Mice*
Zelonsky, Joy. *I Can't Always Hear You*

Category C
Books Provide Stories with a Character with Disability or Illness. Category C Books Are Inclusionary Literature.

Barrett, Mary Brigid. *Sing To The Stars*
Booth, Barbara. *Mandy*
Borden, Louise. *Good Luck, Mrs. K.!*
Borton, Lady. *Junk Pile!*
Bunting, Eve. *The Wall*
Carter, Alden R. *Big Brother Dustin*
Carter, Alden R. *Dustin's Big School Day*
Caseley, Judith. *Apple Pie and Onions*
Condra, Estelle. *See The Ocean*
Cowen-Fletcher, Jane. *Mama Zooms*
Crunk, Tony. *Big Mama*
Damrell, Liz. *With the Wind*
Davies, Patricia. *Brian's Bird*
Derby, Janice. *Are You My Friend?*
Edwards, Michelle. *alef-bet—A Hebrew Alphabet Book*
Foreman, Michael. *Seal Seafer*
Faustino, Lisa Rowe. *The Hickory Chair*
Gainer, Cindy. *I'm Like You, You're Like Me*
Gilmore, Rachna. *A Screaming Kind of Day*
Girnis, Meg. *ABC for You and Me*
Goodwall, Jane. *Mr. White*
Greenfield, Eloise. *William and the Good Old Days*
Hallinan, P.K. *Heartprints*
Harshman, Marc. *The Storm*
Harter, Debbie. *The Animal Boogie*

Heelan, Jamee Riggio. *Rolling Along: The Story of Taylor and His Wheelchair*

Henriod, Lorraine. *Grandma's Wheelchair*

Hesse, Karen. *Lester's Dog*

Hill, Eric. *Where's Spot*

Hines, Anna Grossnickle. *Gramma's Walk*

Hoffman, Eric. *No Fair to Tigers*

Karim, Roberta. *Mandy Sue Day*

Kroll, Virginia L. *Naomi Knows It's Springtime*

Kroll, Virginia L. *Butterfly Boy*

Lakin, Patricia. *Dad and Me In The Morning*

Lears, Laurie. *Waiting for Mr. Goose*

Meyers, Cindy. *Rolling Along with Goldilocks and the Three Bears*

Moon, Nicole. *Lucy's Pictures*

Muller, Gerda. *A Garden in the City*

Newth, Philip. *Roly Goes Exploring*

Okimoto, Jean Davies. *A Place for Grace*

Orr, Wendy. *Arabella*

Pearson, Susan. *Happy Birthday, Grampie*

Rabe, Berniece. *The Balancing Girl*

Rabe, Berniece. *Where's Chimpy?*

Raffi, *One Light, One Sun*

Rickert, Janet Elizabeth. *Russ and the Firehouse*

Rickert, Janet Elizabeth. *Russ and the Almost Perfect Day*

Rickert, Janet Elizabeth. *Russ and the Apple Tree*

Riggio, Anita. *Secret Signs: Along the Underground Railroad*

Rudner, Barry. *The Handstand*

Sargent, Susan, & Wirt, Donna Aaron. *My Favorite Place*

Schar, Brigitte. *The Blind Fairy*

Slate, Joseph. *Miss Bindergarten Celebrates the 100th Day of Kindergarten*

Slate, Joseph. *Miss Bindergarten Gets Ready for Kindergarten*

Slate, Joseph. *Miss Bindergarten Plans a Circus with Kindergarten*

Slate, Joseph. *Miss Bindergarten Stays Home*

Slate, Joseph. *Miss Bindergarten Takes a Field Trip*

Turk, Ruth. *The Doll at the Top of the Shelf*

APPENDIX D

ACTIVITIES FOR TEACHING YOUNG CHILDREN ABOUT DISABILITIES

It is difficult for young children to understand what it means to have a disability because they have not experienced it. It is somewhat easier to comprehend a disability that they can see like a physical disability, but is particularly difficult to understand the invisible disabilities. Participating in simulated activities can make the abstract notion of a disability become more real and concrete, and increase the children's level of understanding. When children participate in these activities, it is important that they demonstrate respect toward persons with the disability throughout the activity (i.e. silliness and laughing should be monitored). The professional should be aware of safety issues with all of the activities, i.e. tripping when blindfolded, and take necessary precautions to keep all activities safe. Activities are included for the disabilities of blind, partial sight, deaf or hard of hearing, physical, and cognitive disabilities.

SUGGESTED ACTIVITIES

Blind or Partial Sight

Feely Beg. Put common and uncommon objects in a bag. The children reach into the bag and identify an object without looking at it. This can emphasize the challenges of not being able to see. Even very young children are able to participate in this activity by limiting the number of objects and by using common, everyday items. Emphasize to the children the importance of their sense of touch (feeling) and the importance of our naming items for children who are blind or partially sighted.

Listening Activity. Have children listen to recordings of environmental or animal sounds and identify what they are hearing. This can point out the importance of the sense of hearing for people who are blind and the importance or our telling the person who is blind what it is they are hearing in order for them to learn.

Blindfold Activity. Have several children blindfold their eyes and move about the room. This will allow the children to have a better feel for what it would be like not to be able to see. This will point out the importance of keeping everything in the room in its place so the person who is blind will not trip or fall. Point out to the children that people who are blind can learn where everything is in a room and become very independent.

It's best to have several children do this at a time so no one becomes embarrassed. This activity should be done respectful of persons who are blind and not with silliness or as a joke.

Tasting Party. Have a variety of bite-sized foods for children to taste. With the children blindfolded, see if they can identify what they are eating from taste and smell only. To make it more difficult have foods that are very similar like a cookie and a cracker or two different kinds of juice. To make it easier, have foods that are very different such as a cracker and a piece of cheese. This will point out the importance of using these two additional senses.

Food Discovery. For children who can tell time, explain the system used by people who are blind to find food on their dinner plate. They pretend the plate is a clock and the food is placed at 12:00, 3:00, 6:00 and 9:00. On each student's plate, place four different kinds of bite sized food at these four respective locations. Each plate should have the food in the same order so you can work with several children at once. Together the children try to identify the food at 3:00, the food at 9:00, etc. This provides the students some understanding of how individuals who are blind learn to locate food on their plates.

Aids and Equipment. Collect as many aids as possible that are used by people who are blind or partially sighted. Provide times when the children can investigate and use each of the aids. Some possible aids are the Braille alphabet (you might be able to get one for each student), Braille pre-reading activities, Braille books or books with print and Braille, bell ball (ball with a bell inside it), tactile ball (ball with each section a different texture), slate and stylus, Braille typewriter and white cane. The best resource is the vision specialist for your district or your special education teacher.

Braille. Young children can learn one or two letters in Braille. A good letter to begin with is the first letter in their names. Older children may be able to learn all of the letters in their names. Children enjoy seeing what their own name looks like in Braille even if learning the entire name is too difficult. A student who is blind and in high school may be willing to put the students' names in Braille. This allows the children to appreciate how challenging it is to learn to read Braille with your fingers. Again your best resource is the vision specialist.

Deaf or Hearing Loss

Story Time With A Hearing Loss. Have the children listen to a taped story or a video with the sound turned down so low it becomes very difficult to understand what is being said. This will simulate a hearing loss. Then listen to the tape or video again with the sound turned up. Talk to the children about what it was like and how they felt when they couldn't quite hear the story.

Story Time When Deaf. Use a taped story or a video with no sound. Then read to the children by mouthing the words. Children will begin to understand what it means to be deaf and why it is important to see a person's face when he or she is speaking in order to read lips.

Aids and Equipment. Provide the children the opportunity to investigate and experience equipment that is used by individuals with a hearing loss (e.g. hearing aids, phonic ear). Your best resource is the teacher of the deaf or a speech and language clinician.

Snack Time With Gestures. During snack time, have several choices of snacks for the children and make the rule that they must communicate with gestures only. They will need to tell you which snack items they want and how many by gesturing. This will help children realize how difficult it is to communicate without speaking and appreciate the need for alternate means of communication, i.e. sign language, lip reading, communication boards, and technology.

Snack Time With Sign Language. Teach the children some simple signs that can be used during snack time such as the signs for drink, cookie, more, thank you and toilet. Require the children to communicate during this period of time with only sign language. Children enjoy learning some signs and come to realize that there are different ways to communicate.

Physical Disabilities

Aids and Equipment. Provide opportunities for children to experience the aids that are used by persons with physical disabilities. Examples of equipment that may be borrowed or rented are: crutches, leg braces, wheelchair, walking sticks, a stander, adaptive eating utensils, etc. Good resources for you are special education, your occupational therapist or physical therapist. Some stores that rent equipment will allow schools to borrow items for short periods of time. If the equipment needs to be rented, contact a local service club for a donation to cover the rental costs.

Wheelchair Maze. If a wheelchair is available, set up a short path for the children to follow including some obstacles. This will help them understand how independent a person in a wheelchair can be until an obstacle in the environment gets in the way. With the children, problem-solve how to overcome the obstacle. By wheeling around the classroom the children become aware of the importance of keeping the room in a particular arrangement to make room for the chair and having items at a height that can be reached by a person in a wheelchair.

Paint With Your Feet. Sometimes when people have a physical disability that takes away the use of their arms and hands, they learn to use their feet for drawing, painting and even eating. Sometimes they learn to draw or type by holding a utensil in their mouths. Children could try painting with their feet by holding the brush with their toes and using watercolor paints and large paper as they experiment. Or, they could try painting by holding the paintbrush in their mouths. These exercises would allow the children to see how difficult it is, yet it can be learned with perseverance.

Cognitive Disabilities: Mental Retardation or Learning Disability

(Simulation for these disabilities is much more difficult.)

Symbols For Letters. For children who can read, substitute symbols for the letters of the alphabet. Give the children a short sentence to read. In order for them to read each word, they must first look up each symbol and find out which letter it stands for. This is difficult and time consuming, which is what happens to students who have challenges with learning.

Reading At A Higher Level. Again this activity is for children who can read. Give them some sentences or a short paragraph to read from a higher reading level than they are performing. Because they won't know many of the words, this task will be difficult and frustrating which again is what happens to students who have challenges in learning.

Resources

Getshow, V., & Konczal, Dee (1996). *Kids with special needs: Information and activities to promote awareness and understanding.* ISBN 0-88160-244-2 ($17.98).

PACER Center, Inc. (Parent Advocacy Coalition for Educational Rights). 8161 Normandale Blvd., Minneapolis, MN 55437-1044 (952)838-0199, www.pacer.org This organization has a set of large puppets representing children with disabilities. The puppets are of exceptional quality and are used by their volunteers who go into local schools and teach children about various disabilities. The PACER puppets are also available for purchase.

Bickert, Grace. (2002). *Including the Special Needs Child: Activities to Help All Students Grow and Learn.* Nashville, TN: Incentives Publications, Inc. ISBN 0-86520-568-4 ($12.00).

APPENDIX E

Publishers of Children's Books

Abingdon Press
201 Eighth Avenue South
Nashville, TN 37203
(615)749-6000

Alyson Publications, Inc.
6922 Hollywood Blvd. #1000
Los Angeles, CA 90028
(323)860-6065
www.alyson.com

American Association for the Care of Children's Health
7910 Woodmont Avenue, #300
Bethesda, MD 20814
(301)654-6549

Augsburg Books
Augsburg Fortress Publishers
426 South Fifth Street, Box 1209
Minneapolis, MN 55440-1209
(612)330-3300
www.augsburgfortress.com

Band of Angels Press
3048 Charlwood Drive
Rochester Hills, MI 48306
(800)963-2237
www.bandofangels.com

Blue Sky Press
555 Broadway
New York, NY 10012
(212)343-6100
www.scholastic.com

Boyds Mills Press, Inc.
815 Church Street
Honesdale, PA 18431-1895
(570)253-1164
www.boydsmillspress.com

Carolrhoda Books, Inc.
Lerner Publishing Group
241-1st Avenue North
Minneapolis, MN 55401
(612)332-3344
www.lernerbooks.com

Centering Corporation
1531 N Saddle Creek Road
Omaha, NE 68104
(402)553-1200

Charlesbridge Publications
85 Main Street
Watertown, MA 02472
(617)926-0329
www.charlesbridge.com

Children's Press
Scholastic Inc.
90 Sherman Turnpike
Danbury, CT 06816
(203)797-3500
www.grolier.publishing.com

Chronicle Books for Children
85-2nd Street, 6th Floor
San Francisco, CA 94105
(415)537-3730
www.chroniclebooks.com

Clarion books
215 Park Avenue South
New York, NY 10003
(800)733-1717

Crown Publishers
Division of Random House
299 Park Avenue
New York, NY 10171
(212)572-2600
www.randomhouse.com

Dawn Sign Press
6130 Nancy ridge Dr.
San Diego, CA 92121-3223'
www.dawnsign.com

Dial Books for Young Readers
345 Hudson Street, 3rd Floor
New York, NY 10014
(212)366-2000

Doral Publishing
10451 West Palmeras Drive, #225
Sun City, AZ 85373-2073
(623)875-2057
www.doralpubl.com

DK Publishing, Inc.
375 Hudson Street, 2nd Floor
New York, NY 10014-3672
(212)213-4800
www.dk.com

Dutton Children's Books
375 Hudson Street
New York, NY 10014
(212)414-3700
www.penguinputnam.com

Farrar, Straus & Giroux, Inc.
19 Union Square West
New York, NY 10003
(212)741-6900

Free Spirit Publications
217-5th Avenue North, #2000
Minneapolis, MN 55401-1260
(612)338-2068
www.freespirit.com

Gareth Stevens, Inc.
330 West Olive Street, #100
Milwaukee, WI 53212
(414)332-3520
(800)341-3569

Garlic Press
605 Powers Street
Eugene, Or 97402
www.garlicpress.com

Greenwillow Books
1350 Avenue of the Americas
New York, NY 10019
(212)261-6500
www.garlicpress.com

Harcourt Brace & Company
525-B Street, #1900
San Diego, CA 92101-4495
(619)231-6616

Hannacroix Creek, Books, Inc.
1127 High Ridge Road, PMB 110
Stamford, CT 06905-1203
www.hannacroix.com

HarperCollins Children's Books
1350 Avenue of the Americas
New York, NY 10019
(212)261-6500
www.harpercollins.com

Harper Trophy
Division of HarperCollins
1350 Avenue of the Americas
New York, NY 10019
(212)261-6500
www.harpercollins.com

Health Press
PO Box 1388
Santa Fe, NM 8750
(505)-474-0303
www.healthpress.com

Henry Holt & Co.
115 West 18th Street
New York, NY 10010
(212)886-9200
www.henryholt.com

Holiday House, Inc.
425 Madison Avenue
New York, NY 10017
(212)688-0085

Houghton Mifflin Co.
222 Berkeley Street
Boston, MA 02116
(617)351-5000
www.hmco.com

Ideal's Childrens books
535 Metroplex Dr. #250
Nashville, TN 37214
(615)333-0478

Jason & Nordic Publishers
PO Box 441
Holidaysburg, PA 16648
(814)696-2920

Kendal Green Publisher
Gallaudet university Press
800 Florida Avenue NE
Washington, DC 20002-3695
(800)621-8476
www.gupress.gallaudet.edu

Alfred A. Knopf, Inc.
225 Park Avenue South
New York, NY 10171
(212)751-2600
www.aaknopt.com

Lee & Low Books
95 Madison Avenue
New York, NY 10016
(212)779-4400
www.leeandlow.com

Lerner Publishers
241 First Avenue North
Minneapolis, MN 55401
(621)332-3344
www.lernerbooks.com

Arthur A. Levine Books
Scholastic, Inc.
555 Broadway
New York, NY 10012
(212)343-4436

Little, Brown & Company, Inc.
1271 Avenue of the Americas
New York, NY 10029
(212)522-8700
www.littlebrown.com

Macmillan Co.
2 Penn Plaza
New York, NY 10121
(212)904-6749

Magination Press
750-1st Street NE
Washington, DC 20002-2984
www.maginationpress.com

McEldberry Books
Simon & Schuster Publishing
1230 Sixth Avenue
New York, NY 10020
(212)698-2761
www.simonsayskids.com

Millbrook Press, Inc.
2 Old Milford Road
Brookfield, CT 06804
www.millbrookpress.com

William Morrow
HarperCollins Children's Books
10 East 53rd Street
New York, NY 10022
(212)207-7000
www.harpercollins.com

Multnomah Publishing, Inc.
PO Box 1720
Sisters, Or 97759
(541)549-1144
www.multnomahbooks.com

North—South Books
1123 Broadway, #800
New York, NY 10010
(212)706-4545
www.northsouth.com

Orchard Books
95 Madison Ave., 11th Floor
New York, NY 10016
(212)951-2600
www.grolier.com

Peachtree Publications
1700 Chattahoochee Avenue
Atlanta, GA 30318-2112
(404)876-8761
www.peachtree-online.com

Philomel Books
345 Hudson Street
New York, NY 10014
(212)414-3610

Puffin Books
Penguin/Putnam, Inc.
345 Hudson Street
New York, NY 10014-3657
(212)414-2000
www.penguinputnam.com

Puffin Pied Piper
Dial Books for Young Children
345 Hudson Street, 3rd Floor
New York, NY 10014-3657
(212)366-2000
www.penguinputnam.com

G.P. Putnam's Sons
375 Hudson
New York, NY 10014
(212)366-2000
www.penguinputnum.com

Raintree Steck-Vaughn
15 East 26th Street
New York, NY 10010
(215)592-1000

Random Books for Young Readers
201 E. 50th Street
New York, NY 10022
(212)751-2600
www.randomhouse.com

Red Deer Press
Mackimmie Library Tower, #813
2500 University Drive NW
Calgary Alberta, TZN1N4, Canada
(403)220-4334
www.reddeerpress.com

Redleaf Press
450 N Syndicate, #5
St. Paul, MN 55104
(651)641-0305; (800)423-8309
www.redleafpress.com

Sasquatch Books
615-2nd Avenue, #260
Seattle, WA 98104
(206)467-4300
www.sasquatchbooks.com

Scholastic, Inc.
555 Broadway
New York, NY 10012
(212)343-6100
www.scholastic.com

Standard Publications
8121 Hamilton Avenue
Cincinnati, OH 45231
(513)931-4050
www.standardpub.com

Star Bright Books
325 West 38th Street, #511
New York, NY 10018
(212)564-3981
www.starbrightbooks.com

Troll Communications
100 Corporate Dr.
Mahwah, NJ 07430
(201)529-4000
www.troll.com

Viking Children's Books
345 Hudson Street
New York, NY 10014-3657
(212)366-2000

Walker & Company
435 Hudson Street
New York, NY 10014
(212)727-0984

Warner Books
1271 Avenue of the Americas
New York, NY 10020
(212)522-7200
www.twbookmark.com

Franklin Watts
A Division of Scholastic
555 Broadway
New York, NY 10012
(212)343-6100
www.scholastic.com

Albert Whitman & Co.
6340 Oakton St.
Morton Grove, Ill. 60053-2723
(847)581-0033
www.awhitmanco.com

Woodbine House
6510 Bells Mill Rd.
Bethesda, MD 20817
(301)897-3570
www.woodbinehouse.com

APPENDIX F

National Disability Organizations and Agencies

Alexander Graham Bell Association for the Deaf and Hard of Hearing. 2000 M St. NW #310, Washington, DC 20036, (202)337-8314, www.agbell.org

Alliance for Technology Access (ATA), 2175 E Francisco Blvd, #L., San Rafael, CA 94901-5524, (415)455-4574, www.ataccess.org

American Association on Mental Retardation, 444 N Capitol St. NW #846, Washington, DC 20001, (202)387-1968, www.aamr.org

American Association of the Deaf Blind, 814 Thayer Ave. #302, Silver Springs, MD 20910-4500, www.tr.wou.edu/dblink/aadb.htm

American Foundation for the Blind. 11 Penn Plaza #300, New York, NY 10001, (212)502-7600, www.afb.org

American Society for Deaf Children. PO Box 3355, Gettysburg, PA 17325, www.deafchildren.org

American Speech-Language-Hearing Association. 10801 Rockville Pike, Rockville, MD 20852-3279, www.asha.org

Arthritis Foundation. 1330 W Peachtree St., Atlanta, GA 30309, (404)872-7100, www.arthritis.org

Arc of the U.S. 1010 Wayne Ave. #650, Silver Springs, MD 20910 (301)565-3842, www.thearc.org

Association for Persons with Severe Handicaps (TASH), 29 W Susquehanna Ave. #210, Baltimore, MD 21204, (410)828-6706, www.tash.org

Autism Services Center. PO Box 507, Huntington, WV 25710-0507, (304)525-8014

Autism Society of America, Inc., 7910 Woodmont Ave. #300, Bethesda, MD 20814-3015, www.autism-society.org

Better Hearing Institute, Hearing Helpline, 515 King St. #420, Alexandria, VA 22314, (703684-3391, www.betterhearing.org

Birth Defect Research for Children (BDRC), 930 Woodcock Rd. #225, Orlando, FL 32803, (407)895-0802, www.birthdefects.org

Brain Injury Association. 105 N Alfred St., Alexandria, VA 22314, (703)236-6000,www.biausa.org

Cancer Information Service. (800)332-8615, www.nci-nih.gov

Candlelighters' Childhood Cancer Foundation. 3910 Warner St., Kensington, MD 20855, (301)962-3520, www.candlelighters.org

Canine Companions for Independence. 4989 State Rt. 37E, Delaware, OH 43015-9682, (740)548-4447, www.caninecompanions.org

Children and Adults with Attention Deficit Hyperactivity Disorder (CHADD). 8181 Professional Place #201, Landover, MD 20785, (301)306-7070, www.chadd.org

Epilepsy Foundation. 4351 Garden City Dr., Landover, MD 20785, (301)459-3700, www.epilepsyfoundation.org

Genetic Alliance, 4301 Connecticut Ave. #404, Washington, DC 20008-2304, (202)966-5557, www.geneticalliance.org

Human Growth Foundation. 997 Glen Cove Ave., Glen Head, NY 11545, (516)671-4041, www.hgfound.org

Immune Deficiency Foundation. 40 Chesapeake Ave. #308, Baltimore, MD 21204-4843, (410)321-6647, www.primaryimmune.org

Institute for Families of Blind Children. PO Box 54700, MS 111, Los Angeles, CA 90054-0700, (323)669-4649

International Dyslexia Association (The). 8600 LaSalle Rd., Chester Bldg. #382, Baltimore, MD 21286-2044, (410)321-5069, www.interdys.org

International Hearing Society. 16880 Middlebelt Rd. #4, Livconia, MI 48154, (734)522-7200, www.hearingihs.org

Juvenile Diabetes Research Foundation International (JDF), 120 Wall St., 19th Floor, New York, NY 10005-4001, (212)785-9500, www.jdf.org

Learning Disabilities Association of America. 4156 Library Rd., Pittsburgh, PA 15234-1349, (412)341-1515, www.ldaamerica.org

Leukemia Lymphoma Society. 1311 Mamaroneck Ave., White Plains, NY 10605, (914)949-5213, www.leukemia-lymphoma.org

Little People of America. National Headquarters PO Box 745 Lubbock, TX 79408, (888)572-2001, www.lpaonline.org

March of Dimes Birth Defects Foundation. 1275 Mamaroneck Ave., White Plains, NY 10605, (914)428-7100, www.modimes.org

Muscular Dystrophy Association. 3300 E Sunrise Dr., Tuscon, AZ 85718, (520)529-2000, www.mdausa.org

National Association for Parents of Children with Visual Impairments, PO Box 317, Watertown, MA 02471-0317, (617)927-7441, www.spedex.com/napvi

National Association for the Deaf. 814 Thayer Ave., Silver Spring, MD 20910-4500, (301)587-1788, www.nad.org

National Center for Learning Disabilities. 381 Park Ave. S, Suite 1401, New York, NY 10016, (888)575-7373, www.ncld.org

National Center for Stuttering. 200 E 33rd St. #17C, New York, NY 10016, (212)532-1460, www.stuttering.com

National Diabetes Information Clearinghouse (NDIC). One Information Way, Bethesda, MD 20892, (301)654-3327, www.niddk. nih.gov

National Down Syndrome Congress. 7000Peachtree-Dunwoody Rd., Bldg. 5 #100, Atlanta, GA 30328, (770)604-9500, www.ndsccenter.org

National Down Syndrome Society. 666 Broadway #810, New York, NY 10012, (212)460-9330, www.ndss.org

National Health Information Center. U.S. Department of Health and Human Services, PO Box 1133, Washington, DC 20001-1133, (301)565-4167, healthfinder@nhic.org

National Information Center for Children and Youth with Disabilities (NICHCY). PO Box 1492, Washington, DC 20013-1492, (202)884-8200, www.nichcy.org

National Library Service for the Blind and Physically Handicapped. Library of Congress, 1291 Taylor St. NW, Washington, DC 20542, (202)707-5100, www.loc.gov/nls

National Organization for Rare Disorders (NORD). PO Box 8923, New Fairfield, CT 06812-8923, (203)746-6518, www.rarediseases.org

National Spinal Cord Injury Association. 6701 Democracy Blvd. #300-9, Bethesda, MD 20817, (301)588-6959, www.spinalcord.org

PACER Center, Inc. (Parent Advocacy Coalition for Educational Rights). 8161 Normandale Blvd., Minneapolis, MN 55437-1044, (952)838-0199, www.pacer.org

Spina Bifida Association of America. 4590 MacArthur Blvd. NW #250, Washington, DC 20007-4226, (202)944-3295, www.sbaa.org

United Cerebral Palsy Association. 1660 L St. NW #700, Washington, DC 20036-5602, (202)776-0406, www.ucp.org

INDEX